FIXED STARS

IN THE CHART

Constellations, Lunar Mansions and Mythology

Oscar Hofman

The Wessex Astrologer

Published in English in 2019 by
The Wessex Astrologer Ltd
PO Box 9307
Swanage
BH19 9BF

For a full list of our titles go to www.wessexastrologer.com

© Oscar Hofman 2019

Oscar Hofman asserts his moral right to be recognised as
the author of this work

Cover design by Jonathan Taylor

A catalogue record for this book is available at The British Library

ISBN 9781910531372

No part of this book may be reproduced or used in any form or by any means
without the written permission of the publisher.

Contents

Preface	v
Word of gratitude	vi
Chapter 1. Spiritual background	1
Chapter 2. Delineation practice	4
Magnitudes, star natures and orbs	
Comets, novae, outer planets	
The Milky Way, the nodal axis and antiscia	
Precession and the Age of Aquarius	
Chapter 3. Mythology of the constellations	21
List of constellations, their stars and mythology	
Short mythological vocabulary	
Chapter 4. List of stars by zodiac sign	75
Chapter 5. The star houses or lunar mansions	83
Chapter 6. 24 Case studies	107
Appendix A. List of keywords per star	189
Appendix B. The 48 traditional constellations	232
Appendix C. Arabic lunar mansions with rulers and boundaries	234
Bibliography	238

Preface

The fixed stars and their mythological life themes are now receiving more attention in astrology after having been ignored for too long. This is well-deserved as they add so much to the chart. Classical astrology, on the rise again since the 1980s, has inspired an increasing interest in the fixed stars, and with the Great Conjunctions of Saturn and Jupiter in the air signs between 1980 and 2020, astrology is making room for reabsorbing 'new' old knowledge. This is a fortunate development as there is so much of value to be found in the gold-mines of the tradition. The method presented in this book is the one most commonly used; it is not the only method to work with fixed stars but it is, in my experience, the most consistent, effective and logical approach, which will, if applied in the right way, lead to amazing results, especially in natal and in mundane astrology.

These results are concrete facts that can be checked, as things indicated in the chart actually manifest in the tangible reality around you; the accuracy of the fixed stars and the star houses, the lunar mansions, will send shivers down your spine. Formula 1 driver Nikki Lauda, for example, had his notorious accident in which he suffered serious burns to his face, when the fixed star *Achernar* was activated by an important progression. This star is connected to the story of Phaeton who, overestimating his powers, tried to steer the solar chariot through the heavens, lost control and came down in flames.

And in the chart of Nicolai Tesla, unsurpassed genius in electrical design and invention, the Sun is on the fixed star *Castor* on the IC; Castor is the dying brother of the famous heavenly twins. One of the critical events in Tesla's youth was the death of his elder brother who was killed by a horse. The heavenly Twins, represented in the zodiac by the sign Gemini, are known as horse tamers. *Castor* and *Pollux* is also the traditional name for a light phenomenon, St Elmo's fire, sometimes seen on the masts of ships and caused by electrical discharge. They are the archetypical symbol of tension between two poles, of which electrical phenomena are just one manifestation.

This kind of proof is very exciting, but to recognise it you need some knowledge of mythology and the ability to translate the symbolism into real life events. Without this you would see nothing special in the progressions over *Achernar* in Nikki Lauda's chart or in *Castor* on Tesla's IC. This book aims to clarify the essence of the mythological stories so you can apply the method in a creative way, based on understanding rather than relying on keywords. However, I've included such a list in Appendix A which can be used as an integral part of the whole method.

Discussion continues on my blog, which you can find at http://www.pegasus-advies.com/blog/category/english-articles/

Expression of gratitude
This book is also based on the workshops given by my teacher John Frawley in 2005 in Den Bosch, The Netherlands and in 2010 in Regensburg, Germany. Without his inspiring ideas and generous support, it would not have been written.

1
The Spiritual Background

The basic theme of the fixed stars and constellations is to indicate how mankind can escape from a state in which he is overly bound to earthly desires and wishes, like success, pleasure, money, power, sex and status – in fact everything that stands in the way of detachment. It is these strong passions that make us unhappy and prevent spiritual development. To be absolutely clear about this, it is completely natural and necessary to have desires, but not to the point where we are subjugated by the more animal side of our nature. In achieving some detachment we will in fact create a greater measure of real freedom for ourselves. The stars and the constellations give an indication of the field of variations and possibilities related to this process of detachment. Sometimes a constellation will show that the passions are deeply ingrained: for example if a star in the constellation of *Hydra* is active then sometimes the desires are easier to control, but they could be accompanied by specific pitfalls like too much pride or ambition. So the stars are, spiritually, an instruction book on how to temper those strong bonds to our animal nature. These instructions are often very specific. For example, royal *Regulus*, the Lion's Heart, on a luminary or an angle would indicate that ambition and pride have to be sacrificed consciously. The Heart of the Lion gives a very strong urge for an immortal name; it will do everything for this, whatever the cost. To understand the essence of these mythological stories, the imagery is important as this imparts direct knowledge by its symbolism. Again an example, the image of Pegasus, the flying horse, will clarify what this story is essentially about, and in this sense the constellations are also like an exhibition of traditional art.

The theme of detachment is central to all great religions. For example, in Christianity it is the crucifixion showing the painful sacrifice of the desire nature, after which Resurrection and Ascension follow. In Buddhism, the same theme is formulated on a more psychological level with the realisation that liberation from suffering comes from the recognition of the essential void of the ego and its desires.

2   Fixed Stars in the Chart

If we act through desire, karma is created that perpetuates samsara, the wheel of suffering and reincarnation. Realisation of a state of non-desire means that the believer will be reborn, not in the samsaric worlds of death and pain, but in one of six Buddha kingdoms. So allowing for cultural, local and temporal variations, Christianity and Buddhism say, partly at least, the same things.

The fixed stars have their own separate level in the delineation of the chart which goes deeper than that of the planets. This is made clear by the traditional model of the cosmos, which is essential to understand astrology. In this model the earth is the lowest and central point, surrounded by the elemental spheres, then by the seven planetary spheres, above which follow the eighth sphere of the fixed stars and then the ninth sphere, the zodiac of the twelve signs. So the eighth sphere of the fixed stars is higher than the planets and closer to the divine dimension of the Empyreum, found behind the sphere of the zodiacal 'Towers', the signs. As Dante suggests regarding the concentric circles of the spheres: "the vaster they are the greater their virtue". His *Commedia Divina* sketches a picture of this traditional cosmology. The spheres represent inner as well as outer structures as the cosmology is macrocosmic and microcosmic at the same time.

This reflects what was said above about the spiritual nature of the stars, which give a picture of the essential work to be done in the life, in the work leading up to the *Empyreum*, 'the place where God lives'. The stars in a chart represent an individual's life-quest in contrast to the planets, which indicate the events and the conditions of the life. For example, if *Alphard* – the main star in the Water-snake – is on the Ascendant, there is likely to be a persistent battle with a strong desire nature which must be conquered, otherwise chaos and unhappiness will result. It is quite different if *Altair*, the main star in the Eagle, is found on the Ascendant, when we may expect that Zeus will come down to carry this Ganymede to Olympus, to the feast of the gods. This star is a good starting-point for acquiring and teaching knowledge of higher things to support further development. These different stars point to individually differentiated essential jobs to be done.

So the planets indicate the events of the life and although the stars are also connected to concrete levels of interpretation, they do reach further. If the 'star work' is done they are an escape route out of the material life governed too strongly by earthly passions, and in a way you could see the planets as precisely these passions. It should be noted though, after all these highly strung spiritual words, that manifesting the down-to-earth meaning of the stars in our mundane lives is just as important as their associated spiritual themes. The concrete is nothing less than the spiritual essence becoming anchored in our lives.

A good example is the chart of the German general and 'desert fox' Erwin Rommel who fought and both dramatically and mythically lost a famous battle in the North African deserts in the Second World War. He has the powerful star *Canopus* on an angle, and one of the elements in the *Canopus* story is dying in the Egyptian desert as the consequence of a snake bite. If the going gets tough, you need more than just smartness to survive. *Canopus* is a very southerly star, far away from the zodiac, most appropriate for a general fighting in the African desert.

The traditional cosmological model of the spheres

2
Delineation Practice

The constellations visible in the sky form families of related stars belonging to the same mythological story. This means that the constellations of which the stars are part are central in their meaning; the stars are nothing more than concentration points of (a part of) the myth, touching the chart and thus the life, through a conjunction of the star with a planet, a cusp or a part. So a delineation which includes the stars should always start with the myth connected to the constellation, as this is the story the individual is inevitably caught up in. An astrologer with this knowledge can give important insights into the life of their client as we are here in the ninth sphere, in the Firmamentum, as close as we can get to the divine Empyreum.

Within the constellations the individual stars have their own specific nature. This is shown by the places they occupy in the image (foot, heel, horn, eye, heart, wing, hand, hoof, shoulder, head, girdle, neck, sword, spear, bow, arrow), clarifying their meaning further. Also every fixed star has its own planetary nature. A star of a pure Venus nature is obviously quite different from a Saturn/Mars star in its effects on the world and the individual. As we are talking about planetary energies here, the dignity of the planets should also be taken into account, as martial stars will have a more harmful effect if Mars is in detriment in the chart (the dignity system is explained in Chapter 6).

Furthermore, the latitude of the star and its vertical distance to the ecliptic will have a bearing on how powerful it is. Obviously, a star in the Dragon encircling the Pole far away up in the North will be less important than a star right on the ecliptic, the path of the divine essence of which the Sun is a visible symbol. A star's power is also indicated by its magnitude – the amount of light it reflects – so obviously the brighter a star is, the more powerful its effects. The scale of magnitudes relevant for astrology runs from first magnitude for the brightest stars up to sixth magnitude for the tiny stars that can just about be seen with the naked eye. The first magnitude stars, of which there are about twenty, form a kind of elite, so if you have a planet or an angle on such a star you have a good chance of becoming prominent in the field concerned. The fixed stars do actually move, transiting the signs at a very slow pace of about 1 zodiac degree every 72 years, which means they will stay in one zodiac sign for about 2200 years. You will always have to correct the star positions for the year you are working in, according to the precession movement to which we will return later. The list of stars per sign given in Chapter 4 was calculated for the year 2010 and can be recalculated to any year using the above-mentioned rate of 1 degree = 72 years.

The final practical point is orbs, which are as follows: 1 degree orb for stars of the magnitude 2 (up to 1.30 degrees on an angle) or higher (a higher magnitude indicates a weaker light power); 2 degrees orb for the 1st magnitude bright elite stars, and 3 to 4 degrees orb for the royal stars: *Aldebaran, Antares, Regulus, South Scale, Pollux, Spica* and for the 'Queen of Darkness', the extremely malefic *Algol*. There is some scope for flexibility in this though, as a second magnitude star on an angle occupied by two planets will have an effect even if it is technically not exactly in orb. Also, for example, for nebulae and star groups a somewhat wider orb may be used as their boundaries are not as sharply defined as single individual stars.

Only conjunctions
In the delineation of the stars only conjunctions with planets, cusps or Arabic parts will be taken into account, with the orbs mentioned above. To get an overview of the main myths, consider any stars conjunct the Sun and the Moon (the luminaries), the Midheaven, the Ascendant, and the ruler of the first house, Lord 1. The lunar mansion – the star house – occupied by the Moon as discussed in Chapter 5 is very important, as this indicates the core mythological direction in our lives. In Chapter 5 you will read how to integrate the lunar mansions in the star delineation system. Sometimes two royal stars on the luminaries or angles suffice to give the general story of a life, as is the case with Princess Diana, for example.

A star conjunct a planet will influence the way the planet works out very much as a general significator and as a house ruler. The same thing applies to the houses themselves, as a star on a cusp cannot be ignored. Arabian parts are also interpreted in connection with the star conjuncting the part. The stars also play a very important role in prediction, as a star can be activated by one of the main predictive factors: the Sun, Moon, Ascendant, Midheaven, Part of Fortune, Part of the Sun and Lord 1 conjuncting it, and its effects will then start to materialize in the life. A star does NOT have to be in a prominent position in the natal chart necessarily, as it can also act through progression only. A star dominating a solar return chart, by being on the Midheaven for example, will also have a considerable effect in the life for the year covered by the return chart; the same thing applies to lunar returns on a monthly scale.

Spiritual AND concrete
The more practical central question in delineating the constellations and the fixed stars is: What can I do to make the mythological story I am caught up in work out in the most positive way and how can I limit any damage done?

More so than planets, the stars give you the opportunity to act consciously in your life story and make the outcome as positive as possible. If you have *Regulus* on your Moon for example, don't try to come across as the great authority at all costs, for blind ambition may bring you down or at least cause you a lot of trouble. So in Chapter 3, after the description and interpretation of the myths, the central theme encompasses recommendations in how to avoid the main pitfalls of the story. Mythical themes are inevitably closely related, and the constellations often indicate diverse phases of development and variations in a similar general story.

If the essence of the myth is understood, the astrologer will grasp the stars' meaning and interpret the traditional texts effectively in a non-literal way. It cannot be emphasized enough that stars and constellations have a concrete meaning too, so don't make it too spiritual, although there will be a spiritual meaning present in the background. For example, someone with Lord 10 of profession on the star *Vega* in the constellation of the Falling Vulture (Lyra), may be happy to work at an airport, whereas someone with *Altair* the main star in the Eagle (Aquila) may be a good pilot. So don't forget that the way stars and their myths work out is closely related to their imagery. The central message of the stars is to act out the myth consciously and knowingly on the concrete and spiritual levels as much as possible, so that we may avoid the typical pitfalls in a story. If we don't actively participate in a myth, the myth may be forced on to us, which is in most cases much more unpleasant.

A boundary of a zodiac sign will always remain just that. A boundary is like a wall, so a planet cannot be conjunct a star on the other side of the wall. Stars are like planets in this sense, as they also transit through the signs. During our lifetime the powerful royal star *Regulus* has moved over the sign boundary from Leo into Virgo, and the period when this happened is therefore important (January 2012). As soon as *Regulus* entered Virgo it made a conjunction with planets in the first degrees of Virgo and not with the planets at the end of Leo, and this is significant. However, *Alcyone*, the main star of the Pleiades, has moved from Taurus into Gemini, but as *Alcyone* is the centre or the leader of the whole nebulous pack of Pleiadean stars, we have Pleiades on both sides of the Taurus/Gemini boundary.

It will often happen that two stars are very close to each other when projected onto the zodiac. In this case, for delineation we select the star closest to the planet or cusp, the star with the highest number of magnitude (the brightest of the two) and the smallest latitude, or the one whose nature corresponds most to the planet it is conjunct. In some cases one powerful star will dominate the other, for example *Capulus*, the Sword-hand of Perseus, is very close to *Algol*, the Demon's Head, and will seldom be delineated separately as *Algol* is extremely powerful. The same applies in the case of the stars *Adhafera* and *Algieba* in the Lion, which are close to *Regulus*, the most royal star amongst royals.

Being too technically precise can lead you astray, as like all things precision has to be appropriate, and here it certainly is not. A solution to the issue of proximity can be found by applying the criteria mentioned above or in other creative ways. The stars *Almach* in Andromeda and *Menkar* in the Whale are for example extremely close, but as they belong to the same mythical story, you know what is going on when a planet is exactly between them. This issue only arises because we are trying to give form to a system which cannot be pinned down so exactly. The only thing in astrology that is perfect is the 12-fold energy girdle, of the 12 invisible signs or zodiacal Towers.

The 48 constellations

In ancient astrology there were originally 48 constellations, but since the 16th century many more have been added. The International Astronomical Union (IAU), which decides the official names for all sky objects, recognizes as many as 88 constellations, but many of these border on being silly, and aren't relevant to astrology. The whole process of adding and subtracting constellations is so artificial and arbitrary that we can safely ignore all new constellations and limit ourselves to the 48 traditional constellations listed in Appendix B. Are we really missing anything by leaving out the 'Printer's Office', the 'Chemical Furnace' or the 'Pendulum Clock'?

The 48 traditional constellations were logically subdivided according to their positions relative to the zodiac. There are 12 constellations on or very near the zodiac band, or the Sun's path, and they are obviously related to the 12 signs bearing their names. Furthermore, there are 21 constellations to the north and 15 southern constellations. It is important to understand that the 12 zodiacal constellations are related to 12 signs but they are not the same thing. The zodiacal constellations are visible star groups found near the zodiac, you could say in some sense more or less by accident, whereas the 12 signs bearing the same names are invisible zones of energy. Our ancestors could have avoided a lot of trouble by calling the constellation Aries "William" for example to distinguish it clearly from the sign Aries. As constellations and signs belong to totally different separate spheres in the astrological model of the cosmos, they should not be confused – despite the fact they have the same names. For anyone working within the traditional model, this is obvious: the visible-imperfect (constellations) is not the same as the invisible-ideal (signs). But the zodiacal constellations bear the same name as the signs precisely because they are posited near/on the zodiac. This marks them as special constellations but it does not turn them into signs.

Projections

The projections of fixed stars onto the zodiac has been increasingly criticised over the past years. This condemnation stems from the idea that you cannot use projected positions because the stars are not physically in the zodiac. This isn't a very strong argument as the planets aren't found exactly in the zodiac either. If we have a conjunction between two planets, they are very rarely right on top of each other in the sky, but by using projection they can be in the same zodiacal degree. Planet positions projected into the zodiac is standard practice and it has always been so. The Moon may be even more than 5 degrees latitude away from the zodiac, so there does not seem to be a valid principal argument against projection as an astrological method.

Outer planets – star-like factors

The outer planets don't have a role of great importance in classical astrology; they cannot be seen as planets, they don't act as sign rulers and they don't have a signature. There are no Pluto organs in the body and no Pluto plants or stones in nature. The outer planets are not included in the seven basic energies structuring our world, as are the seven classical planets. But the outer planets can be included in the classical method of chart interpretation as a separate important category of fixed stars, in which case we will not then only count the conjunction of a traditional planet with an outer planet, but also the opposition.

Neptune as a star-like factor is Poseidon, the mighty god of the oceans and it will literally or figuratively flood a situation (a city by a tsunami or your life by desires) and its main theme is uncontrollable chaos. Poseidon makes the earth shake with his famous trident, and the aim of the perpetually bad-tempered sea-god is to conquer dry land (will and consciousness) by flooding it with his element, the wild waters of desire.

Uranus as a star-like factor is the castrated primordial sky god, a symbol of unlimited potential that vehemently resists the painful enforcing of limitations. It was Saturn who castrated Uranus, so this story is about accepting earthly practical forms instead of always reaching for the sky. The drops of blood from the castrated sky god fell into the sea, leading to the birth of Venus, illustrating that discipline and limitation lead to harmony and love; it's not for nothing that Saturn is exalted in the Venus-ruled sign of Libra.

Pluto as a star-like factor is Hades, the malefic ruler of the underworld, and is connected to subterranean activities, general nastiness and sudden overwhelming confrontations. The delineation of the outer planets will technically proceed as in the case of real fixed stars, except that we also count the opposition with a planet. The three star-like factors have a status comparable to first magnitude fixed stars, so it is a good idea to include them.

Comets and novae
Other star-like factors are comets, the infamous 'hairy stars', which are always seen as malefic as a comet is something that dramatically breaks through all normal order and development. A comet's meaning is further interpreted on the basis of the sign in which it first appeared, although the signs it will move through are also taken into account. These signs indicate the parts of creation harmed by the malefic effects of the comet. Its colour in terms of planets is also important to clarify its effects. A red colour points to a Mars nature, blue and great brightness is associated with Venus, a grey and faint tint with Saturn, gold-yellow with the Sun and silvery brightness with Jupiter. If the comet is only visible at sunrise and sunset this points to a Mercury or Venus nature as these planets are always close to the Sun. The nature of the planet indicates the specific fields the malefic effects of the comet will manifest in, and this can be combined with the signs the comet first appeared in and moves through. A red comet appearing in Aquarius, a human sign, could point to a dramatic war, while a red comet in animal Taurus could show cattle affected by a dangerous illness or a fever epidemic.

Comets were regarded as hot and dry, strongly unbalanced exhalations of the Sun, and categorized into several types by their forms: sword-like, lamp-like or even beard-like. Earthquakes, floods, wars, and epidemics are mentioned among the great disasters a comet could bring. This is not limited to natural disasters – it includes all dangerous developments or harmful events. It will be clear that only the very brightest of comets will be relevant, so not every little comet indicates a disaster!

It seems that novae, new stars flaring up in the sky, can be given a meaning in more or less the same way. Novae and the most spectacular and extremely bright new stars, the supernovae, point to a total and dramatic new direction because of their signature. The two most famous supernovae are Brahe's Star which appeared in 1577 and Kepler's Star in 1604. Both supernovae were so exceptionally bright that they were visible even in daylight. This coincided with a major turning-point in European history: the Renaissance and the birth of modernity. A supernova is an exploding star going down in flames, so as a signature this is most appropriate for the end of the Middle Ages, a dramatic and profound change in spirit and culture.

The Milky Way, the antiscia and nodal axis
One of the most striking phenomena in the skies is the Milky Way, that beautiful ribbon of stars which can be best admired outside the light pollution of modern cities. It can be seen to consist of an enormous multitude of stars and this connects to its symbolic meaning. According to tradition this is the gateway for souls to be born on earth. So the Milky Way is a gate or doorway in and out of material life on earth. It mirrors the complete potential of souls to take on, at a certain moment if their time has come, a material form as a body and live an earthly life for a period of time.

The mythical image of the Milky Way is that of milk generously overflowing from the udder of the heavenly cow standing with its four legs on the four corners of the earth. This represents the four elements of material reality. The Milky Way crosses the zodiac in two zones at 22° Gemini – 2° Cancer and at 14 –21° Sagittarius – 0 – 7° Capricorn. If one of the luminaries, Sun or Moon, is found here it is traditionally said to bring blindness, as the Milky Way is a door through which you cannot see to the other side.

In what is left to us of Aztec mythology, the Milky Way appears as the Cloud Snake, pointing to an important parallel image of itself, the nodal axis; the axis that falls between the points where the solar and the lunar orbits cross each other. This axis can be understood better by its other names, the Head and the Tail of the Dragon, because it essentially represents the pure energy of the Dragon, or as the Aztecs called it, the snake. The snake symbolism can be summarized as 'dualism'. The splitting of an original unity into two contrary parts expresses the fundamental tension in earthly life. The snake is therefore one of the main symbols of desire, as we can only have desires if we are not one but two; only if there is a point different from our own can we covet something. We strive to move to the other point to get rid of the tension that the separation creates.

This explains why the effects of the expansive Jupiter-like North Node and of the limiting Saturn-like South Node are so extreme. This is the pure energy of the snake; on the North Node it is a craving for life to be satisfied and often accompanied by a considerable amount of success, while on the South Node it is a the 'narrow gate', a harsh limitation of your possibilities in life in order to redirect attention to the higher worlds of spiritual origin. Planets or cusps in narrow conjunction with the nodes are strongly influenced by the raw Dragon energy. On the difficult South Node the essential task is expressed by the traditional image of St George killing the dragon and getting the upper hand over desire. In this symbolic perspective it is not the North Node that has to be 'developed', as you hear said so often, it is on the contrary the South Node that needs special attention, as on this point we can make great progress in happiness, detachment and tranquility by sacrificing the areas connected with it.

The snake symbolism of duality is also found in the story of the Garden of Eden where the Tree of Knowledge of Good *and* Evil grows. Immediately following the snake's suggestion to take a bite from an apple from this tree, Adam and Eve lose their primordial unity as they become aware that they are opposites and fall into the tense heaviness of matter; they have to hide their sexual organs because these organs are the physical expression of their difference. It will be only after the snake (duality) is killed in the final battle, Armageddon, and the New Jerusalem descends to earth that man and woman will be able to return to unity. Until that time the gates to Paradise are guarded by *tetramorphs*, the angels with flaming swords whose 'fourfold form' symbolises the elements. So it is material life in duality that blocks the way back into Paradise.

The theme of duality is also strongly emphasized in Vedic mythology. The Dragon's Head and the Dragon's Tail represent what is left of Vasuki, the son of sage Kashyapa and the demon lioness Simhika. This demon assisted the gods in preparing the elixir of life that would make them immortal. However Vasuki succeeded in drinking from the elixir too and was punished for this by Vishnu who cleaved his body into two parts. Because he had already become immortal his Head and Tail remained alive and are known in Vedic astrology as Rahu and Ketu. They are even seen as two extra planets, indicating how important their effects are. If we have the South Node conjunct the MC for example, there will be painful limitations in the career, as it cuts you off from success.

The snake also plays a role in diverse constellations: The Snake, The Snakebearer, The Hydra or Watersnake, The Wagon-driver (with his snake feet) and the Dragon around the pole (not discussed in this book as it has no astrological effect, but it is a symbol) which can be understood by the dualistic symbolism, just like its positive counterpart the fish, pointing to divine non-duality. A fish is said to be always awake, to have its eyes always open, so it is not part of earthly rhythms, an indication of its connection to the divine unity. It can also move around unharmed in water, which is a symbol of desire, so it is free of desire. This is also why Christ is Ichtus, the fish.

So the nodal axis and the Milky Way are very closely connected symbolically – they both represent on their own levels the gate through which we enter and leave life. An activation of the nodal axis in a progression or solar return chart indicates that radical changes can be expected. The antiscial positions of the planets in the chart have a similar meaning, which is why antiscia are often active around the time of death; they represent the nodal axis in yet another way. This is because antiscia are found by mirroring planet positions around the solstitial axis, 0° Cancer/0° Capricorn.

This axis is again another representation of the nodes and the Milky Way but now on a zodiacal level. Cancer, called Octopus in ancient times, is the parallel to the North Node, the sign of an unlimited desire for life, whereas the Saturnian winter sign Capricorn, once called the Dolphin, which is the liberation of leaving material life behind, corresponds with the South Node. So in this sense antiscia are also nodal points and that is the reason their meaning is somewhat hidden and does not work out in the most obvious way. The Milky Way, the nodal axis, the solstitial axis of Cancer/Capricorn and the antiscia are all images of the dualistic nature of the snake, of going in and going out, and thus can be understood at a deeper level by the mythology of the snake.

Via Combusta – not a path of stars!
In traditional astrology the somewhat mysterious Via Combusta is a zone of 30 degrees from 15° Libra to 15° Scorpio where the Moon, and only the Moon, is very weak and unstable. Every horary astrologer will confirm this traditional idea as in many charts of questions asked in periods of emotionally difficult times, the Moon will be found in exactly this zone.

Also the secondary progressed Moon moving through this zone is often an indicator of a period of extra emotional tensions, especially at the moment of entering its fall in Scorpio.

It is a bit unclear why this is so and it is often said that the reputation of the Via Combusta can be explained by the malefic fixed stars once found in this part of the zodiac. This however seems somewhat illogical as these malefic stars have now precessed out of this zone and yet the Via Combusta still works in the way it always did.

A more sensible explanation of the Via Combusta is that 15° Libra to 15° Scorpio is opposite to the place where the Sun has its exaltation, namely the nineteenth degree of Aries. It is here that the power of the cardinal fire sign Aries erupts in its full glory. That means that the zone in opposition will be very much harmed, effectively under heavy fire from the Sun. It is only the Moon that is affected when it is in the Via Combusta because it is like a zodiacal-symbolic Full Moon – and a Full Moon is always a weak moment for the Moon as it is totally dependent on the Sun for its light. So the Via Combusta is explained by the structure of the zodiac itself, and hasn't got much to do with fixed stars at all.

This is also underlined by the length of the Via Combusta, which is exactly 30 degrees like a sign. If the fixed stars were really the explanation for the reputation of this zone, it would not have been exactly 30 degrees, and its length would have been determined by the precise star positions. So again it is made clear that this is something zodiacal, not constellational. The Via Combusta is an expression of the fact that all lunar processes have their phases of extreme instability; we could also think of the spring tide or the menstruation cycle. What it mirrors is that the rank of the Moon as the second and lesser luminary, is dependent on the Sun, the symbol of divine presence in the cosmos. The Moon also represents terrestrial instability and changeability in general, whereas the greater luminary, the Sun, is independent, never changes its form and always remains what it is.

On yet another symbolic level of twelvefoldness, there is always a twelfth part of the whole that causes trouble, and this could be called the Judas principle. Judas also represented the unstable earthly weakness opposing the solar light of the Messiah and that is why Judas was paid out in silver coins – silver being the metal of the Moon. In the structure of the zodiac you can see this illustrated in the fall of the Moon in

Scorpio, the fixed Water sign where the desire nature reaches its deepest intensity, and therefore the Moon is in a bad condition here. In this part of the zodiac it cannot fulfill its essential function of purely mirroring the solar light because it is controlled by the intense desires of Scorpio. For clarity: the Scriptures make clear that Judas is a necessary part of the divine plan, so there is nothing intrinsically bad about him in this sense. If we have a creation, we will have earthly weakness; it is inherent in creation, which is essentially a separation from God.

The precession and the Age of Aquarius
As mentioned before, the fixed stars move very slowly, and this movement is known as the precession. In understanding the precession – essentially the movement of the fixed stars through the signs – the vernal equinox point is all-important. This point is the exact position of the Sun when it crosses the celestial equator heading north at the start of spring in the northern hemisphere, beginning the months of greater light and heat across the 'top' part of the globe. It is called the equinox because at the moment that the Sun is overhead at the equator night and day have the same duration; *equi* is Latin for equal and *nox* means night. There is another equinox moment six months later in the year, at the start of autumn, when the Sun again crosses the celestial equator, but now on its way 'down', heading south, beginning winter months for the northern hemisphere and summer months for the southern hemisphere. The vernal (spring) equinox point can be defined with precision astronomically. It is also by definition a starting-point, as it determines the position of 0° Aries, the commencement of the tropical zodiac used in western astrology.

This means that the zodiac with its twelve signs will always start here. This will never change – it is a metaphysical necessity, also based on numerological symbolism to divide the zodiac band by twelve. The zodiac contains twelve signs because in this way all the possibilities of the cosmos can be described; it is four multiplied by three. The number 4 corresponds to the more material level of the elements, it is an expression of tension, because it is two times two and the number 2 means separation, opposition and contrarity. Furthermore, there are three crosses or modalities describing how the elements work out. The number 3 is the number of the spirit, it reconnects the two poles that resulted from the first separation. So in the zodiac we see all possibilities, symbolised by 3 multiplied by 4, of the interpenetration of matter and spirit. It will be clear that any thirteenth zodiac sign, as for example Ophiuchus the Snake-bearer which is sometimes mentioned, is an impossibility because of this basic symbolism. There have to be twelve signs, regardless of the way you might wish to join up the dots to form the star constellations above us.

The three modes or crosses indicate the way the elements manifest on earth: the cardinal mode is the first impulse, the fixed mode is an exploration of all the possibilities in a situation, and the mutable mode points to closing off and going to the next phase, therefore representing the duality of the mutable signs. A similar symbolism of the number 3 can be seen on a different level in the trinity of the Father, the Son and the Holy Spirit in Christian theology. It will be clear from this extensive description that the zodiac is a metaphysical concept, a cosmic blueprint for the whole material-spiritual cosmos. The tropical zodiac is a 12-fold energy girdle that does not precisely correspond to the star groups of the same names and cannot be seen in the sky, and this is because of precession. The gradual movement of the Earth's globe on its axis means that our planet points to a slightly different part of the sky each year. From our point of view the equinox point slips backwards against the position of the stars taking thousands of years to complete the circuit and encompass the energy of each of the zodiac signs in a so -called 'Age'. More on this below.

The implication of this is that the stars you can see are not the signs. What is visible belongs to a lower more material level in the astrological scheme of the cosmos. The signs of the zodiac can be found above the cosmic sphere containing the visible constellations of the stars. The spheres of the planets are found below the level of the visible constellations, in other words between earth and the heavens. This also demonstrates what the function of the planets involves; they are messengers bringing the blueprint potencies of the signs to earth. They are the dynamic structuring forces of the world which by the way do contain the same elemental energy as the signs, only in another more dynamic form. The more essential dignity a planet has, the better it can fulfill this messenger function.

So in the traditional cosmology every sphere will always move within a vaster sphere. The planets move around within the highest sphere of the zodiacal signs as do the stars contained within it. Astrologically the zodiac and the vernal equinox point at 0° Aries do not move at all, they will stay fixed for ever. But from our earthly point of view the stars and constellations move just like the planets through the signs of the zodiac, only much slower, at a pace of 1 degree in 71.6 years. They go around the whole circle in 25.920 years and this is known as a Platonic year. This movement is the precession seen in a cosmological perspective; it is the movement of the lower sphere of the fixed stars and constellations **through** the higher sphere of the twelve signs.

From a more material perspective, the precession is a result of the wobbling of the earth on its oblique axis, called 'nutation'. The visible result of the nutation is indeed the movement of the vernal equinox point seen against the background of the fixed stars. This movement is only apparent because you have to measure a movement against a background. So if you measure the equinox point against the sky year after year you will see it has gradually moved from star to star. But this is only a movement over the stars or constellations, it cannot move through the signs as the equinox is the starting point of the zodiac by definition. There is a lot of confusion about this which has led to the idea of the Age of Aquarius and other Ages characterized by signs. This is based on the confusion between the signs and constellations which should be distinguished clearly, because they are really very different things.

The vagueness of the Age of Aquarius
The vernal equinox point is found on the straight line, which is the zodiac, and it has precessed up to the supposed, but imaginary, boundary between the constellations of Pisces and Aquarius – not between the signs Pisces and Aquarius of course! Please note that the precessional movement is reversed, the vernal equinox does not move from Aquarius to Pisces like the planets and stars but in a retrograde motion through the zodiac.

The insurmountable problem however is that the boundary of the constellational 'cusp' – is totally artificial and not grounded in any principle; it has no deeper astrological meaning at all. It is like the

18   Fixed Stars in the Chart

demarcation of the border between Libya and Algeria, it was drawn somewhere on a map by the authorities because there had to be a border somewhere. So no one can say with any accuracy when the Age of Pisces will be left behind and the Age of Aquarius will start. Has it started already or will it have to wait for another 700 years? This makes the whole idea of the Ages somewhat questionable.

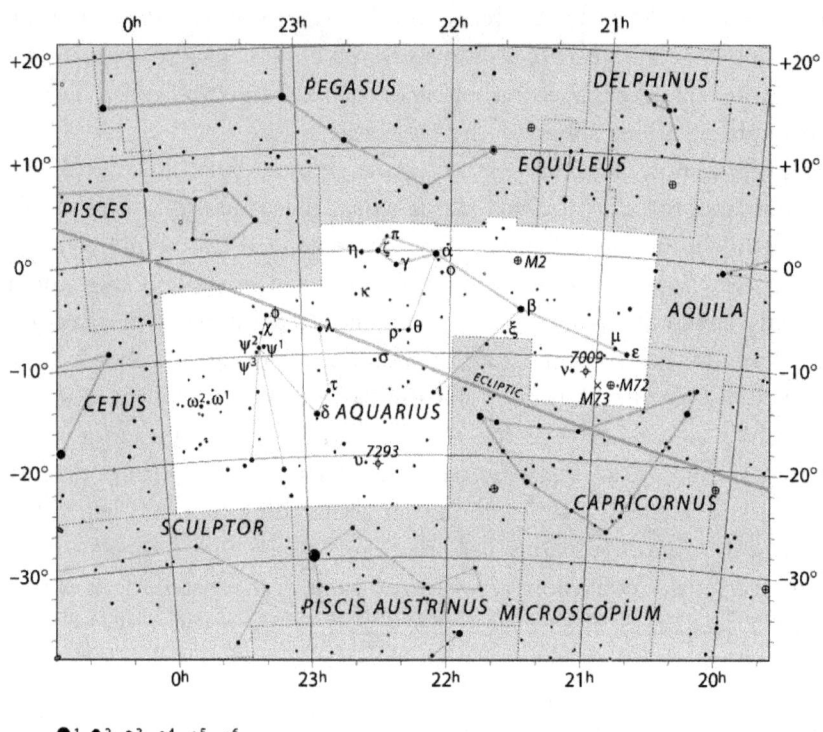

Precession of the Equinoxes

Because the vernal equinox point is seen moving against the background of the stars, the idea of a (New) Age of Aquarius was launched by Theosophy and later also taken over by modern astrologers following Carl Gustav Jung, who wrote a book about it (*Aion*). The problem is that nobody knows where Pisces ends and Aquarius starts (see picture above). The whole idea is a bit illogical and in fact astrologically untenable, as it is based on a confusion of the levels of the twelve signs and the twelve zodiacal constellations in diverse ways. The constellation of Aquarius is something quite different from the sign Aquarius, although the sign functioned as a kind of archetype from which the constellation arose. The fundamental point is that a sign is an energy zone of exactly 30 degrees with sharply defined boundaries; a visible constellation of stars does not have such boundaries and this leads to many inconsistencies. The whole general idea of 12 Ages connected to the signs is to a certain degree obvious, and it is also found in authentic traditional texts but in a very different way.

Another insurmountable problem is the duration of the Ages if you take the precession of the vernal equinox point through the constellations as your starting-point. The constellation of Aries is much shorter than the constellation of Pisces for example. The Piscean Age would have to be about four times longer than the Arien Age if you follow the logic of the system. This is at least very strange if not a decisive argument against the whole idea of the Ages. If we have 12 Ages of very different durations, in what sense could we speak about Ages as periods connected with signs? It is certainly not completely absurd but there are too many inconsistencies in the idea as it is usually presented.

Also the clear and fundamental changes in our times do not require a dawning of the Age of Aquarius to be explained effectively. The entry of the Great Conjunctions of Saturn and Jupiter (GCs) into the Air triplicity is the astrological indicator of a major shift of power in the world and of the massive Air processes like digitalisation, globalisation and mass migration. The GCs will stay in one element for about 220 years and the entry into a new element always brings profound political, economic and cultural change. So we don't need an Aquarian Age to explain this and even if we accept the idea, could a time in which everything becomes flexible and unstable point to an entry into a fixed sign?

A very important precessional movement connected to the developments in our times is the entry of the last of the four Watchers into a mutable sign. The four Watchers are the stars *Aldebaran* (spring – start), *Antares* (autumn – end), *Regulus* (summer – summit), *Fomalhout* (winter – rest), and their precessional entry into a new sign indicates changes on a vast scale. These four stars constitute a kind of cosmic cross, as they are so clearly connected to the starting-points of the seasons. When the

Aldebaran – Antares axis moved into Gemini/Sagittarius we saw the first stirrings of the Renaissance; *Fomalhout* into Pisces brought the Enlightenment, and at the moment we have the last Watcher *Regulus* which has moved over into Virgo.

So all the fixity has disappeared now and we have entered the third phase of total mutability. The entry of *Regulus* into Virgo is certainly also an indicator of the great changes taking place in the world. It is to be expected that the whole process of Renaissance – Enlightenment will be completed and in a way repeated. Of the four Watchers, only *Fomalhout*, the Mouth of the Southern Fish, is not a royal star associated with worldly success. *Fomalhout* is the winter star of the birth of Christ, or Ichtos the Fish, and as it is clearly stated, His Kingdom is not of this world.

3
The Myths of the Constellations and their Stars

Here are the guidelines for the correct use of the list of mythical stories per constellation in this chapter.

1. Look up in the list of the fixed stars per sign in Chapter 4 which stars are in conjunction with a natal planet on a chart you are delineating (or less importantly if they are in conjunction with a cusp or an Arabian part). Start with the luminaries (Sun and Moon), the angles (Ascendant and MC) and Lord 1. Note down the stars' planetary natures, their magnitudes, and of course the constellation they belong to.
2. Look up the constellation that the star is part of in the list of myths and constellations that follow.
3. Delineate the mythical theme in combination with the planet (or cusp or part) on it.
4. Look at the star's planetary energy and take into account the dignities of these planets in the chart. The more dignity, the more positive the star tends to work out.
5. Also look at the exact place of the star in the constellation, a foot is not quite the same as an eye, a heart or a horn.
6. Only then, and not before this, you can look up the star in the list of keywords in Appendix A to check what these keywords have to add to your interpretation.
7. As a last point look up in Chapter 5 which lunar mansion or 'star house' the Moon is placed in. This can be seen as the individual core myth.

ANDROMEDA

When Perseus was on his way home after decapitating Medusa, he saw on the coasts of Libya (Africa is a symbol of being bound to matter) a young girl (symbol of the soul) chained to a rock in the sea. This was the princess Andromeda who was punished by the sea-god Poseidon (the sea is the symbol of untamed, wild desire) because her mother Cassiopeia had boasted her daughter was more beautiful than the Nereids, the servants of Poseidon. Andromeda was to become the bride of the sea and a horrible monster that had first ravaged her father's kingdom was on its way to devour her. Perseus produces Medusa's head (conquered desire) which he carries with him in a bag and petrifies the monster with it, frees Andromeda and marries her. So the quest to liberate the soul from material bonds is fearlessly continued.

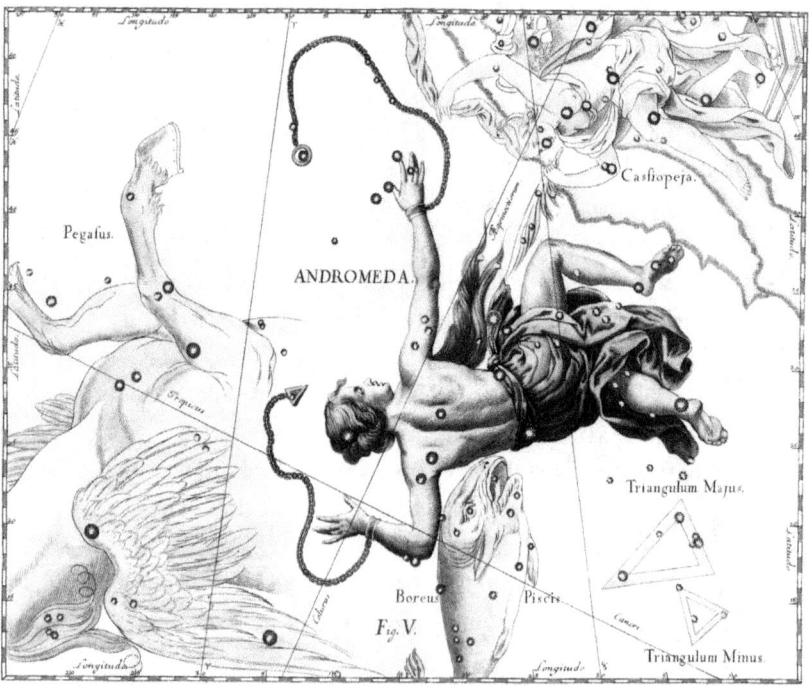

Alpheratz is the most important star in Andromeda as it marks her head, and has a positive Venus/Jupiter nature. Also *Almach* is a pleasant Venus star in the left foot, which is the contact point with the concreteness of the earth. *Almach* gives artistic talents, it is the soul that sings and creates beauty because it has been liberated, and the star *Mirach* has a similar meaning. *Vertex* however is the Andromeda nebula and as always a nebula has a darker meaning. In this case it blinds, and allows the soul to become the victim of the sea monster. Andromeda is strongly connected to the arts; stars in Andromeda/Sea Monster are also often found in charts of naval disasters.

Theme: protection of something of value in a difficult situation, confrontation with trouble caused by over-confidence; the possibility to connect by purity with higher worlds and show the beauty of these dimensions in artistic creations. The essential battle is to liberate the soul from material bonds. The aesthetic and the arts are a central theme in Andromeda, the protection and preservation of beauty and truth in a difficult and hostile environment. She is the ultimate 'damsel in distress'.

AQUARIUS

This is said to be the most human sign, the Cup-bearer pouring out sweet water. It is the only zodiacal constellation in which we find sweet water. This indicates the meaning of the myth, the purified sweet water can be drunk and is not the wild salt water of desire. This purification theme associates Aquarius with Ganymede, the most beautiful – that is the purest – of mortals, who was carried to Olympus by an eagle to serve the wine at the feast of the gods. So in this way sweet water (purified desire) is transformed into the pure wine of the spirit, a theme echoed in the Bible in the story of the wedding at Cana. It is all about purifying the desire water by distilling it until the water is pure and ready to be poured out as healthy sweet water. The tamed desires are turned into wine.

This is a precarious process and the right and left shoulders of the Cup-bearer, *Sadalmelek* and *Sadalsuud*, are rather negative in their effects. The whole purification process is in full action and may still go wrong. Only *Skat* on the right leg has the positive effect to be expected from a constellation representing the most beautiful among mortals, as the right leg (positive realisation) stands in the stream of sweet water that is poured out. This constellation is associated very much with secrets in a positive or negative sense, with esoteric/occult matters; the jar filled with valuable sweet water and the process of making it

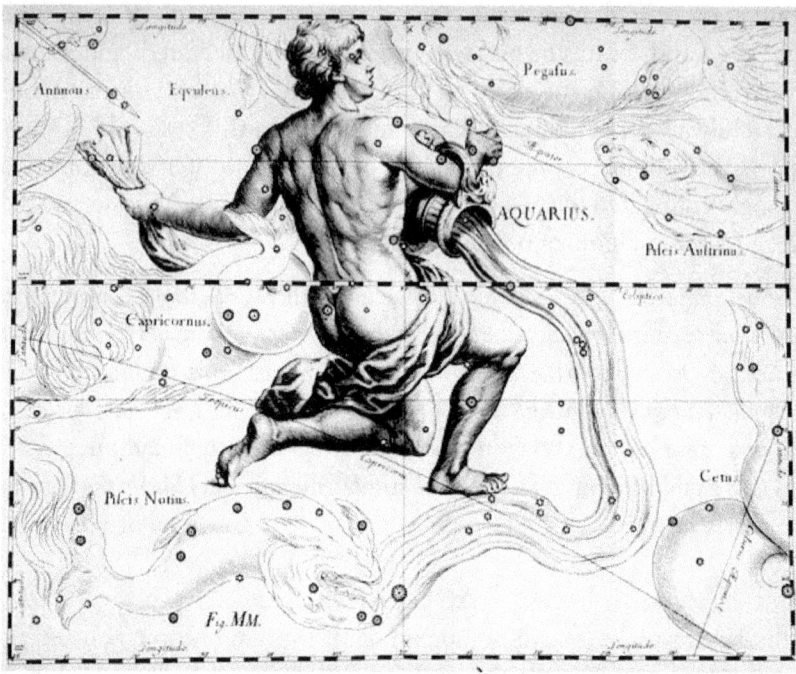

have to be protected from the impure environment. The sweet water poured by the Cup-bearer streams into the Mouth of the Southern Fish or *Fomalhout*, representing the birth of Christ, so the taming of the water is the preparation for spiritual birth.

The symbol of the zodiacal sign of Aquarius clearly illustrates this theme. We have two waves of zigzag lines, repeating the twofold glyph of Libra, also an Air sign and associated with the same theme of human and divine dimensions. In Aquarius, a fixed sign, the process of purification is up and running, with the zigzag lines pointing to activity driven by the heat of the Sun. Aquarius can be seen as a part of the traditional water cycle, the raw water evaporates and comes down as purified sweet water fertilizing the earth. Purification is painful and requires sacrifice and therefore Saturn rules the sign of Aquarius. The Sun that drives the process from the outside is not at home here, so is in detriment in Aquarius.

Theme: painful purification into a condition of real humanity as a preparation for spiritual birth, hidden things, the occult.

ARGONAUTS' SHIP – ARGO NAVIS

The ship of Jason and the Argonauts is the first to navigate the oceans, and savage Poseidon was not exactly amused when he suddenly saw the ship's shadow above him, defying his dark domain of desire. The Argonauts are on their way to capture the Golden Fleece and this constellation describes the first phase of this quest in which you distance yourself from the desire nature. The aim of Jason's quest, the Golden Fleece, is the skin of the Ram sacrificed by Phryxis and hung on a tree; it is the solar animal representing the divine energy realised on earth. To capture the Golden Fleece, Jason, among other things, has to control a plough pulled by fire-breathing bulls (a symbol of matter) and to outwit a dragon (symbol of duality). The Ram as a symbol of the spirit can clearly be associated with the Lamb, also sacrificed on a tree.

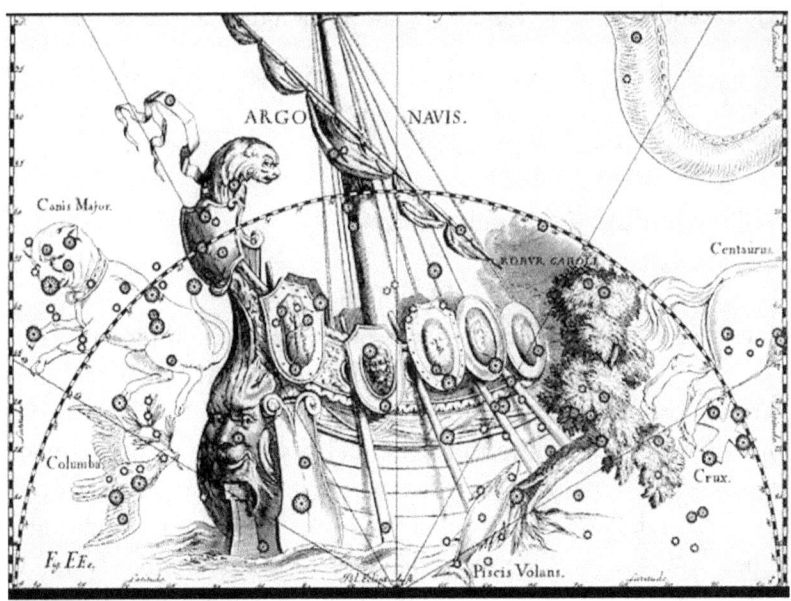

The very bright elite star of the first magnitude *Canopus* in this constellation stands for worldly wisdom which is sufficient for only a part of the quest. *Canopus* is the name of Menelaus' capable helmsman who led home the Greek fleet after the Trojan war, and was killed by a snake in Egypt. When the going gets tough, you need a bit more than worldly smartness in order to survive. The worldly wisdom of this capable helmsman could not save him from the snake in the desert, so this star pushes us further towards real knowledge, which may connect us to the spirit. A very clear example of the effect of *Canopus* is the German general Erwin Rommel who had Canopus on an angle in his chart, and was known as the cunning 'desert fox'. But in the end he was beaten along with his Africa Corps in the North African deserts in World War Two. Later he was forced by the Nazis to commit suicide, which he did with all possible dignity. This seems to repeat the whole mythical theme in another way.

The star *Markeb* (29° Virgo) successfully sails over the waters of desire and therefore gives knowledge, travels and educational work. *Foramen* (22° Libra) is a nebula and so has malefic effect; it is connected with handicaps and blindness and of losing your way during the quest. The modern subdivisions of this constellation should of course be ignored.

Theme: development of higher knowledge by keeping yourself aloof from desire, worldly wisdom is insufficient, also literally connected to navigation, education, knowledge and travelling.

ASSES – ASELLI – see under CANCER

BOÖTES

Boötes is a herdsman and the guardian of the bear. According to the myth he changed into a bear to pursue his mother into the temple of Jupiter, where the priests threatened to kill him for unlawful trespass. The bear is an old symbol of the warrior caste and Boötes mirrors the theme of the warrior's action unconnected to higher guidance and goals. It refers more to the rebellion of warriors against priestly authority. Traditionally the bear and the boar are often juxtaposed, the boar representing the priestly caste of the druids. The image of King Arthur, who accepted Merlin's guidance, shows the correct relationship between spiritual and temporal authorities. On a different level this constellation symbolises the over-appreciation of concrete action, shown by the many weapons Boötes always carries. One of the stars in Boötes is aptly called *Princeps*, Latin for 'prince'; the domain of corrective action and violence was always the privilege of royal, temporal power. Basically Bear and Boar mirror the well known antithesis of action and contemplation.

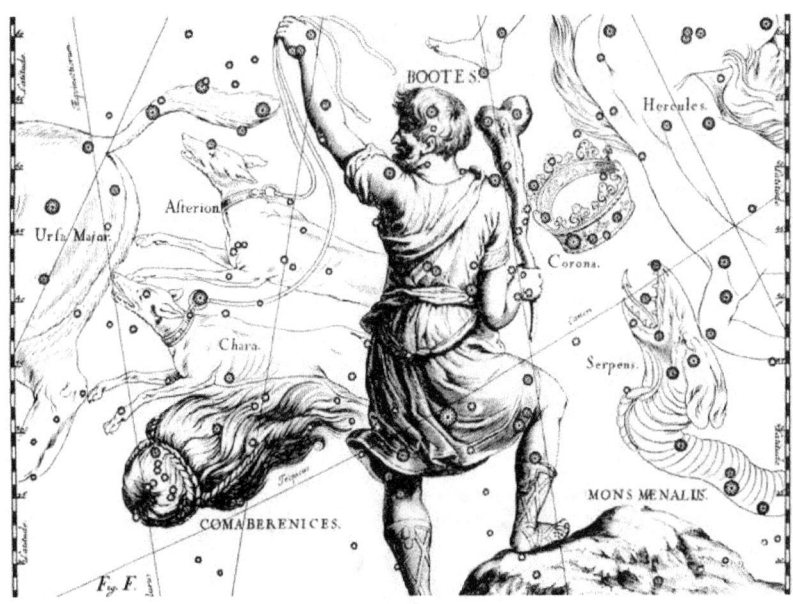

Arcturus is the very bright Guardian of the Bear, it has a warlike Mars/Jupiter nature and gives success and effective vigorous action. However, it is very close to royal *Spica*, and to decide which star of the two is activated by a planet in a particular chart, you can use the method given in Chapter 2.

The star *Princeps* on the shaft of Boötes' spear, and especially *Seginus* on his left shoulder, are much less positive than the main star *Arcturus*; success will be accompanied by many problems. *Seginus* is a star of losses and bad endings, the problem being exactly this rebellious unguided action.

Theme: concrete action should be guided and moderated, impulsive actions lead to problems, literally connected to agriculture and hunting, over-appreciation of concrete actions, crusading and the misleading idea that a treatment of symptoms constitutes a real solution.

BULL – TAURUS

This is Zeus who in the shape of a bull abducts the young girl Europa, an image of the soul, from Asia to her place of origin in Crete. It shows that the soul should return to its origin through matter without getting stuck in it, and symbolises the necessity of experiencing the material world, thus being enabled to develop further.

The big star in Taurus is royal *Aldebaran*, one of the four Watchers, the star of spring and of new beginnings. It is the left eye of the Bull, fixed on earth and life in matter; the right eye looks the other way towards the divine. It is a powerful star of success, and placed on its own in an influential position in the chart *Aldebaran* can make careers. Nevertheless, it is also a suitable starting-point for a more spiritual quest, reaching through matter to the land of the soul, the spiritual origin of humankind symbolised by Crete. *Aldebaran* is an intensely red star, which points to its purely martial nature, its effective material action and the spring energy of growth and expansion. It is not a star of much harmony. The danger of all the material success it provides, is that it stops there and does not go on. Money and success are pleasant but there are more things between heaven and earth, and the Taurus myth requires you to go on. If this is not done it may have nasty effects in the life. The bull is a dangerous and aggressive animal, a rough piece of material steaming storm-power. Activation of *Aldebaran* in progression sometimes leads to violence, and people with a prominent *Aldebaran* may be troublemakers, as there is a lot of Mars in this star.

El Nath and *Al Hecka* are the North and the South Horn of the Bull respectively and as always the South Horn, strongly associated with accidents, is the meanest of the two. Although neither of them is really pleasant, as they are after all the Bull's weapons. Stars in the Bull will work in a more positive way if you can leave behind the attachment to wealth and success and go looking for your own personal symbolic Crete. If you stay completely attached to your success, it will bring endless struggle as bulls are fierce animals.

Another ritual image of the Bull myth is the bull-fight. The toreador illustrates how to handle matter; he plays with it, dances with it and finally kills the beast, which is returning to Crete, the land of the soul. Simply standing in the Bull's way would not work; you cannot deny its existence or it will crush you. But you can dance with it without getting attached, exhaust it and become its master. The Bull has to be killed after the fight, just as we have to leave strong attachments to our success behind. It is this relationship with matter that is the central theme of Taurus, also shown by the lunar horn in the glyph of the sign. It is a second phase of the first fire horns of Aries, the first initial (Aries) impulse of manifestation has now materialised. The Moon is the fundamental symbol of earth as opposed to heaven and is very appropriately exalted in earthly Taurus.

The star groups Pleiades and the related Hyades are found in the Taurus constellation and their themes are also much connected to a confrontation with brutal, material reality.

Theme: great material success, necessary experience of the physical side of life but also leaving behind the attachment to it, sheer material force, violence, sensuality, a new successful start.

CANCER

When Hercules is fighting the Hydra, he is bitten by Cancer the crab on his heel, symbolically indicating a vulnerable blind spot. Cancer represents desire in man, the basic impulse without which no action or life would be possible. The fact that Hercules kills the crab by crushing it shows that right action is the solution, desire is channeled into correct deeds. Cancer's remains after having been crushed are represented by the many stars in the *Praesepe* cluster, which is part of the whole Cancer myth.

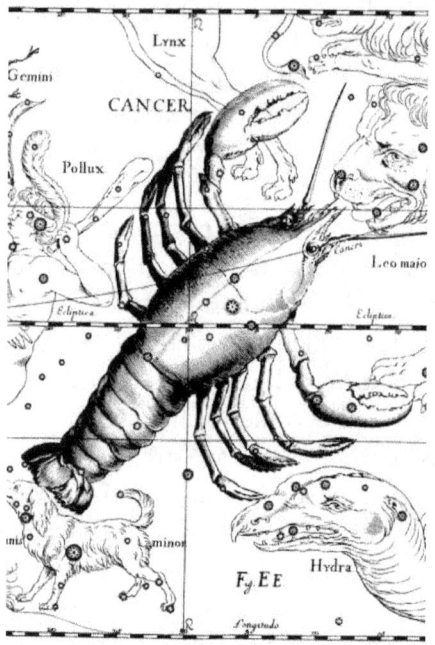

Acubens is the main star in Cancer. It is the Southern Claw of the Crab which bit Hercules, therefore its meaning is negative; it is trying to distract him from his essential battle with the Hydra, the small desires tending to disturb the important work. In ancient times Cancer was also known as the Octopus, the malefic monster pulling you into the wild seas of desire. It was associated with the North Node too. The symbolism of the Octopus and the Crab are similar in that they are both animals living in the sea water without choosing their own direction, they just go with the flow.

The Asses

A typical but important part of Cancer are the *Aselli*, the Northern and Southern Asses, and within their midst the Crib, supermalefic *Praesepe*. The Asses were ridden by the gods Vulcan and Bacchus in the battle of the gods against the Titans; the noise the asses made is said to have scared off the Titans. So subjugation of the animal nature brings victory over the Titanic forces which are inimical to life. The ass is an ancient symbol of satanic power and this is the reason Jesus rides on an ass when He enters Jerusalem; it shows that He has subjugated evil. Therefore the people lay palm leaves on the road, to represent the Tree of Life, the eternal unity and counter-image of the Tree of Knowledge. In the Tree of Life there is no snake, no duality.

The *Aselli* therefore also have the meaning of 'listening to the master'. In Christian symbolism we find them as the Ass and the Ox present in the stable (or better the cave as the symbol of the human heart). The divine light is born on earth as the Son of God that will master evil (ass) and matter (ox). Of course, this service may also have negative results in practice as it all depends on the master you are following. As usual the Southern Ass has a more malefic effect than the Northern Ass.

The most malefic part of Cancer is the Crib itself, known as the Beehive or the Manger. It is called by the Chinese 'the exhalation of piled-up corpses'. It is nothing but an empty manger, a trough to feed animals, and so has a very material symbolism. The king that is to be born is not found in it and this cannot be a good sign. You can see *Praesepe* as a second Algol – it is very malefic. It could be called the Heart of the Crab, but the Crab has no heart, nor will it resist the wild waves of desire, it will simply go with the flow. Because Hercules kills the Crab by crushing it, it also points to slaughtering and shattering. Together with *Algol*, *Praesepe* plays an important role in mundane astrology.

The Crib and the Asses from 7°–9° Leo constitute an integral thematic unity of gradations of disaster. It is not for nothing that they are so close together. *Praesepe* is free-moving boundless malice, the Asses represent malice controlled to a certain extent, as the gods ride on them. The Northern Ass is most firmly under control, and in the Southern Ass the dark forces are stronger and it threatens to escape its rider. This is symbolically emphasized by the fact that the Southern Ass is the she-ass and feminine lunar forces are always seen as more easily seduced by evil, as in the symbolic role of Eve. It is to be understood clearly that this is purely symbolism, and the feminine Moon is simply seen as the more earthly side of humankind, that is all.

The zodiacal sign of Cancer is the water element in its cardinal mode, the first fast-moving impulse. It says: 'yes I want this'. This in turn corresponds to the constellational symbolism above; the twelve signs are the inspirational backgrounds to the zodiacal constellations bearing the same names; it does not mean they are identical. Traditionally Cancer is the shell containing all the seeds and possibilities for the developments to come, and is therefore associated with the North Node, the gate through which we enter life, thirsty for experience. That Jupiter, the principle of expansion and fruitfulness, has its exaltation in Cancer is understandable seen from this perspective.

The central message of Cancer is to stay focused on the goal, the battle with the Hydra, and not be distracted by the bites of the crab in your heel, your vulnerable point. You must crush it by taking the right action. The Asses are an integral part of this as they illustrate, more or less, the subdued material forces and the idea of serving the master, hopefully the divine principle. The Crib is the darkest point, unleashing the boundless desire nature which may lead to bloodshed, chaos and fragmentation.

Theme: concentration on the main work, not allowing oneself to be distracted from the goal by the crab of small desires biting at your heel, taking the correct vigorous action, chaos, boundless satisfaction of desires with disastrous consequences.

CAPRICORN

The enigmatic goat with a fish tail or the Goat-Fish, is an image pointing to a kind of transition state or process. It is said to be connected to the story of the earth god Pan, half-goat, who suddenly came upon horrible Typhon (Death) and only escaped by jumping into the Nile, turning into a goat-fish. As a zodiacal sign Capricorn is connected with the winter solstice, a picture of starting a new cycle on another level. And this is what the myth also shows – Pan as a symbol of natural down-to-earth life escapes death by transforming himself into another form. Life continues on another level in a more spiritual form, as the fish is

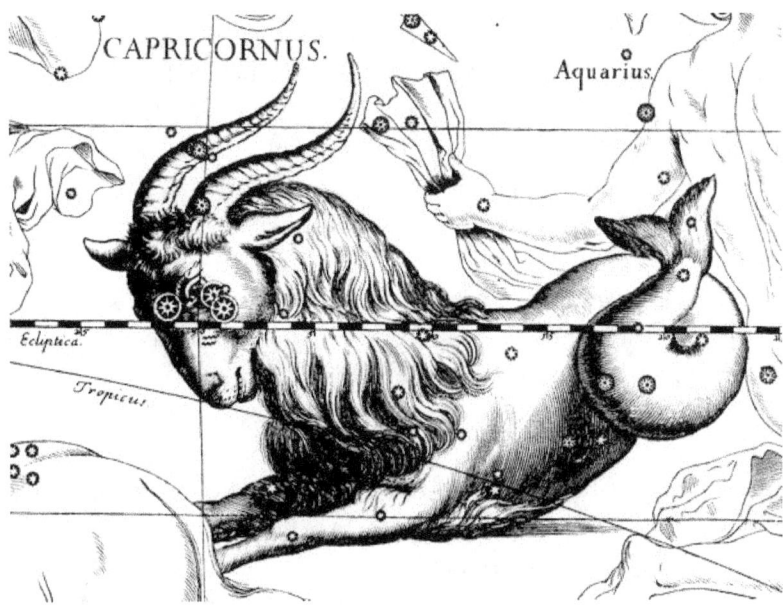

a symbol of higher consciousness – fishes never sleep and move freely in the seas of desire. Christ is also called Ichtus the Fish for the same reason; fishes have mastered the dangers of the wild waters.

Dabih and *Deneb Algedi* are the most powerful stars in Capricorn. They are of the third magnitude, with other stars in the constellation having even less light. This fits with the winter solstice symbolism and the idea of a seed moment for a new cycle. Nothing is moving yet but the change to another level has been made behind the scenes; it only seems that there is a stand-still. Some stars in Capricorn have remarkably positive effects: sharp intellect and preparedness to sacrifice, explained by the connection with the higher dimension to which Capricorn is the gate.

The Capricorn stars give little outward action as they are connected to the stand-still of winter and so they represent dying on some level to bear fruit on another level. In ancient times Capricorn was also called the Delphin, liberating you from material fetters. It is the counterpart to Cancer's pure lust for life, associated with the image of the dark Octopus. The Cancer-Octopus energy belongs to the demonic ambitious North Node; Capricorn-Delphin belongs to the painful limitations of the South Node with a liberating effect as it cuts you off from life.

As the name suggests there is a connection between the Delphin and the famous oracle of Delphi, shown by the contact made there with a higher dimension at the next level by Delphin-Capricorn, and this contact gives knowledge. In the zodiacal solstitial winter sign of Capricorn, dark and painful Saturn rules and Mars is exalted, pointing to the courage you need to go through the darkness.

Theme: liberation and birth on another higher level, endings and death, standstill, winter solstice, little outward action, flight from an enemy who threatens you, painful changes under pressure of imminent danger.

CENTAUR – PHOLUS

Centaurs are half-horse and half-human, an image of powerful instincts led by the conscious will, although there is always the danger that the instincts will get the upper hand. The constellation Centaur in the heavens represents Pholus, who like Chiron was a more civilized centaur in whom the human upper half dominates. We see him in many pictures piercing a wolf. Pholus was also the guardian of a wine cask he opened when Hercules visited him. The other non-civilized wild centaurs smelt the wine and came storming to Pholus' cave, upon which Hercules killed them all with the arrows he had dipped in the lethal venom of the Hydra. Pholus, fascinated by the power of the poison arrows, pulled one out of a dead centaur, wounded himself and died.

So there is a chance that the Hydra poison – the desire nature – will strike with dire consequences, if we are tempted by the mysterious deadly poison that attracted and fatally wounded Pholus. Contrary to immortal Chiron, mortal Pholus is not a gifted teacher of heroes but just very curious.

Even if their human nature is strong, as in Chiron and Pholus, the centaurs remain unsavoury and unpredictable creatures, with a very tense combination of knowledge and desire. The danger that the instincts will get the upper hand despite all the civilized parts is an important theme in both stories. Because the small point of a poisoned arrow turns out to be fatal, the myth of Pholus is connected to seemingly small actions having dangerous consequences. Pholus is simply curious and kills himself when he picks up the poisoned arrow to take a closer look at it.

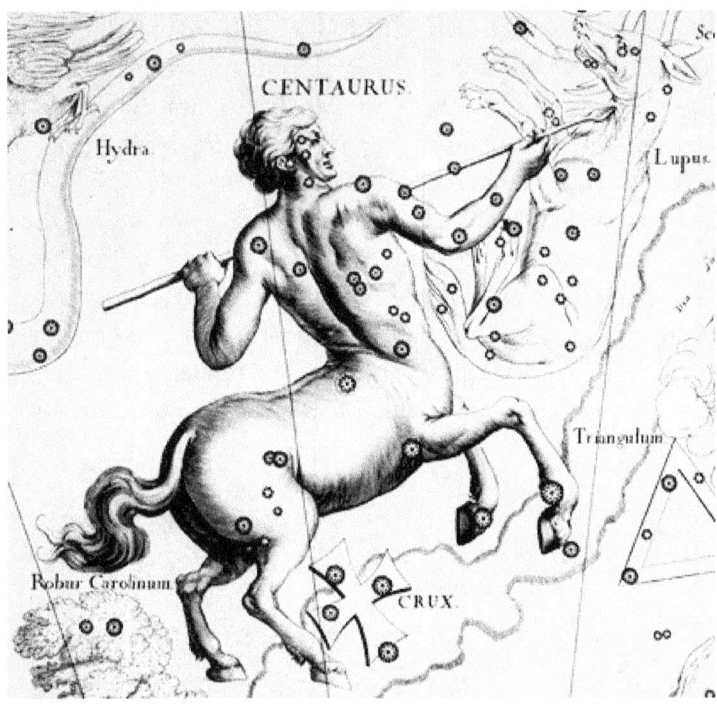

The Centaur star *Bungula* often indicates licentious behaviour; the instinctive animal part of the centaur is strong and *Bungula* is the left leg, and the left – *sinister* in Latin – is always seen as unfavourable. *Agenaon*, the more positive right leg, represents the better half of the Centaur; it has a Jupiter/Venus nature and it is said to bestow honour, refinement, morality and health. Both stars belong to the first magnitude elite and so can have powerful effects on the life.

Theme: resisting powerful instinct, small things which seem not be dangerous may have dire consequences, strong tension between desire and will, the desire nature may strike in an overpowering way, naive curiosity will lead to great problems: 'curiosity killed the cat'.

CHARIOTEER – AURIGA

This is Erichtonius, the son of the lame god Vulcan, pictured standing in a war chariot, with snakes as his feet. In his arms he carries a little she-goat, said to be Amalthea, Jupiter's wet-nurse. The image points both to correct action and speed, but with the possibility that this swift, correct action will be undermined because of the weakness of the snake feet. So it can represent being led astray by desire, and be associated with the image of 'feet of clay'. We see the smart charioteer making an instrument by which he can overcome the snake feet through swift action. The she-goat Amalthea points to the tenderness accompanying all the action; without this the charioteer will turn into a hard-luck pilot or a merciless activist.

The powerful first magnitude star *Capella* is the little she-goat, so this star suggests an element of tenderness. *Capella* is close to the heart of the charioteer. This is the star on the Ascendant of Formula 1 driver Nikki Lauda. Also Donald Trump's Sun conjuncting the North Node is on *Capella*. The other astrologically relevant star in the Charioteer constellation, *Menkalinan*, is placed on the Charioteer's shoulder and is much more malefic; it is pure swift action without tenderness.

Theme: speed and innovative action should be accompanied by tenderness and compassion, avoid fanaticism, often literally connected to transportation and traffic.

CUP (Crater) and CROW (Corvus)

This is the crow who forgot the divine task given to him by Apollo, the solar god, to fill a cup with water at a well. On his way to the well, the crow saw some nice ripe figs in a tree and decided the fruits were too attractive for him not to stop and eat them. As a result he returned to the Sun-god too late and lied to Apollo that the Hydra-snake had blocked his way to the well. The cup in this story is also Bacchus' cup and this points to the forgetfulness of our glorious divine origin, so the cup may be filled with poison, but is also the Grail. The question is, will we forget how it once was before we were born into the flesh or will we be able to keep that memory in mind? This is indicated by the Crow's quest which did not succeed because he saw those figs.

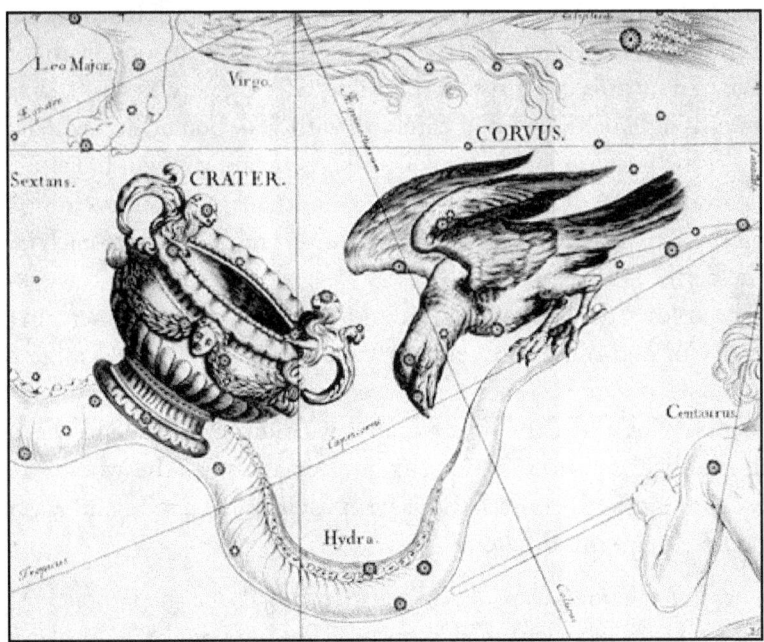

According to myth, the Grail Cup was made by angels from emeralds once set on the brow of Lucifer, the Angel of Dawn; he fell to become Satan through his disobedience to God. The exact place of these precious stones associates them with the third eye, the non-material eye that can see, without matter interfering, the original unity and so the truth. The filling of the Cup by the Crow is a clear parallel with the Grail Cup in which Joseph of Arimathea collected the sacrificial blood of Christ, bringing salvation and the return to the primordial unity of non-duality. The Grail is often pictured together with a lance. This is the lance of Longinus with which Christ's sides were pierced on the Cross. A lance is a symbol of the pole, or God as the supreme centre. Water and blood, spirit and psyche pour out of the wounds and are purified by the sacrifice and collected in the Grail Cup. The alchemical allusions are clear. Also the Cup represents feminine receptivity and can again be alchemically associated with the black earth – blackness pointing here at pureness, a complete readiness to receive.

The main star in the Crow, *Algorab*, is strongly connected to finding your way through the earthly dirt, towards the gold and beauty of heaven, but a crow that stops to eat figs will be punished by Apollo. *Labrum*, the main star in the Cup, is also associated with the cup that will not pass you by, and rates alongside *Terebellum* and *Al Pherg* as one of the stars of fate. The words of Christ in the Bible refer directly to this theme; if *Labrum* is activated, fate will catch up with you. Something which has been in the air for a long time will strike now and you will have to face the consequences. The Crow has to ignore the figs and pursue his quest to fill the cup, so the Cup and Crow are inseparably linked to each other in the myth.

The role of the desire snake is underlined by the placement in the skies of Cup and Crow right on the Hydra; the central theme is forgetting your mission because something more attractive appears. It will also be clear now why the Crow is associated with unreliability and the Cup with intelligence, success and religion. But as always the whole theme plays a role in both constellations with their stars *Labrum* and *Algorab*, only the emphasis is different.

Theme: foster the knowledge of man's divine origin, do not give up your mission because you see something more attractive, fateful events, lying, looking for divine beauty in the dirt of the earth.

DOG – GREATER AND LESSER – CANIS MAJOR and CANIS MINOR

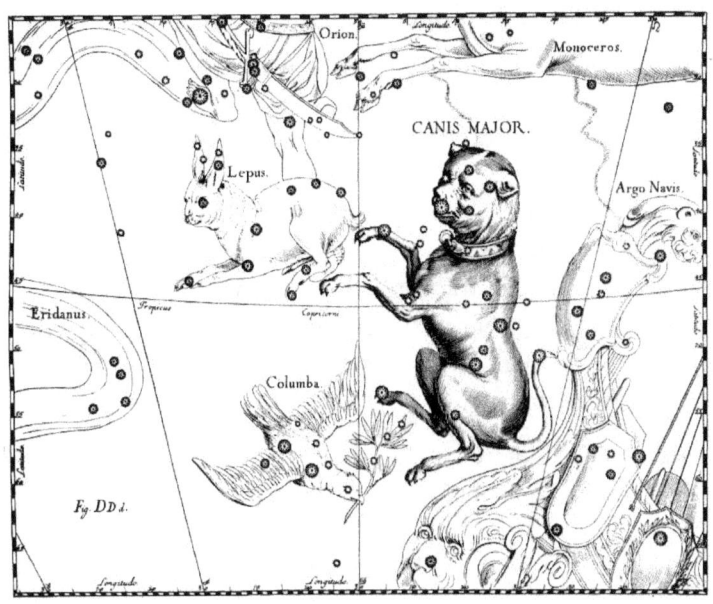

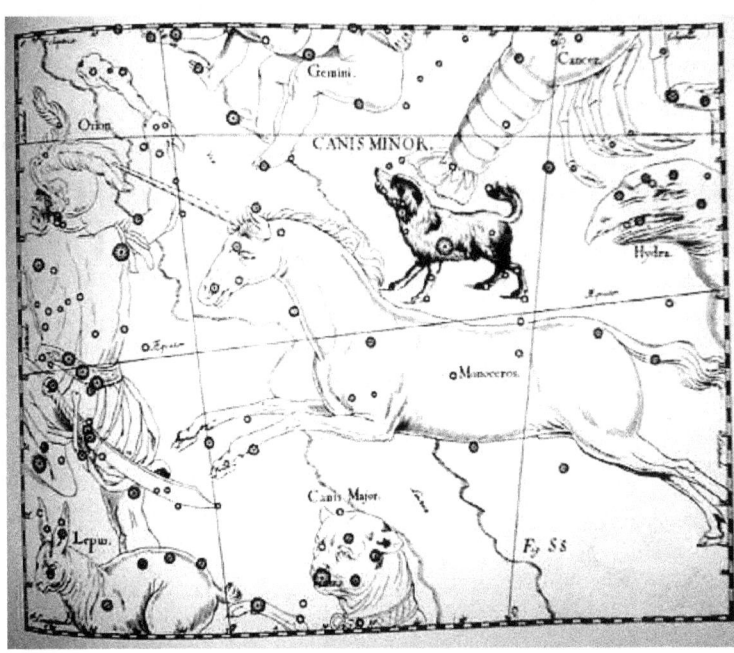

These are fierce and wild beasts who need clear external guidance and orientation. The Greater Dog is a heedless dangerous animal that makes a lot of noise and openly intimidates, attacks and bites everybody; the Lesser Dog is a nasty fierce little yapper that causes a lot of trouble, but it is more clever and dexterous than its big brother. *Sirius* in the Greater Dog's mouth can give great success because of its readiness for battle, but the fiery energy has to be led in the right direction. *Sirius* is the guardian of Europa, the soul. It is too stupid and aggressive to be in charge itself but it can be a very useful general or guardian. The same is true for *Procyon* the main star in the Lesser Dog. Both stars are very bright and will have a powerful effect in the life, giving much success. The Lesser Dog is often found in charts of people who do it their own way, defying the powers that be.

Theme: avoid heedless aggression, discipline combative spirit, accept guidance, the essential second-in-command, lots of success.

DOVE – COLUMBA

This is a lovely constellation but because it is so far from the ecliptic it does not have much power to act. Its only star of astrological importance is *Phact* with a pleasant Venus/Mercury nature. The Dove is not a traditional constellation as it was artificially constructed as late as 1679, but it is mentioned here only because the star *Phact* is part of it. It can be assumed that the Dove was a new constellation formed around *Phact*, whose effect was known traditionally, and therefore the meaning of the Dove and its main star coincide.

Theme: to consciously and actively express the lovely and the beautiful.

EAGLE – AQUILA

This is Jupiter, who in the shape of an eagle swoops down to take up Ganymede, the most beautiful among mortals, to the divine Olympian World. Ganymede has been working with all his powers on his purification and he receives grace from the gods. This constellation was called the Flying Grype, and vultures were always seen as holy birds. Although they put their heads into rotting meat they stay pure, the dirty earthliness does not stick to them. An eagle is able to look directly into the sun, the symbol of truth and unity. This is the real intellect, a direct connection with the source of truth.

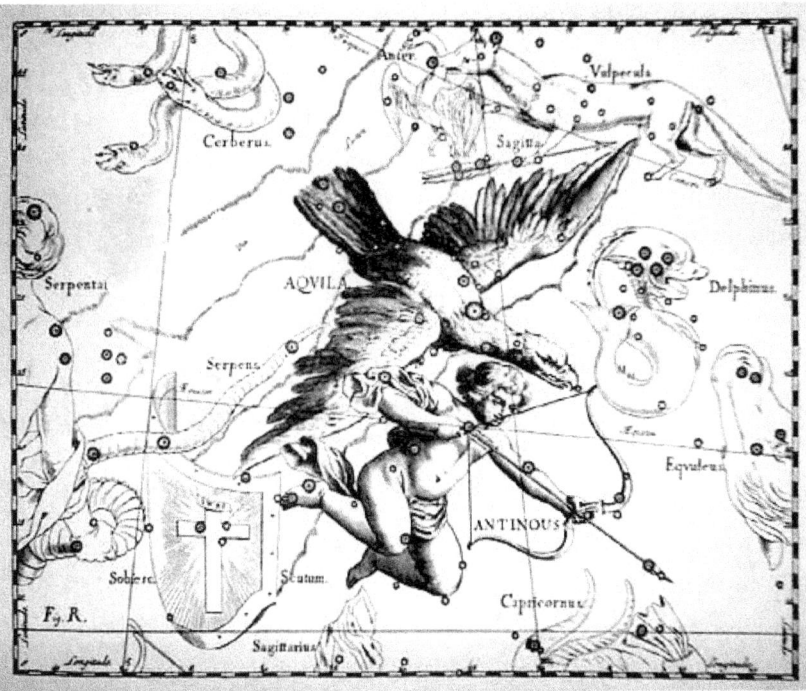

The main star is *Altair* in the neck of the Eagle (the essential point of purity of the vulture) and it gives a powerful aspiration, mostly spiritually. The danger is spiritual arrogance, looking down on the common people who have no idea of higher knowledge, with disdain. The Eagle is also the nasty Scorpion transformed and the symbol of St John the mystical

Evangelist (see further under Scorpio). A second star of importance in astrology in the constellation is *Deneb Okab*, the Eagle's Tail.

Theme: fruitful spiritual aspiration, strong fiery dedication, higher knowledge, purity, literally upward movements, danger of spiritual arrogance and disdain.

FISHES – PISCES

This constellation is associated with giving up what you love, otherwise no progress can be made. The image of the two fishes swimming in opposite directions, up and down, indicates that if the sacrifice is made, divine mercy, of which the fish is the symbol, will come down. It can also be connected to the biblical image of the two fishes and the five loaves of bread, feeding the multitude and representing the two luminaries and the five planets controlling everything that happens on earth. The connection between Sun (the upper vertical Fish) and Moon (the lower horizontal Fish), between solar-divine and lunar-earthy energies, is the central point here, clearly expressed by the enigmatic cord tying the two fishes together.

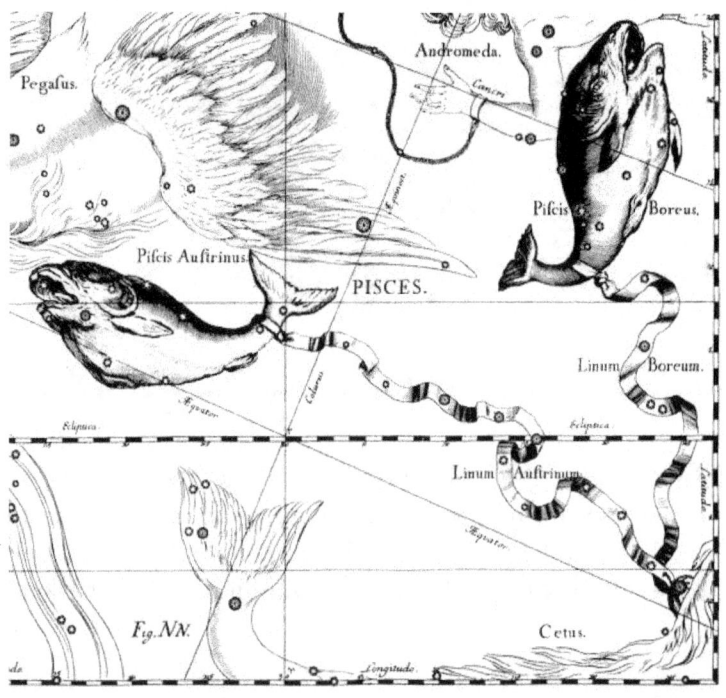

On a constellational level this gives again a picture of the nodal axis, the points where solar and lunar orbits are united, functioning as gates into and out of life. This is the reason *Al Pherg*, the only astrologically relevant star in Pisces, traditionally has a bad reputation as it works as a star of fate, associated with the Head of Typhon (Death) and is understandable in this perspective. The nodes always point to important fundamental changes in the life if they are activated by progression; they represent beginnings and endings.

Pisces is the last sign of the zodiac and this also points to a decisive, fateful moment. It is a last chance. If the sacrifice is made at this juncture things will go on, if not you will get stuck and things will end, as the fateful nature of Al Pherg shows. Venus is exalted in the sign of Pisces, indicating the disappearance of oppositions at the end of the cycle

Theme: sacrifice something you would really love to keep, fateful events, the last phase of a cycle, a last chance.

HYADES

The Hyades are a nebulous group of stars in the constellation of Taurus; they are the seven half-sisters of the Pleiades. The central theme of both groups is similar: disappointments and good intentions that go wrong. They were entrusted with the care of the infant wine-god Bacchus who grew up to be an irredeemable drunk, so the intentions have to be critically analysed – how realistic are they? Their father is Atlas, the famous Titan who carries the massive weight of the whole world on his shoulders, illustrating the same theme. The star *Prima Hyadum* – the first Hyad – is the main star in the group. As a part of Taurus they also represent the necessary experience of these disappointments in life in matter.

Theme: good intentions go wrong unexpectedly, disappointments.

HYDRA – WATER-SNAKE

This constellation is found in the skies right next to the Lion, and its central theme is similar. Leo is the raw lust for power while Hydra is the essential image of desire itself, a many-headed monster exhaling clouds of deadly poison. This shows the true nature of our attachment to matter; it reveals desire in its shocking nakedness. It is difficult to defeat

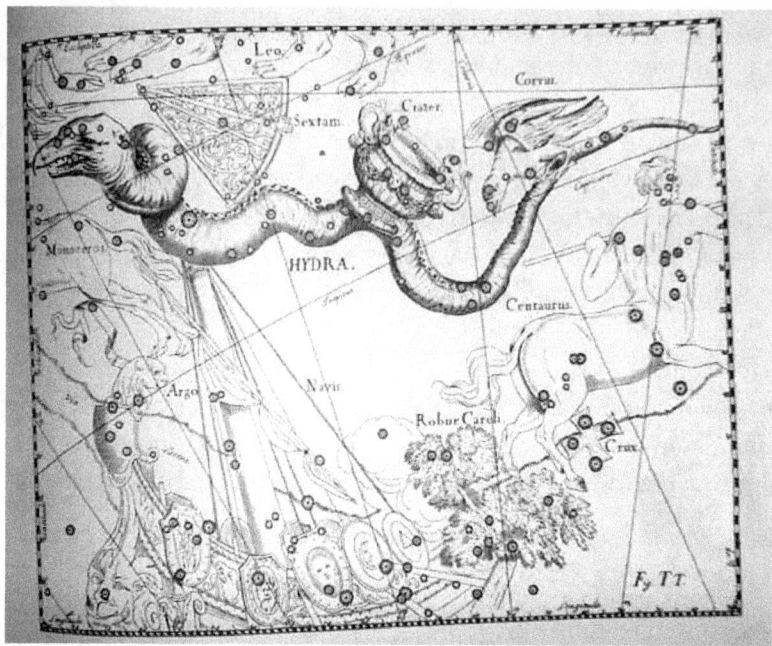

the Hydra beast, because it has many heads. If you succeed in cutting off one head, another one will soon grow to replace it. If one desire has been conquered another one will soon take its place. The Hydra is a sprout of the ill-fated union of Typhon (death) and Echidna (earth, half-woman/half-snake).

It is Hercules, man in his essential heroic role of the conqueror of desire, who defeats the monster. Cutting off its heads one by one does not work; the only way to stop the heads reappearing is to cleanse the wounds with fire (representing an internal spiritual battle). The last immortal head must be pulled off with bare hands and buried under a stone, as Hercules demonstrates. Some core of desire cannot be extinguished in man in his earthly condition, but it can be controlled by the heavy immovable weight of a stone (ethical norms like the Ten Commandments).

The star *Alphard* is the Hydra's heart, its essence, and the only star in the Hydra known to play a role in astrology. It understandably indicates lack of self-discipline and perverted morals, but it may lead to wisdom through experience, if the Hydra is defeated. Often there is a sharp insight into the psychology of desire and a good judgement of character at the same time, therefore the ability to manipulate others. We see this star popping up in many a politician's chart.

Theme: conscious radical sacrifice of strong yearnings, internal battle against desires, control by moral rules and choices, sharp insight into the psychology of desire and manipulation by this knowledge.

HUNTING DOGS – CANES VENATICI

A nebulous cloud near to Boötes indicates the dogs that he seems to be holding on a leash. This is not a traditional constellation and the reason it is mentioned here is that *Copula* in this nebula is a star of marriage and good for relationships ('copulation'). Apparently it gives a healthy blindness to the partner's less attractive sides. This theme does not seem to be connected to the myth of Boötes or the image of the Hunting Dogs. But *Copula* does have the effect mentioned. A star like this, not connected to a traditional constellation, is called 'amorphous'.

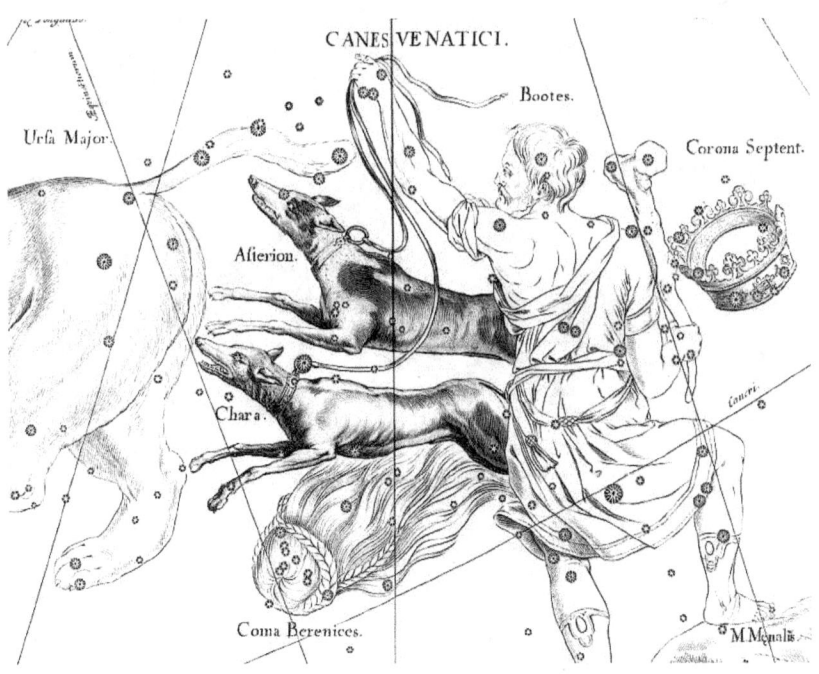

LEO

Leo is the Nemean Lion, again one of many fruits of the illicit union of Typhon and Echidna, the lethally dangerous opponents of the gods, who strive to extinguish the Olympic light of the spirit. The Lion is the fierce beast representing a merciless ambition and a fanatical lust for power, it wants to be the king, Number One, no matter what the costs will be. It is again Hercules, the hero, man as he is supposed to be, who kills the monster, strips off its skin and wears it on his shoulders. This is to indicate that he makes use of the ambitious power and decisiveness, it is not the other way around any more, the energy does not use him. It should be this way, otherwise it will lead to many, many difficulties as the Lion's raw ambition is blinding and will not allow for any guidance or temperance.

All the stars in the Lion, *Algenubi* in the mouth, *Adhafera* in the manes, *Al Jabha* on the head, *Regulus* as the heart, *Zosma* on the back and *Denebola* in the tail, have unpleasant effects, although things will become much better if the raw boundless ambition is consciously sacrificed and tempered, if you follow Hercules and kill the Lion to direct its power. *Regulus* is the Heart of the Lion, so its concentrated essence, and is the best known and most powerful royal star which leads to the throne. It gives lots of success but there is the danger of a fall from this high position through blind and fanatical ambition. *Regulus* means little king, it is also the name of a Roman general who too stubbornly and for too long pursued his battle with Carthage and was cruelly executed by his opponents. He ends his life chained under a scorching desert sun with eyes wide open in the merciless light, and so becomes the victim of what he wanted to be for others. It is a warning that planets on *Regulus* may give you a position of great power but if you fail to make the sacrifice of raw ambition there is a probability of some form of downfall.

A dramatic example is the influential Dutch journalist and film director Theo van Gogh who insisted on bluntly provoking his opponents, fundamentalist Muslims, and who was murdered by one of them. He had the ruler of his first house on *Regulus* and indeed his famous family name, which considerably helped him in his career, is not unconnected to this placement; he was the great-grandson of the painter's brother. Leo is the child of death (Typhon) and earth (Echidna) and it tries to escape this transience by heroically acquiring an immortal name ("I am the greatest, they will have to see this in the end"). So he can do, even in inhuman ways, what he deems necessary for this glory. This may also take on the form of a connection with a glorious past, with the authority of a tradition.

Denebola is the Tail of the Lion, and like all stars in Leo shares in the same theme, but here the specific warning is against provocation and impulsive action. *Zosma* is the Back of the Lion on which no one will ride, *Algenubi* the Mouth which will be heard, like it or not, and *Adhafera* and *Algieba* the Manes are very close to *Regulus* and are often not delineated separately.

Theme: sacrifice, blind destructive lust for power and ambition, it is not possible nor desirable to acquire an immortal name, it is not necessary to become Number One at all costs.

LYRE – LYRA

The Lyre is the counterpart of the Eagle and is also called the Falling Grype. Even an eagle has to return to earth after a high flight and this constellation brings back down to earth what it has seen above, therefore its connection is to art and education. The Lyre is the first musical instrument, made by Mercury, with three strings tightened on a square tortoise shield. This is an image of the cosmos, three and four as matter and spirit are also at the root of astrology. So on the Lyre the complete music of the cosmos is played, but as this is the eagle coming down to earth, it is less spiritually aspiring than *Altair* in the Flying Grype. The positive keywords often given for its main star *Vega* have to be put into perspective: in some mundane contexts, a vulture coming down can be quite sinister, but in general *Vega* points to artistic abilities.

Theme: to give a picture of the higher divine worlds on earth through art and education.

NORTHERN CROWN – CORONA BOREALIS

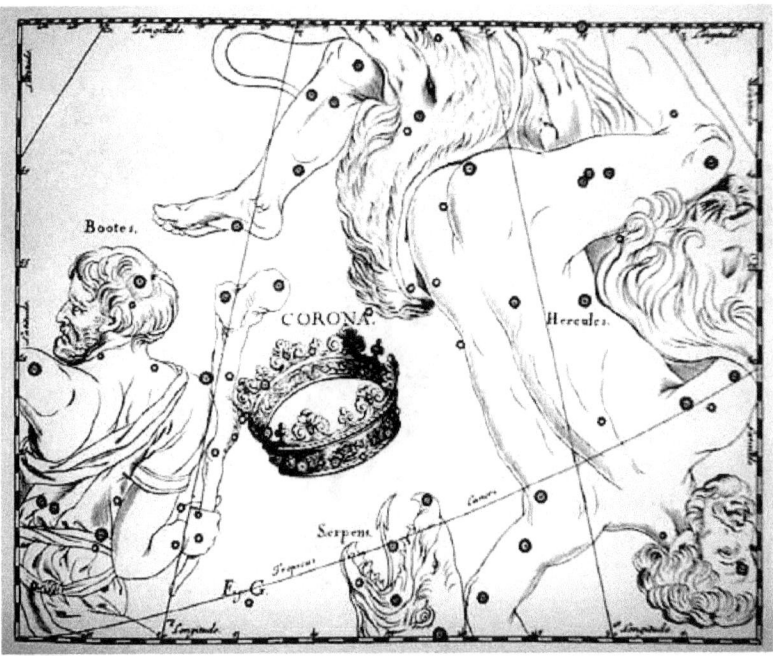

This is Venus' wedding present, a flower garland to Ariadne who, forsaken by Theseus, marries Dionysus. Therefore this constellation is associated with artistic abilities and beauty.

The crown points to success, and this is the meaning of its only astrologically relevant star *Alphecca*.

Theme: expression of beauty.

ORION – THE HUNTER

Orion is easy to find in the skies, being much bigger than most constellations. This indicates its important meaning for us, and sometimes it is even said that souls pass through Orion on their way to manifestation in material form. Orion is the mythical hulk, the arrogant bragging hunter, who in the end over-estimates his own powers. He is successful in his hunting and therefore thinks he can do everything, defeat everyone and hunt down every animal, a boast that finally triggers the wrath of the gods. Orion was created from an oxhide, showing he only has a material nature, and he is stupid because he thinks he is the

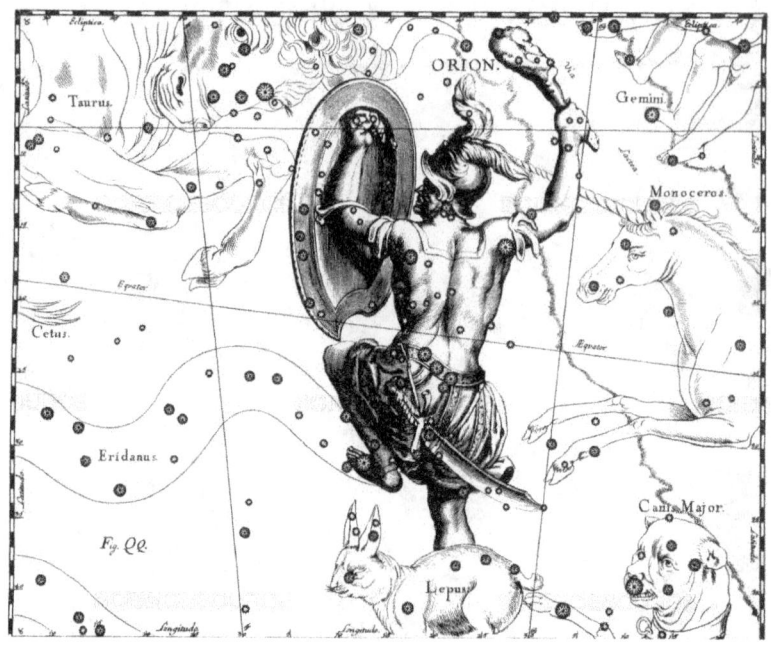

strongest. Orion is the anti-hero, we cannot expect him to sacrifice his desires, he will only do his best to satisfy them.

The most powerful stars in *Orion*, *Betelgeuse* and *Rigel*, give much success because of this material strength, but it does not lead to further development, it all gets stuck at the purely material level. So these stars are very useful to realize success, but the really important things are to be found elsewhere. There is also the danger that an Orion who becomes too sure of his success will meet his Scorpio (see under Scorpio), which will kill him. The central message is that time and death will soon overcome Orion's success. If for example the Orion star *Betelgeuse* is activated by progression, be quick and dirty: hit and run.

Theme: great material success but not more than that, successes of short duration, beware of overestimation of your powers, Scorpio is on its way to kill you.

PEGASUS

The winged horse Pegasus arises from the blood of Medusa, the sacrificed desire-nature. Horses are symbols of strong instinctive forces but this horse has wings so it is rising up to Olympus, to the spiritual world of the gods. The powerful energy of desire is directed towards the heavens by the wings of wisdom. It is the hero Bellerophon who tames Pegasus and flies on its back above his enemies. From this lofty position he defeats his opponents, one among whom is the Chimaera, a hideous mixture of a lion, a goat and a snake – again one the children of Typhon and Echidna, of Death and Earth. The arrows shot by Bellerophon at the Chimaera do not manage to kill it, so he throws a chunk of lead into the monster's fire-breathing mouth which then melts and kills it. Not for nothing is it lead, as this is the metal of Saturn, the planet of sacrifice, wisdom and discipline.

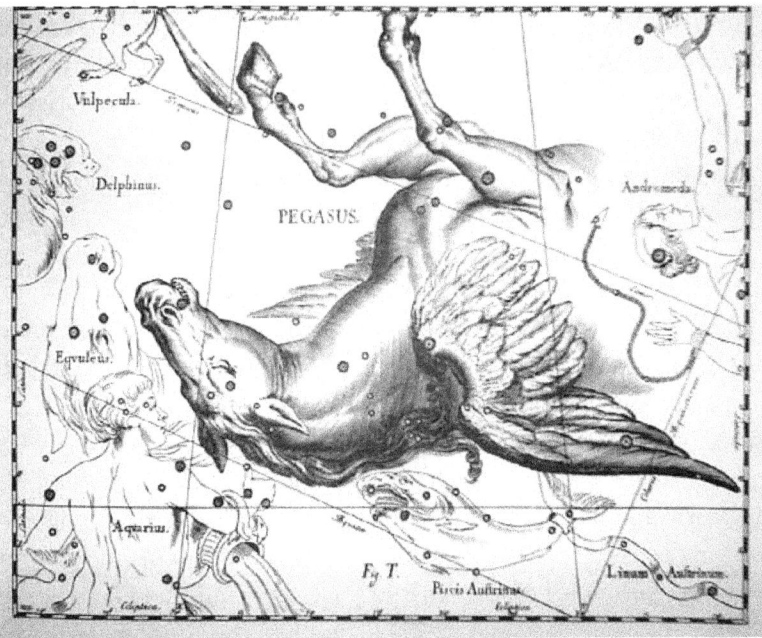

The warning is in the second part of the story, because Bellerophon, inspired by this first success, decides to make his way to the world of the gods on his own initiative. Zeus is not amused by such arrogance and sends a horsefly which stings Pegasus, and Bellerophon is thrown off and falls to earth. Blind and alone Bellerophon roams the face of the earth for the rest of his life without any orientation or goal.

From Pegasus' hoof flow the streams from which the Muses drink, so this is the source of all arts and sciences based as they are on foresight and trust in human powers alone. Bellerophon is quite appropriately a son of Sisiphus who deemed himself smart and ingenious, but is punished in Hades where he endlessly pushes a rock up a hill only to see it come rolling back down as soon as he almost reaches the top. Bellerophon is the heir to this curse of his father. Another association with the same theme at its core is with Prometheus (Greek for 'foresight'), the Titan – an earth giant – who stole fire from the gods and was chained by Zeus in the Caucasus for this crime. Every day Zeus sends an eagle to peck out his liver, symbolising the pain which foresight brings. The liver is the Jupiter organ and represents foresight and oversight, necessarily creating the urge to act and trust your human ingenuity.

It is the centaur Chiron who frees Prometheus by giving up his immortality and taking his place, indicating the similarity of the corresponding myths. Sagittarius (= Chiron) also has association with shooting arrows (plans) into the future, with foresight. Chiron's pain is the tension between knowledge and desire, and the impossibility of solving this tension by his own smartness. On every level, esoteric or concrete, the central theme of Chiron's story is the same as those similarly connected with Bellerophon, Prometheus and Sisiphus. It does not mean that arts and sciences are meaningless but it does point to their essential limitations and dangers. We only need to think of the dangers lurking in modern science to see the important truths in these myths.

Scheat, *Markab* and *Algenib* are the stars in Pegasus which represent this story, and as expected they have quite malefic effects. *Markab* on the wing of Pegasus is the most positive, while *Scheat* on the contrary is placed on the left leg much closer to the earthly mud, and is clearly more malefic. All three stars give the opportunity to rise above material reality and desires, but it will go wrong if human limitations are not humbly observed and accepted.

Theme: avoid overestimation of spiritual or scientific powers, observe human limitations, accept guidance, do not trust in your ingenuity and techniques alone.

PERSEUS

The story of Perseus is intimately connected to the star *Algol*, the 'Queen of Darkness', which is the head of the Gorgon Medusa who has snakes as her hair. Anyone who looks at Medusa without protection will become petrified, an image of the soul dying by giving itself up to desire. It is important to point out that Medusa is not only pictured as a hideous monster but also as a beautiful woman. This shows that the desire nature is extremely attractive, and we often do not see its harmful essence.

Perseus is the great hero who succeeds in decapitating this hideous monster because he has a helmet making him invisible (the too material human nature is left behind), he has wings (abstraction, clear thinking) and a mirror-shield (protective wisdom and religion). He approaches Medusa when she is asleep and using his mirror-shield to observe her (you cannot approach her head-on, you need the help of spiritual reflection), cuts off her head which he uses later to petrify his enemies. This shows what gain *Algol* may bring you, a radical detachment by which you liberate yourself from all manipulations; others can only have power over you if you lock up yourself in your desires. If you are prepared to sacrifice them, you are free.

Algol is the central star in this constellation, it is the petrifying head of Medusa. It is the most malefic star in the heavens, although its negative effects may be tempered by voluntarily giving up something you desire very much. The choice is: will you cut off its head or will it cut off your head? *Algol* is extremely mean; if it is active all beautiful appearances will finally be taken away and you will be confronted with the rough unadorned realities of life. But if you have the courage to take up the sword of Perseus, there is a lot to win here. *Algol* astronomically is a star with a fluctuating magnitude, it is like a sun that is continually eclipsed, a signature for its extremely malefic effect on the life. An activated *Algol* calls for clear distinctions; cut off what you don't need even it looks attractive, and only keep the essence.

In Mick Jagger's chart the Moon is on *Algol*, in Donald Trump's chart it is on the MC. So don't make the mistake of seeing only literal bloodshed and disaster in *Algol*. While it does have these effects especially in mundane astrology, it also has more subtle ways to work out in the life. In a way this is the star that contains the very essence of our spiritual problem on earth, and that is why *Algol* has this huge power.

Capulus is the star that represents the sword-hand of Perseus but is so close to *Algol* that it is strongly overshadowed by Medusa's Head. They are of course part of the same story. *Capulus* is also a cloudy star cluster so it will afflict the eyesight, literally or figuratively.

Theme: radical sacrifice of material bonds and intense desires, glamorous and seductive appearances, making others lose their heads or losing your own head (or both), bloodshed, throw away everything you don't really need, clear distinctions of the essential, liberation from manipulation.

PLEIADES

The Pleiades are a famous group of seven stars in Taurus. They are the daughters of the Titan (earth giant) Atlas, which points to their outspoken material nature. It is not for nothing that there are seven of them, as this refers to the planets of course – the connectors between heaven and earth – and the Pleiades are the factors that pull you into the material world. They are chased by the cosmic hulk Orion, the anti-hero without any spiritual dimension, and this shows that the Pleiades are connected with things that go wrong, and with disappointments. Their effect is very malefic. *Alcyone* is the main star of the group, cutting us off from what we really want, namely the divine dimension behind the planets. Therefore the Pleiades can also be responsible for the blindness they cause.

This is further indicated by the fact that the whole group is embedded in a large nebula, the Nebula of Tears. As they are sisters this may sometimes literally point to problems in the family. *Alcyone* itself has entered Gemini in our times, while others of the Pleiades are still in Taurus. In Vedic mythology the Pleiades are the wives of the seven Sages who can be seen in the Great Bear circling the pole, always a symbol of the divine centre. The sages' wives were seduced and as a consequence fell away from the God-Pole, to the distant zodiac, which explains their effect of disappointment and cutting off in yet another way. With *Algol* and the strongly related seven Hyades, the Pleiades form a kind of prolonged crisis zone between 25° Taurus and 5° Gemini, clearly working out in progression.

Theme: disappointments, tears, things going wrong, confrontations with blunt material reality, problems in the family, blindness, also see Taurus.

RAM – ARIES

This is the ultimate solar animal, a symbol of the spirit, and quite appropriately in the myth it is a Ram who saves brother and sister Phryxis and Helle from their bad stepmother Ino – a symbol of material bonds. On the back of the Ram, Phryxis and Helle fly up to the heavens, but Helle does not attain the goal, she looks down and falls into the sea (the Hellespont is Greek for the Sea of Helle). Brother and sister represent two parts of the soul, the feminine sister-part, always more

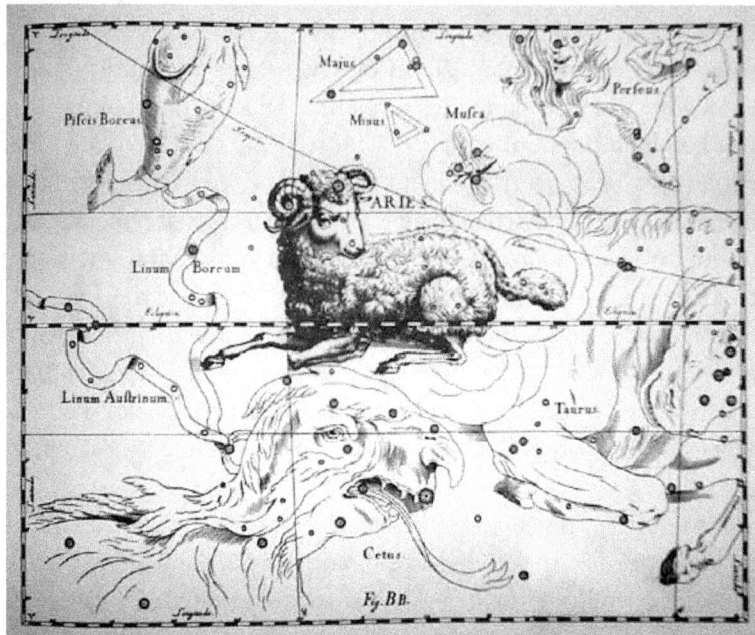

earth–bound, does not succeed in the spiritual flight, the brother-part without his earthly side does, precisely because he got rid of rid of this side. It is an instruction like all myth. You have no use for this part of the soul if you are on a flight on the back of the Ram, because it drags you back down.

The story goes on and Phryxis arrives at his destination, sacrifices the Ram and finds his peace. He gives the Ram's hide to king Aëtes, a son of the Sun-god Helios, underlining the theme of returning to the source for which a sacrifice is necessary. This could also be translated more concretely as knowing when to stop. Even if a battle is tough you don't need your weapons any more when it is over. On a higher level it shows a kind of economy of the spirit; you will receive tools and insights for life from the gods but you must return these to the source as they were only granted you for a while to be used effectively. The Ram's Hide kept by King Aëtes is also the Golden Fleece, the aim of the Argonauts' quest. It is a symbol of the divine realised on earth.

Hamal and *Sharatan* are the Southern and Northern Ram's Horns respectively. The north is always the better side of mercy, while the south is the harsher side of justice. But both stars have a Saturn/Mars nature and neither of the two is very pleasant. The whole idea is not to fall into the Hellespont but to succeed in sacrificing the fiery Ram power at the right moment. This points to resolute fiery action without allowing yourself to be distracted by overly earthly considerations (Helle's fall). But it also highlights the danger of going on too long and too fiercely, and this may be the main thing here. Remember that these are the Ram's horns, and this impulsive storm-power clearly indicates the effect on life and how to interpret the stars, as well as the necessity of controlling this wild energy and using it purposefully.

The symbol for the zodiacal sign of the Ram shows this fresh fiery impulse clearly. The original line of unity is split for the first time into two lines indicating horns. The abundance of solar fire in Aries can be seen in the exaltation of the Sun in this sign; exaltation always points to exaggeration. The Ram's Hide or the Golden Fleece is kept appropriately by King Aëtes in a cave dedicated to Mars, and it is in the house of Mars (Aries) that the Sun is exalted. The Golden Fleece is hung on a tree and the story of the Ram can be associated with that of the Lamb who also leads human souls out off material bounds and back to the source.

Theme: the right use of the fiery Ram power (vigorous goal-oriented action, the wish to conquer) and its sacrifice when the goal has been attained, it also connects to a dedicated quest for truth and the essence of things.

RIVER – ERIDANUS

This is the river into which Phaeton fell when he tried to steer the solar chariot through the skies. He could not control it, and paid for this blatant over-estimation of his powers with a scorching fall into Eridanus. This indicates the meaning of the constellation, getting rid of pride and personal over-estimation and learning the lesson of real humility. Therefore all stars in Eridanus have a Saturnian nature except for the Mouth of the River which is *Achernar*, described as a great benefic. At this point the lessons of bitterness and the fall are poured out as wisdom and experience. But despite the positive description in the texts, Achernar has a darker side of usurpation, of stealing a kingdom, of spiritual over-estimation of your powers by which the development of the kingdom is harmed. The River is traditionally a symbol of the boundary that has to be crossed to reach a better level, or the Promised Land as in the case of the River Jordan.

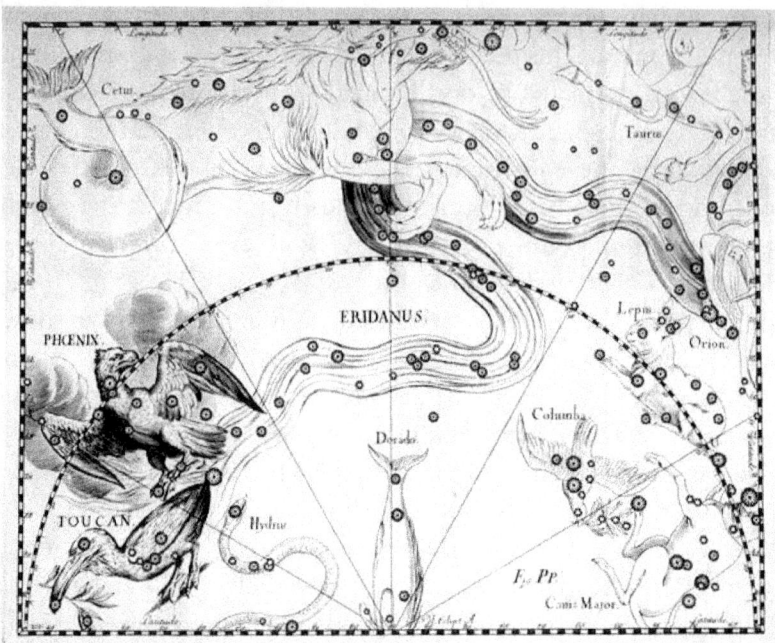

Theme: conquer your (spiritual) pride, learn to be humble, avoid usurpation and over-estimation of your limited powers, teaching of wisdom won through bitter experience.

SAGITTARIUS – CHIRON

Chiron is the wisest among the centaurs and was for many heroes like Hercules and Jason a teacher and a tutor. But there is still a danger, because Chiron is accidentally wounded by the poison on one of Hercules' arrows that came from the Hydra, the many-headed snake of desire. A centaur, even civilized Chiron, will always be only half-human, so he has to be careful to remain master of his instinctive nature, particularly if he is with friends like Hercules. The Hydra poison represents the danger of being totally overwhelmed by the chaotic instinctive forces from the infrahuman unconscious. In the skies we also find another centaur, Pholus, with a similar but slightly different meaning.

It will be clear that the half-human Chiron's fiery passionate nature points to a painful tension in the soul. The Hydra poison is a kind of desire virus infecting him and he suffers enormously because all his knowledge is not sufficient to heal himself. It is his horse part that is

The Myths of the Constellations and their Stars

always pictured with pronounced sexual organs to indicate this strong instinctive side. Because Chiron, who is suffering so much from the poisoning, is immortal, he changes places with the Titan Prometheus, chained by Zeus in the Caucasus mountains (see under 'Pegasus') and gives up his immortality for him. Prometheus ('foresight') is a mythical character also strongly connected to knowledge and human ingenuity. There is a clear mythical kinship between Chiron and Prometheus.

The arrow of Sagittarius is a symbol of the world axis or the Pole, traditionally the divine centre around which everything turns. A link with this centre is to gain knowledge of the essence. The sign Sagittarius, which provided in a way the model for the constellation with the same name, is the mutable fire sign pointing at reaching further to the next phase (mutable) of the flame (fire). An appropriate image of knowledge and teaching.

Polis, a star on the arrow, gives optimism, success, ambition and sharp insights. *Pelagus*, also on the arrow, gives optimism, sincerity and spirituality. *Ascella* is found in the armpit, pointing at vulnerability for manipulation; the moment you shoot the arrow this is the place on your body which is unprotected. *Facies* is a nebula in the face of the Archer and gives blindness, accidents and a violent death. You can't see what you are shooting at, and the same thing applies to the nebulae *Manubrium* and *Spiculum*.

These stars show both sides of the Sagittarian medal (animal-human), and by their exact place in the constellation they indicate the kind of effect they have. A remarkable star in the tail of Sagittarius is tiny *Terebellum* of the sixth magnitude, which despite its faint appearance is an influential star of fate associated with prophecies coming true.

Theme: wisdom, dedicated teaching, painful tension between knowledge and desire, the failure of knowledge, being painfully harmed despite all the knowledge.

SCALES – LIBRA

This most enigmatic zodiacal constellation used to be known as the Scorpion's Claws, the Chelae, only later receiving the name of Libra the Scales. Libra is also a zodiacal sign and this does not mean that the zodiac changed essentially in any way when the constellation was renamed. The *South Scale* and the *North Scale* are a pair of stars concerned with justice and mercy (south – harsh justice, north – mildness and mercy). The *South Scale* is one of the royal stars, the extremely powerful Fist of Justice that restores the balance in the Scales, just as the actions of men are weighed in the balance and if necessary corrective measures or punishment follow (therefore the Scales are also the Claws).

As men and women fallen with Adam we are necessarily sinners and our moral efforts are always below standard, but as is clearly stated in the Bible, mercy will always outweigh justice. This can be seen in the zodiacal glyph for Libra where the lower line indicates justice and the upper line mercy. It is also a picture of the upper divine waters and the lower earthy waters. The bend in the upper line symbolises the rainbow, the sign of God's merciful covenant with Noah. Venus is the ruler of the zodiacal sign of Libra suggesting that mercy is the dominant part, while Saturn is exalted in Libra showing the justice required to restore the balance.

The Scales are, as mentioned above, the same as the Scorpion's Claws, the Chelae. The Southern Claw, also called *Lucida Lancis* (South

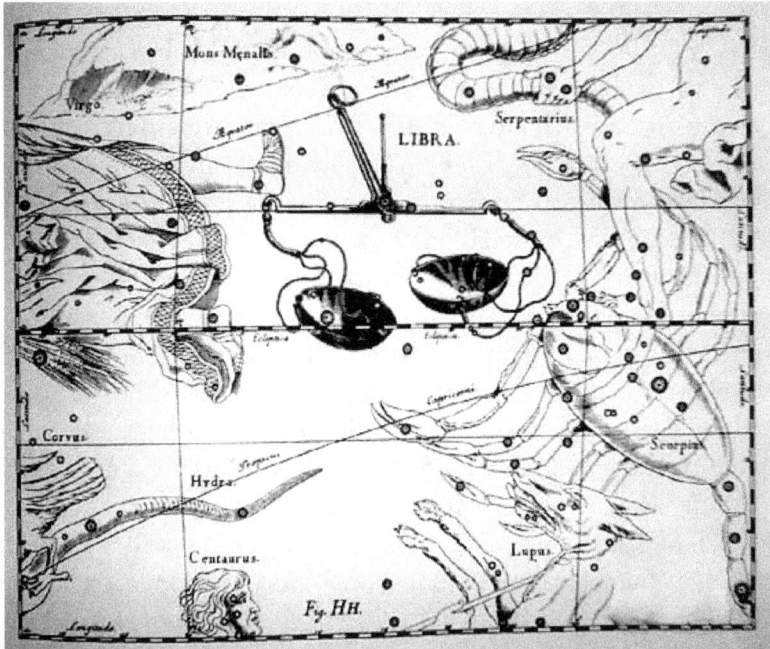

Scale) is harsh and malefic, its punishment merciless, a rock-hard claw that will get you; a cosmic Dirty Harry. Both Scales are part of the same theme but the *North Scale* (the Sufficient Price) is milder than the *South Scale* (the Insufficient Price). On the *South Scale* what you pay is never enough, it relentlessly goes on till the work is done. It is said that in the old days the Scales were placed on the pole, underlining the justice/mercy theme as the pole is where all forces are in balance; it indicates the whole idea of corrective action. At a certain moment the balancing Scales came down from their dominant position on the pole and took their zodiacal place as the Claws of the Scorpion/Libra. This coming down of the Scales from the pole refers to a profound change in circumstances and ambience on earth, going back a very long time. Nothing much is known about these ancient times in our present day.

Theme: avenging justice and mercy, restoring the balance, harsh corrective action.

SCORPIO

Cosmic hulk Orion is killed by the Scorpion, a nasty ball of lethal poison sent by the gods to get even with the stupidity and arrogance of this otherwise successful hunter. It shows how the overestimation of his material powers ends; the Scorpion finishes him off in an unpleasant and vicious way. *Antares* in Scorpio is a powerful royal star, the counterpart of *Aldebaran* in the constellation of Taurus. *Antares* represents the heart of the Scorpion and its ruthless essence; it is the cosmic killer, the star of autumn ending-cycles. The best way to use it is to sting to death your external or internal Orions. Its name is derived from Anti-Ares, the Rival of Ares, because the star is as fiery and militant as the war god.

All stars in Scorpio (*Graffias, Isidis, Lesath, Aculeus, Acumen*) are unpleasant and associated with poison, sudden attacks and malice. If an important factor in your chart progresses over the Heart of Scorpio, a nasty ball of poison will cross your path and something will dramatically end. Orion humbles himself or is killed. Such a progression in some cases will bring the real death of the person themselves or of someone in their near environment. The Scorpion is sent by Moon goddess Diana, and the Moon is the great symbol of earthly transience to which Orion is extremely sensitive as he is made out of matter alone. With *Antares* activated the Scorpionic desire should be directed towards a higher goal, the lowly dark beast has to be transformed into the royal eagle.

See also above under SCALES, the Scorpion's Claws are also the Scales, royal *Lucida Lancis* the Southern Claw is the *South Scale*.

Theme: stop over-estimating your powers, something is brought to an end in a nasty vicious way, sharp sudden attacks, poison, death.

SEAMONSTER or WHALE – CETUS

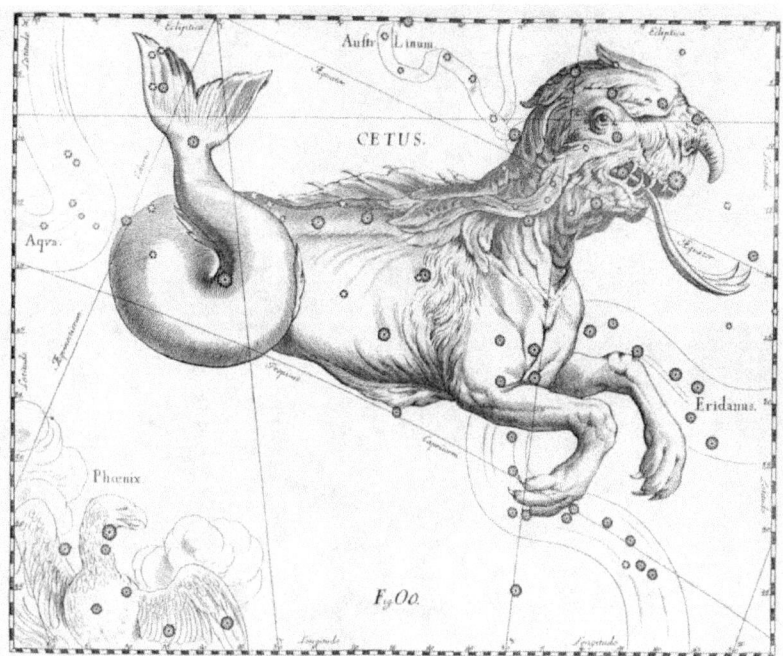

This is the monster sent by Poseidon to devour King Cepheus' daughter, Princes Andromeda, and create chaos in the kingdom. The stars *Menkar* in the jaws, *Baten Kaitos* in the belly and *Difda* on the tail all have a purely Saturnian nature and are all malefic. Symbolically they point to the soul which is threatened to be devoured by hungry wild desires, or more concretely it indicates imprisonment or being chased away. See also ANDROMEDA.

Theme: difficult unfavourable circumstances, exile, being driven or dragged away, overwhelming desires leading to trouble, compulsory change, chaos, naval disasters.

SOUTHERN FISH – PISCES AUSTRALIS

This is a different big fish from the Seamonster – which isn't actually a fish. This one is a real fish associated with spiritual initiation and with being spiritually born from matter. It is Jonah's whale who devoured him but also spat him out later when he had been transformed. The Mouth of the Fish is in Arabic *Fom-al Hut* or *Fomalhout*, one of the Four Watchers and the star of the winter solstice marking Christmas, the birth of Christ. It is a very powerful star but as Christ's Kingdom is not of this world, it does not give success in the material sense. It cannot therefore be said to be a royal star. It is also connected to the story of the goddess of lust, Venus who changes into a fish, indicating a transition to a more spiritual level. This fish is not part of the constellation of Pisces, but their themes are of course somewhat related. The stream of sweet water received by this fish comes from Aquarius' Cup, showing that purification of the desire nature is a preparative phase in the initiation process.

Theme: spiritual birth, a kingship not of this world.

SNAKE – SERPENS

The only star in the Snake – the one held by the Snake-bearer Ophiuchus – that is astrologically relevant is *Unukalhai*, the Heart or the Neck of the Snake. The meaning is clear, as the snake's heart it is the essence of duality and of seductive earthly desire, and the image of the snake is also associated with the continuous shedding of the skin. This points to the necessity of not getting stuck in one earthly form and deliberately changing to stay ahead of petrifying desire. A snake as the pure life energy of duality has to shed its skin in order not to lose its flexibility, otherwise it would get stuck in matter without a chance to evolve. It will be clear that the effect of the Snake star will not be very positive; it stands for immorality, poison, violence and accidents.

Theme: avoid the seductive snake desires which may lead to immoral behaviour, the shedding of the skin is a pointer to continuous change, taking on a fresh new form again and again in order not to get desperately stuck in material desires.

SNAKEBEARER – OPHIUCHUS

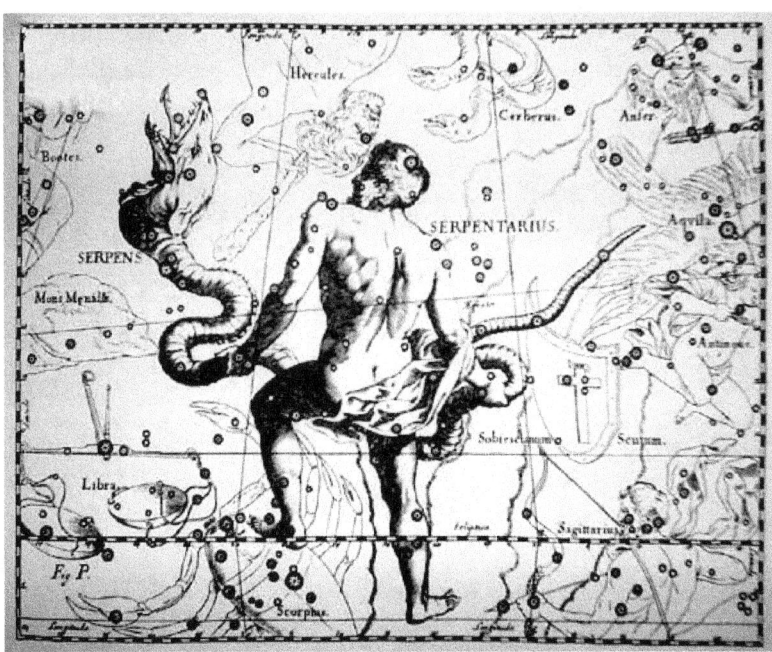

This, according to some versions of the myth, is Hercules as a baby who strangled the snakes sent by Juno to kill him. Killing the snake is the theme of this constellation but all stars in Ophiuchus (*Yed Prior, Han, Rasalhague, Sabik* and *Sinistra*) are morally dubious and weak. If you want to hold or bear the snake, you have to take care or it will bite you. More concrete is the role of the constellation as Aesculapius, the ancient medicine god, as healing is harmonizing and balances the dualistic life energy of which the snake is a symbol (the Caduceus staff has two snakes). This can clearly be seen in the diverse forms of traditional medicine in which the central point is always re-balancing two opposite energies; Yin-Yang, Sulfur-Mercury or fire-water. The symbolism of the snake shedding its skin also points to going though the process of disease in order to achieve healing. It is the Snake-bearer who can guide the life energy through these processes and this is why this constellation is associated with medicine. Another image expressing essentially the same thing of guiding the life energy is snake-charming.

Theme: medicine, destroy evil as soon as soon it shows itself, immoral tendencies and dishonesty.

As the Sun in our time also moves through a small part of the constellation of Ophiuchus you sometimes hear astrologers talking about the Snake-bearer as the thirteenth sign. It will be clear that this is impossible as was explained in Chapter 2.

SWAN – CYGNUS

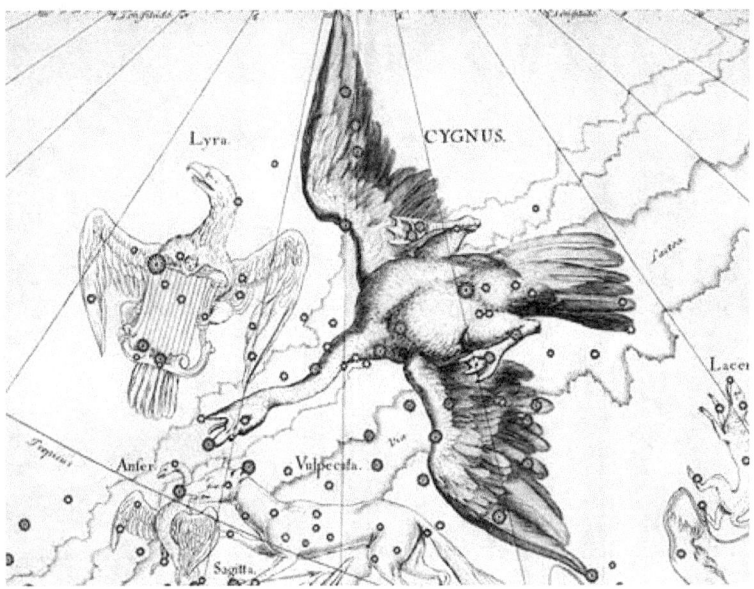

This is Jupiter who mated with Leda in the shape of a swan and it shows the great creative impulse taking on a beautiful gracious form. The Swan is therefore strongly associated with art and beauty, although there is some lack of energy and it requires conscious expression. *Deneb* (*Adige*) is a powerful first magnitude star in the Swan; another weaker star is *Albireo*.

Theme: expressing art and beauty.

TWINS – GEMINI

This is the famous pair, Castor and Pollux, the heavenly Twins, and its essence can be expressed simply as polarity, the basic tension between two poles which is one of the founding principles of the whole cosmos. All this is mirrored in the Twins; there is a mortal brother, Castor, the part of the soul that wants to get involved in earthly action, and an immortal brother, Pollux, the part of the soul that wants to return to its divine origin above. The brothers are fighters, tamers of horses and protectors of sea-men, themes that point to the taming of the waters of desire, and in these battles Castor is killed. After his death the brothers change

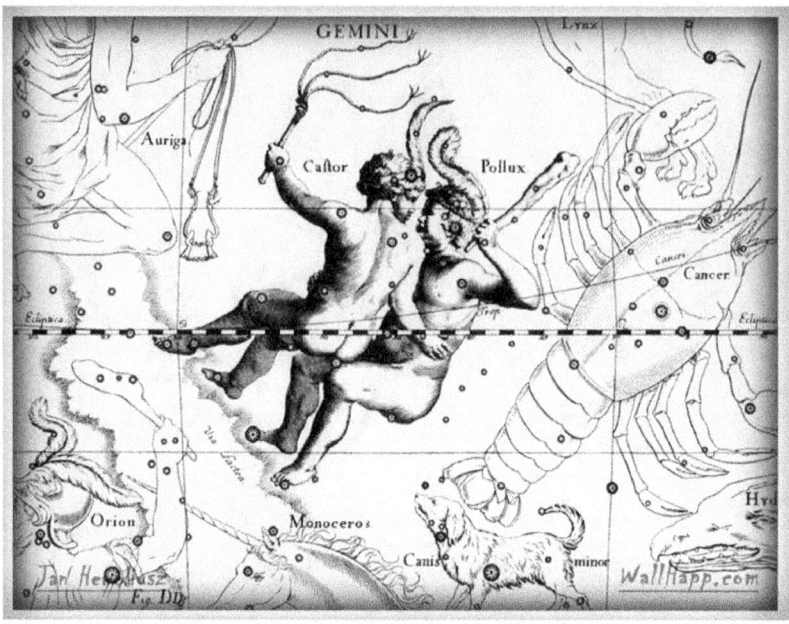

their abodes, sometimes they are together on Olympus, sometimes they are together in Hades. This underlines the polarity. Pollux, the immortal part, is so attached to his mortal half that he will stay with Castor even in the darkness of Hades. It shows the mission of humankind in life, which is to retrieve the part of the soul fallen into matter and avoid the danger of getting stuck on earth.

The brothers are also crew members of the Argo. They sailed with Jason in the quest for the Golden Fleece, the hide of the Ram sacrificed by Phryxis and a symbol of the divine realised on earth. This shows again that the Twins are here for action, with their goal to establish a connection with 'above' for the whole soul. Pollux should not allow himself to be dragged down into Hades by mortal Castor. The polarity symbolism is also found in their origin of being born from the World Egg laid by Leda. The World Egg is the primordial unity giving birth to the polarity expressed by the Twins. There is also a connection with the Pillars of Hercules placed on both sides of the Strait of Gibraltar symbolically representing the boundaries of the world, the poles between which all things happen, and the association with the solstices is also clear. If you sail past the Pillars, and out of the world, you will find the golden Apples of the Hesperides on the tree of life. This could be one of the reasons that New York is called the Big Apple.

In the symbol for the zodiacal sign Gemini we can see these two pillars, the basic polarity. You cannot go past these points and live; a human being is caught in the high tension between the two forces symbolized by Castor and Pollux, earth and heaven, mortal and immortal, matter and spirit. The very powerful royal star *Pollux* – sometimes also called Hercules – gives success and decisiveness; mortal *Castor*, less bright, is still powerful but more impure because of his earthbound mortality. The Twin theme is often expressed in life as a struggle/relationship between (not always symbolic) brothers, one of whom dies. Or it is an outspoken double ambivalent nature which has very 'mortal' and 'immortal' sides. The strong tension between two related poles gives a double nature, as for example in knowledge and action combined, and it may be expressed almost literally as in the case of Nicolai Tesla, the inventor for whom electricity was the central theme of his life.

The star *Alhena* gives artistic talents (the connection between mortal material form and immortal essence). It is found in the foot, therefore suggesting concrete artistic form. The other stars in Gemini have a varying influence on life. Some are clearly positive like *Propus* and *Dirah* while others like *Wasat* and *Tejat* are of a darker nature. This mirrors the ambivalent tension between the mortal and immortal parts of the soul.

Theme: doubleness, don't get stuck in the earthly world with all its fascinating opportunities for action, ambivalence, tension between two poles, (symbolic) brother theme, choose Olympus over Castor's Hades, combination of knowledge and action.

VIRGIN – VIRGO

This is an image of purity and is obviously also associated with the Christian symbolism of Mary, the Holy Mother of God. Virginity indicates liberation from material bonds; Christ is born without any involvement of matter or sin, and there is the Roman Catholic dogma of the Immaculate Conception which applies to Mary underlining her purity. In the black Madonnas, for example in Chartres and in Czestochowa, the purity stands out. Blackness, apart from its association with Saturn as wisdom born through suffering, indicates purely passive potentiality, readiness to receive the divine impulse. It is also the black earth of alchemy, described as the fruitful Egyptian soil after flooding by the Nile.

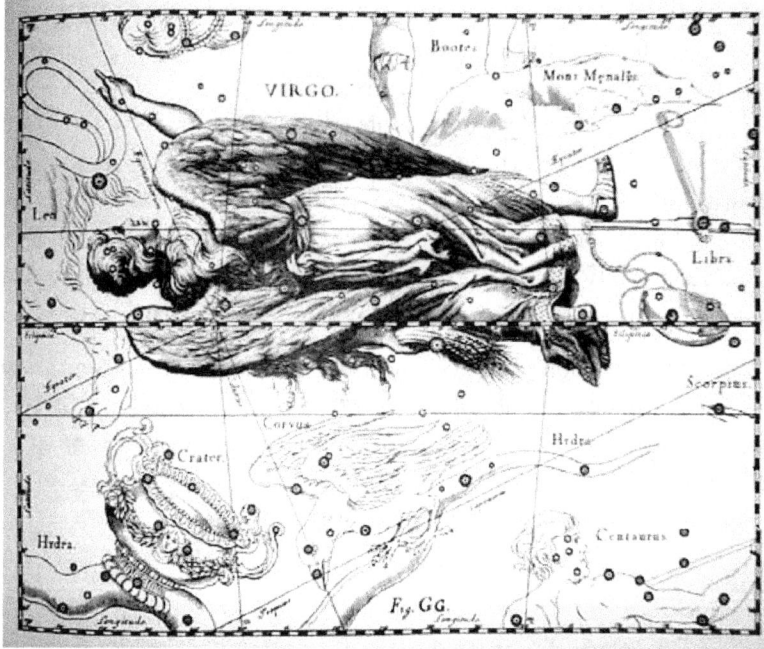

All in all, this makes Virgo one the most important myths of the West. Mary is traditionally connected to the Holy Spirit, the feminine part of the Trinity, which she receives because of her purity. The main star in Virgo is royal *Spica*, which has a powerful protective influence and gives great success. As the star of the Virgin, *Spica* is also *Stella Maris*, the Star of the Sea, shining above the waves as a protective beacon for those who contend with the wild waves of desire. *Spica* represents the Wheat Ear, the concentration point of the harvesting process, the purification and selection, when the wheat is separated from the chaff. *Spica* is much happier than the royal Heart of the Lion, always burning with unsatisfied ambition, because for *Spica* success is not the most important thing in life. In antique mythology Virgo is Astraea, a Titan's daughter who chooses the side of the Olympic gods (spirit) against her own ancestry. This is of course exactly the same theme as Mary's myth.

Most stars in Virgo have a positive meaning, however with the star *Khambalia*, found in the foot of Virgo, decisive action is required to retain the purity. This dubious aspect is indicated by the star's name the 'Crooked-clawed'. A special case in Virgo is the malefic star *Vindemiatrix*, that represents Amphelos who climbed a vine, fell and broke his neck. This indicates the Sorcerer's Apprentice theme, over-estimation of one's powers and freeing uncontrollable forces harming everybody. It is also the Widowmaker, a star of divorce. It points to the assumption that you posses the knowledge before you really do, also to arrogance and taking something that does not belong to you. Amphelos tries to gather the grapes at the wrong time, it is a premature harvesting process, a purification which fails.

Vindemiatrix is one of the few fixed stars used in horary astrology (see the list in Chapter 4).

Theme: purity, critical selection of useful elements, separating the wheat from the chaff, to become receptive by distinction of the pure and the impure.

WHALE – see SEAMONSTER

'Apocryph' and ineffective constellations

Constellations like the Dragon, the Greater Bear and the Lesser Bear, Cepheus, the Southern Cross, (not a traditional constellation) and Cassiopeia are situated far from the ecliptic and therefore have a negligible astrological effect. In astrology, the zodiac, the royal path of the Sun, has a central role and the nearer to the zodiac a star is positioned, the greater its power. There are also some traditional constellations, like the Hare and the Delphin, which we could call 'apocryph', as they contain no stars that according to traditional sources have an astrological effect worth mentioning, and therefore they have been left out of the list. It does not mean that they are unworthy of any attention, but too little is known about them. The Delphin holds a position in the middle, as it does rule a lunar mansion whose effect is clear and it is mentioned by William Lilly, although he didn't name the stars within it. Until more is known about these apocryph stars it seemed wiser not to discuss them in the above list.

Only conjunctions
A myth associated with a constellation is that it will only become active in a life if a planet or an angle (and to a less degree an Arabian part or another house cusp) is conjunct a star which is part of that constellation. However, there is also an definite effect if one of the main hylegical progressions (Sun, Asc, MC, Moon, PF) move over a star. To trigger the star there is no need for it to be conjunct a natal factor as the progressions are enough to activate it. In prediction this is one of the most powerful tools.

You do not need a specialized program to work effectively with the stars. The positions you need are those projected into the zodiac and they are found in the list in Chapter 4 per sign. These are the positions for the year 2010 and with the simple precession key of 1 degree forward through the zodiac in 72 years you can find the star position at any time.

Concise Mythological Vocabulary

Africa – the land of desire and dominance of matter
Arrow – see sword
Ass – force creating chaos
Brothers, sisters – two parts of the soul, different but very closely
    connected, the material-spiritual nature of humankind
Bull or Ox – gross material reality
Changing place – similarity
Dragon – see snake
Eye – focus of attention
Foot – contact point with the earth, concrete form or action, where you
    get your hands dirty

The Myths of the Constellations and their Stars

Fish – non-duality, divine consciousness, a fish never sleeps and it moves through the waters of desire without being affected
Girl – the soul, which made pure receives the spirit, Mary in Christianity
Head – the consciously guiding and controlling principle
Heel – vulnerable point
Heart – concentrated essence of the energy
Horn – dangerous impulsiveness
Horse – desire which can be directed but not totally controlled
Left – the wrong, dark side, 'sinister' in Latin
Lance – see sword
North – positive side connected to mercy
Parents – the root energies composing some mythological character
Right – the better positive side
Shoulder – forcefully pushing on
Sisters – see brothers
Snake or Dragon – the great symbol of duality or the life energy itself
South – negative side, connected with justice, merciless and harsh
Sword – the pole, the balanced divine centre which gives the knowledge of acting in the right way
Titans – the bad guys, opponents of the gods, demons
Water, salt – the instinctive desire nature
Water, sweet – drinkable water, desire distilled and purified

BASIC MYTHOLOGICAL THEMES

Confrontation with gross materiality: Taurus, Pleiades, Hyades, Orion, Scorpio
Duality human/divine: Gemini, Libra
Openness for beauty and purity: Andromeda, Swan, Dove, Virgo, Cup
Spiritual birth and knowledge: Eagle, Southern Fish, Capricorn, Fishes, Lyre
Shortcoming of human knowledge and ingenuity: Pegasus, Sagittarius, Centaur
Lust for power and gross decisiveness: Leo, Boötes, the Dogs, Aries, the River
Handling desire: Hydra, Snake, Snakebearer, Seamonster, Cancer, Charioteer, Crow, Perseus, Aquarius, the Argonauts' ship

It is helpful to remember that stars are little Suns, not only astronomically, but they are made of the same light as that of the Sun. This means they can be seen as a variation or detailing of the solar light, which is a symbol of the divine presence in our cosmos. So they show something of the process of reconnecting with the primordial divine unity from which everything has arisen and to which everything will return. This is just another way of saying what a myth essentially is, now based on the signature of solar and stellar light.

4
List of Fixed Stars per Sign for 2010

Star positions given for 2010 (precession key one degree in 72 years). Information stated:

Name – Degree – English Name – Planet Nature – Magnitude – Constellation – Latitude (north or south)

The following key is also used:
- F   Star of fatefulness
- N   Nebula or nebulous star cluster
- M   Extremely malefic star
- R   Royal star
- H   Star also relevant in horary astrology

ARIES

2.46 – *Difda*, The Seamonster's Tail – Saturn – 2 – Seamonster – S 20.46

9.20 – *Algenib*, Pegasus' Wing Tip – Mars/Mercury – 3 – Pegasus, the Flying Horse – N 12.36

14.29 – *Alpheratz*, The Princess' Head – Jupiter/Venus – 2 – Andromeda – N 25.41

22.08 – *Baten Kaitos*, The Seamonster's Belly – Saturn – 3.5 – Seamonster – S 20.20

26.59 – *Al Pherg*, The Fishes' Cord – Saturn/Jupiter – 4 – the Fishes – N 5.22 **F**

27.58 – *Vertex*, The Andromeda Nebula – Mars/Moon – nebula – Andromeda – N 33.21 **N**

TAURUS

00.35 – *Mirach*, Andromeda's Girdle – Venus – 2 – Andromeda – N 5.22

4.09 – *Sharatan*, The Northern Ram's Horn – Mars/Saturn – 3 – Ram – N 8.29

7.50 – *Hamal*, The Southern Ram's Horn – Mars/Saturn – 2 – Ram – N 9.58

14.24 – *Almach*, Andromeda's Left Foot – Venus – 2 – Andromeda – N 21.48

14.30 – *Menkar*, The Mouth of the Seamonster – Saturn – 2.5 – Seamonster – S 12.34

24.20 – *Capulus*, Perseus' Sword-hand – Mars/Mercury – Perseus – nebulous cluster – N 4.02 **N**

26.21 – *Algol*, The Demon's Head, Medusa's Head – Saturn/Jupiter – variable – Perseus – N 22.25 **M H**

GEMINI

00.10 – *Alcyone*, Main star in the Pleiades – Moon/Mars – 3 – Taurus/Pleiades – N 4.02 **N H**

Around 0 Gemini – *Pleiades*, The Weeping Sisters – Moon/Mars – nebulous cluster – same latitude as Alcyone **N**

5.59 – *Prima Hyadum*, Main star in the Hyades – Saturn/Mercury – 4 – Taurus/Hyades – S 5.44 **N**

Around 6 Gemini – *Hyades*, Bacchus' wet-nurses – Saturn/Mercury – nebulous cluster – Taurus – same latitude as Prima Hyadum **N**

9.58 – *Aldebaran*, The Bull's Eye – Mars – 1 – Taurus – S 5.28 **R H**

17.00 – *Rigel*, Orion's Left Foot – Jupiter/Mars – 1 – Orion, the Hunter – S 31.08

21.07 – *Bellatrix*, Orion's Left Shoulder, the Amazon – Mars/Mercury – 2 – Orion – S 16.50

22.02 – *Capella*, The Charioteer's Goat – Mars/Mercury – 1 – Charioteer, Auriga – N 22.25

22.21 – *Phact*, The Dove's Right Wing – Venus/Mercury – 2 - Dove – S 57.23

22.32 – *Mintaka*, Star in Orion's Girdle – Saturn/Mercury – 2 – Orion – S 23.37

22.45 – *El Nath*, The Bull's Northern Horn – Mars – 2 – Taurus – N 5.23

23.00 – *Ensis*, Nebula on Orion's Sheath – nebula – Mars/Moon – Orion – S 28.42 **N**

23.38 – *Alnilam*, Orion's Girdle – Jupiter/Saturn 2 – Orion – S 28.42

24.58 – *Al Hecka*, The Bull's Southern Horn – Mars – 3 – Taurus S 2.11

28.47 – *Polaris*, The Pole Star, the Bear's Tail – Saturn/Venus – 2 – Lesser Bear – N 66.05

28.56 – *Betelgeuse*, Orion's Right Shoulder – Mars/Mercury – Orion – S 26.02

CANCER

0.05 – *Menkalinan*, The Charioteer's Right Shoulder – 2 – Mars/Mercury – Charioteer – N 21.30

3.34 – *Tejat*, Castor's Left Foot – Mercury/Venus – 3 – Gemini – S 0.54

5.26 – *Dirah*, Pollux's Left Foot – Mercury/Venus – 3 – Gemini – S 0.50

9.04 – *Alhena*, Star in Pollux's Left Foot – Mercury/Venus – 2 – Gemini – S 6.45

14.15 – *Sirius*, The Big Dog's Mouth – Jupiter/Mars – 1 – Big Dog, Canis Major – S 39.25

15.08 – *Canopus*, The Helmsman – Saturn/Jupiter – 1 – The Argonaut's Ship – S 75.50

18.41 – *Wasat*, Castor's Right Arm – Saturn – 3 – Gemini – S 0.11

19.05 – *Propus*, The Twins' Shoulders – Mercury/Venus – 4 – Gemini – N 10.05

20.15 – *Castor*, Castor's Head – Mercury – Gemini – 2 – N 10.05

23.23 – *Pollux*, Hercules. Pollux's Head – Mars – 1 – N 6.40 **R**

25.57 – *Procyon*. Star in the Lesser Dog's Body – Mercury/Mars – 1 Lesser Dog, Canis Minor – S 16.00

LEO

7.22 – *Praesepe*, The Crib, the Beehive – Mars/Moon – nebula – Cancer – N 1.33 **M N**

78   Fixed Stars in the Chart

7.43 – *North Asellus*, Northern Ass – Mars/Sun – 6 Cancer – N 3.11

8.54 – *South Asellus*, Southern Ass – Mars/Sun – 6 – Cancer – N 0.04

13.46 – *Acubens*, The Crab's Claw – Saturn/Mercury – 4 – Cancer – N 9.43

20.52 – *Algenubi*, The Lion's Mouth – Saturn/Mars – 3 – Leo – N 9.43

27.27 – *Alphard*, The Hydra's Heart – Saturn/Venus – 2 – Hydra, the Water-snake – S 22.23

27.44 – *Adhafera*, The Lion's Manes – Saturn/Mercury – 3 – Leo – N 11.52

28.04 – *Algieba*, Star in the Lion's Manes – Saturn/Mercury – 3 – Leo – N 4.52

29.59 – *Regulus*, The Lion's Heart – Mars/Jupiter – 1– Leo – N 0.28 **R H**

VIRGO

11.29 – *Zosma*, The Lion's Back – Saturn/Venus – 2 – Leo – N 14.20

21.47 – *Denebola*, The Lion's Tail – Saturn/Venus – 2 – Leo – N 12.16

25.13 – *Copula*, Nebula – Moon/Venus – Hunting Dogs (non-traditional) – N 50.55 **N**

26.51 – *Labrum*, The Cup – Venus/Mercury – 4 – Crater/Cup – S 17.34 **F**

27.20 – *Zavijava*, The Virgin's Head – Mercury/Mars – 3.5 – Virgo – N 0.42

29.03 – *Markeb*, The Ship's Bow – Saturn/Jupiter – 2.5 – Argonauts' Ship – S 63.43

Libra

5.00 – *Zaniah*, The Virgin's Wing – Mercury/Venus – 4 – Virgo – N 1.22

10.06 – *Vindemiatrix*, The Widow Star, the Magician's Apprentice – Saturn/Mercury – 3 – Virgo – N 16.13 **H**

10.18 – *Caphir*, The Virgin's Left Arm – Mercury/Venus – 3.5 – Virgo – N 2.48

13.37 – *Algorab*, The Crow's Wing – Mars/Saturn – 3 – Crow – S 12.11

17.50 – *Seginus*, Boötes' Left Shoulder – Mercury/Saturn – 3 – Boötes – N 49.33

22.18 – *Foramen*, Nebula in the Argonauts' Ship – Saturn/Jupiter – Argonauts' Ship – S 58.55 **N**

23.58 – *Spica*, The Virgin's Wheat Ear – Venus/Mars – 1 – Virgo – S 2.03 **R H**

24.22 – *Arcturus*, Boötes' Left Knee – Mars/Jupiter – 1 – Boötes N 30.47

Scorpio

3.19 – *Princeps*, The Spear-shaft, the Prince – Mercury/Saturn – Boötes – N 48.59

7.00 – *Khambalia*, The Virgin's Left Foot – Mercury/Mars – 4 – Virgo – N 0.28

12.02 – *Acrux*, The Southern Cross (non-traditional) – Jupiter – 1 – S 52.52

12.28 – *Alphecca*, The Knot in the Ribbon – Venus/Mars – 2 – Northern Crown – N 44.20

15.15 – *South Scale*, Lucida Lancis, the Southern Claw – Jupiter/Mars – 1 – Libra N 0.20 **R M**

19.32 – *North Scale*. Northern Claw – Jupiter/Mercury – 2.5 – Libra – N 8.30

22.14 – *Unukalhai*, The Snake's Heart – Saturn/Mars – 2.5 – Snake – N 25.50

23.57 – *Agena*, Pholus' Right Foot – Venus/Jupiter – 1 – The Centaur, Pholus – S 44.09

29.38 – *Bungula*, Pholus' Left Foot – Saturn/Venus – 1 – The Centaur, Pholus – S 42.43

SAGITTARIUS

2.28 – *Yed Prior*, The Snake-bearer's Left Hand – Mars/Jupiter – 3 – Ophiuchus, the Snake-bearer – N 17.15

2.44 – *Isidis*, Star in the Scorpion's Right Claw – Mars/Saturn – 2 – Scorpio – S 1.58

3.21 – *Graffias*, The Scorpion's Head – Mars/Saturn – 3 – Scorpio – N – 1.1

9.24 – *Han*, Star in the Snake-bearer's Left Knee – Saturn/Venus – 3 – Scorpio – N 11.24

9.56 – *Antares*, The Scorpion's Heart – Mars – 1 – Scorpio – S 4.34 **R M H**

12.07 – *Rastaban*, Nebulous star in the Dragon's Eye – Saturn/Venus – 3 – Dragon – N 75.17

18.08 – *Sabik*, The Snake-bearer's Left Knee – Saturn/Venus – 2 – Ophiuchus – N 7.12

22.37 – *Rasalhague*, The Snake-bearer's Head – Mercury/Mars – 2 – Ophiuchus – 35.51

24.11 – *Lesath*, The Scorpion's Sting – Mars/Moon – 3 – Scorpio – S 14.00

25.54 – **N** *Aculeus*, Nebula in the Sting – Mars/Moon – nebula – Scorpio – S 8.50 **N**

28.42 – *Acumen*, Nebula in the Sting – Mars/Moon – nebula – Scorpio – S 11.12 **N**

29.55 – *Sinistra*, Star in the Snake-bearer's Left Hand – Saturn/Venus – 3 – Ophiuchus – N 13.41

CAPRICORN

0.47 – *Spiculum*, Nebula on Chiron's Arrow point – Mars/Moon – nebula – Chiron, Sagittarius – N 0.01 **N**

3.23 – *Polis*, Star on Chiron's Bow – Jupiter/Mars – 4 – Chiron, Sagittarius – N 2.21

8.27 – *Facies*, Nebula in Chiron's Face – Sun/Mars – nebula – Chiron, Sagittarius – S 0.43 **N**

12.33 – *Pelagus*, The Arrow's Vane – Jupiter/Mercury – 2 – Chiron, Sagittarius – S 2.36

13.48 – *Ascella*, Chiron's Arm-pit – Jupiter/Mercury – 3 – Chiron, Sagittarius – S 7.10

15.10 – *Manubrium*, Nebula in Chiron's Face – Sun/Mars – nebula – Chiron, Sagittarius – N 0.52 **N**

15.29 – *Vega*, The Falling Grype – Venus/Mercury – 1 – Lyre – N 61.44

23.49 – *Deneb Okab*. The Eagle's Tail – Mars/Jupiter – 3 – N 36.12

26.44 – *Terebellum*, Star in Chiron's Tail – Venus/Saturn – 6 – Chiron, Sagittarius **F**

AQUARIUS
1.57 – *Altair*, The Eagle's Neck, The Ascending Grype – Mars/Jupiter – 1 – Eagle – N 29.18

3.31 – *Albireo*, The Swan's Head – Venus/Mercury – 3 – Swan – N 48.59

4.02 – *Giedi*, Capricorn's Southern Horn – Venus/Mars – 4 – Capricorn – N 6.58

4.13 – *Dabih*, Capricorn's Left Eye – Saturn/Venus – 3 – Capricorn – N 4.36

4.51 – *Oculus*, Capricorn's Right Eye – Saturn/Venus – 5 – Capricorn – N 0.54

5.18 – *Bos*, Star in Capricorn's Head – Saturn/Venus – 5 – Capricorn – N 1.12

15.22 – *Armus*, Capricorn's Heart – Mars/Mercury – 5 – Capricorn – S 2.59

13.58 – *Dorsum*, Capricorn's Back – Saturn/Jupiter – 5 – Capricorn – S 0.36

20.20 – *Castra*, Capricorn's Belly – Saturn/Jupiter – 5 – Capricorn – S 4.58

21.58 – *Nashifa*, Star in Capricorn's Tail – Saturn/Jupiter – 4 – Capricorn – S 2.33

23.34 – *Sadalsuud*, Aquarius' Left Shoulder – Saturn/Mercury – 3 – Aquarius – S 8.37

23.43 – *Deneb Algedi*, Capricorn's Tail – Saturn/Jupiter – 3 – Aquarius – S 2.35

PISCES

3.31 – *Sadalmelik*, Aquarius' Right Shoulder – Saturn/Mercury – 3 – Aquarius – N 10.39

4.02 – *Fomalhaut*, The Fish's Mouth – Venus/Mercury – 1 – Southern Fish – S 21.08

5.30 – *Deneb* (*Adige*), The Swan's Tail – Venus/Mercury – 1 – Swan – N 59.55

9.03 – *Skat*, Aquarius' Right leg – Saturn/Jupiter – 3 – Aquarius – S 8.11

12.59 – *Achernar*, The River's Mouth – Jupiter – 1 – The River, Eridanus – S 59.22

23.40 – *Markab*, Pegasus' Wing – Mars/Mercury – 2 – Pegasus – N 19.24

29.33 – *Scheat*, Pegasus' Hoof – Mars/Mercury – 2 – Pegasus – N 31.08

As will be clear going through this list there are many stars close together, so the following criteria can be used to effectively select the best star working through a planet: choose the brightest, the closest in latitude and longitude, the star whose nature is the same as that of the planet concerned. Often two stars close together will be part of the same mythical story and then we choose the exact star to provide an emphasis. In a very few cases where it will not be possible to select just one star, then we can consider both stars.

5
Lunar Mansions: Star Houses

The lunar mansions are a kind of missing link in the traditional delineation of the chart. In the old texts of the Western tradition the lunar mansions are mentioned, but there is hardly any information to be found about their effects on the life. There is in fact so little and it is clearly so corrupted that it is impossible to work with the lunar mansions in a way that is clear enough to check their astrological efficacy in an acceptable way. In many cases, texts were copied without their authors apparently testing the methods rigidly in practice or without noting anything about this practical application. However, it is possible to reintegrate the lunar mansions into the Western traditional method on the basis of their clear understanding as star houses.

There are three traditional systems of lunar mansions: the Vedic system from India, the Chinese system and the Arabic western mansions. These three systems differ on some points, for example as regards the exact starting point of the first mansion, the length of the mansion, the number of mansions and the amount of information about their effects available. The three systems and their differences will be critically compared with each other in this chapter, but there is something they all have in common. This is not too surprisingly the fact they are based on the daily movement of the Moon, and not on the Sun, as in the zodiacal houses of the signs.

So a parallel comes to the fore. If we have twelve celestial houses known as the twelve zodiac signs and we have twelve mundane houses – the fields of concrete activity and realisation known as the first house, the second house etc. – we could or should also have lunar houses in the 'middle'. This idea of three kinds of astrological houses fits in well with traditional alchemy, the ancient science so closely related to astrology. In alchemy there are three principles: the fiery Sulfur impulse, (the solar level), the lunar Mercury in the middle and the material form as the alchemical Salt. The tripartition in this structure of manifestation from the fiery essential impulse through an intermediate to a material 'salinic' form, would very much fit with three house levels of comparable functions. In this division the solar zodiac is the first impulse, the divine blue-print, and the lunar mansions are the filters in the middle through which the original impulse is passed on to manifest concretely on the level of the salinic mundane houses on earth.

The term house or mansion is also very instructive. A house is a space with clearly defined boundaries where somebody lives who is the master of the house and who gives this space a particular nature and atmosphere. This picture of a house as a clearly delimited space with a particular quality and an owner/ruler can be used well as a comparison to the method of reintegrating the lunar mansions into the delineation of the chart. It is important to realise that in the lunar mansions we follow the daily movement of the Moon through the skies in the same way as we follow the movements of the Sun in the zodiac. But there is an important difference: the lunar movements are measured against the visible stars, so they are of a lower more material nature than the movements of the Sun through the twelve celestial and invisible houses. In traditional cosmology the twelve solar houses occupy the highest place, below them we find the more materialising factors of formation like the fixed stars, and further on downward are the planets. So it is in the sphere of the fixed stars right *below* the zodiac that the lunar mansions can be envisioned. They are in the middle, between the zodiac above and the planets below. There are still other systems of the mansions and these are shown in Appendix C.

The lunar mansions have a lunar role. They are in the middle, they transfer the essential light impulse of the Sun to earth. The Sun is the spiritual origin but this impulse has to pass through a lunar filter to reach the earth, and this filter gives the solar impulse a certain individual nature, which amounts to the core business of your earthly existence. It indicates the deepest goals connected to your incarnation, the goals of the unique life described by your natal chart. It is the general picture of the specific form the soul will take in material existence. As the original impulse passes through a lunar mansion connected to fixed stars and a constellation with its own mythology, you could call this the individual core mythology. In practice this system turns out to be very effective and very concrete. In many cases it is almost creepy in the accuracy of its details.

The three systems

As mentioned previously, there are three traditional systems of lunar mansions, differing on several points. The best option would be to use 'our own' Arabic mansions if they had survived until today. Unfortunately this is not the case; what we find in the old texts is clearly not a living system intensively used in practice, but dead and limited knowledge copied from even older books. The first big problem confronting us in the reconstruction of the Arabic mansions is the exact starting-point of the first mansion. It is not really clear where this should be, although several authors place the cusp of lunar mansion number 3 on the fixed star *Alcyone*, which at the moment is found on 0° Gemini. Other authors simply copy the texts and take the starting point as 0° Aries, the point where the tropical zodiac starts. This last choice shows a misunderstanding of the nature of the lunar mansions which are so clearly and closely connected to the fixed stars with their mythology and the daily movement of the Moon from to star to star. The lunar mansions cannot, if you use them as part of a practical astrological system of chart delineation, be coupled with the tropical zodiac of the twelve heavenly houses of the Sun. It is another sphere, a different level. The twelve solar houses give the general structure of the cosmos, like a blueprint actualised and brought to earth by the planets as messengers. But this blueprint of possibilities is not the same thing as the sphere of the fixed stars, which is a lower, and more concrete level of manifestation. The starting-point of the lunar system has to be somewhere in the fixed stars sphere, it has to be connected to some logically acceptable fixed star. If the third lunar mansion starts on *Alcyone*, the first mansion must begin on the star *Mesarthim*, the 'Fat Ram' in the constellation of Aries, traditionally mentioned as the first star in the first Aries lunar mansion. So *if* we decide to work with the Arabic mansions, it would be reasonable to start here (see also Appendix C for the resulting mansion boundaries). It is true that the tradition also gives the 28 lunar mansions as building-blocks of the 12 signs and so starting at 0° Aries, but this is only theoretically-metaphysically important, for all practical purposes we have to take into account the precession. So whatever mansion system we use it cannot possibly start at 0° Aries.

The lunar mansions can also be seen as a system relatively independent from the 12-fold zodiac because they are so connected to the fixed stars.

Sometimes it is even seen as a lunar zodiac said to be older than the solar zodiac. This cannot be correct, because the lunar mansions are not really a fundamental blueprint from which everything else is derived. They are themselves subordinate to the higher ninth sphere of the solar zodiac, and within this ninth sphere they perform their precession cycle. The lunar mansions are a **relatively** independent part of the system but they are not a real zodiac and are certainly not older than the solar zodiac. This is impossible as can be seen on the basis of the model of the spheres. But from a purely practical point of view you can see the lunar mansions as an autonomous system because of their strong connection to the stars. This also means that they can function in different zodiacs; if the Moon is on a star, it is on a star, and by which zodiac you measure this, does not matter at all.

The Vedic system

It is not surprising that it is Vedic astrology from India that has retained the clearest information on the lunar mansions. Vedic astrology does not use the tropical zodiac with the vernal equinox point as 0° Aries, but the sidereal zodiac – and *sider* means star. The sidereal – sideric – 'staroid' – zodiac finds its starting point of 0° Aries, not on the basis of the vernal equinox point, but by the position of a fixed star. This star is *Spica*, the Virgin's Wheat Ear, found at the moment in tropical 23° Libra, and it is the point exactly opposing *Spica* that is defined as 0° Aries of the sidereal zodiac. This is much more a star zodiac, and you could even see the sidereal zodiac as a part of the eighth sphere, along with the fixed stars. It also means that a lunar mansion system of 'star houses' fits elegantly with a sidereal 'star' zodiac, easier than with the solar tropical system.

The symbolism of the starting-point of the sidereal zodiac exactly opposing *Spica* is very appropriate. *Spica* is the Virgin's Wheat Ear, pointing to harvesting, and the constellation is also the Virgin Mary in Christian symbolism through whom the divine is born on earth. An image of salvation. She is also the quintessential purity, Virgo is about selecting what is worthwhile, what is good enough to be taken to the next phase, therefore the harvest symbolism of which the Wheat Ear *Spica* is the concentration point. But the starting-point of the sidereal zodiac is not *Spica* itself, not the harvest brought in or the finished purification, it is the point exactly opposing it that begins the process.

Here there is a lot of tension, symbolically pointing at the harvest work in progress in material reality. The crops are still in the fields and the rainy season is fast approaching.

The Vedic symbolism associated with the Virgin's Mansion connected to *Spica* tells much the same story. In Indian astrology this lunar mansion is called *Chitra* and its god is Vishvakarma, also called the heavenly architect, the constructor of the illusion of material reality that acts as a veil between us and the divine. So we see the same essential meaning, the mansion gives the ability to see the essence behind the material illusions and allows us to distinguish what is really valuable. It is the same thing as purification and harvesting. And this is typical for the whole Vedic mansion mythology; it is possible to translate the Indian mythology into Western myth as their essences turn out to be the same. Because Vedic astrology uses the sidereal star zodiac there is no uncertainty about the starting-point of the first lunar mansion, it is simply also at 0° Aries – sidereal. This also shows how the confusion about the starting-point of the lunar mansion system arose in Western astrology. About 1700 years ago *Spica* was at 0 Libra in both zodiacs. At this moment both the zodiacs started at the same point, 0° Aries tropical **was** the same as 0° Aries sidereal. But because the stars precess through the (tropical) zodiac the stars and their constellations/lunar mansions corresponded less and less with the signs, and the mansions were forgotten. Vedic astrology does not have this problem as the sidereal zodiac itself precesses, so the correspondence between stars and signs is preserved. It seems a good idea to follow Vedic astrology and fix the starting-point of the mansion system at 23 Aries – tropical. (0° Aries sidereal). Another problem is the exact length of the mansions and on this the three traditional systems do not agree. The Chinese and Arabic systems use mansions of unequal lengths. The whole idea of following the Moon in its daily course past the fixed stars is taken very literally here, and attention is focused on the boundaries of the mansions marked by the next important fixed star. This seems to be quite inappropriate for a system of houses or mansions; it would be strange if one house is much bigger or smaller than another house, as a system implies strict regularity. It is also rather poor taste to have mansions of 3 and of 19 degrees in length (see Appendix C); it looks like a corruption of the original system, a change made because the principles were no longer properly understood.

So this idea has to be rejected, and we must accept that lunar mansions are of equal length. And this immediately leads to the next problematic point – the number of mansions. The Moon takes 27.3 days to make the full round through the zodiac of 360 degrees, so it is clear there is not too much choice, we either have 27 or 28 mansions. Naturally 28 would be preferred as it is a highly symbolic number. It is 4 times 7, 1 to 7 added together, and it has an important role to play in astrology. Not only is it the number of days the Moon needs to go round, but also the number of years that Saturn goes round, and everything is governed by the planets between Saturn and the Moon. As it is 4 times 7, and as 4 is the number of matter and 7 the number of dynamic active realisation, we see all seven planetary powers going through the four elements. This is a complete cycle.

It would be a good idea therefore to have 28 mansions, and in the traditional Arabic division of the zodiac there are indeed 28 mansions. But as explained previously, this cosmological blueprint is of theoretical importance only, and from a practical perspective there are further considerations. As the system of the lunar mansions is based on the cycle of the Moon, it is strongly connected with the final manifestation of energies on earth. The Moon is the great symbol of the cycles of earthly growth and decay. This implies the possibility of a slight imperfection, deviating a little from the rigid fixed theoretical ideal, for which the traditional Hindu spirit seems to have a preference.

This possibility is indicated by the fact that the Moon takes 27.4 days to go through the circle and not 28 days. So there are good reasons to express this lunar imperfection in the system by using 27 mansions, and this is what Vedic astrology does. There is, by the way, a 28th mansion in Vedic astrology found inside one of the other mansions, but it is not a full part of the whole system on the same level as the others. This mansion is called Abhijit, associated with the star Vega in the Lyre, and is said to have come down unseen to take its place among the other mansions. When this was discovered, it was chased off and put in its proper place. This was done, it is said, because the heavens can only be measured for earthly purposes by 27 mansions, and this is exactly what is meant by the possibility of imperfection inherent in a lunar system.

This is not to suggest that one of these two ideas is correct and the other is not. 27 and 28 are both valid possibilities of systematisation underlining different aspects. In choosing a 27-fold division the earthly aspect is emphasized; in choosing 28 the connection with metaphysical rigidity comes to the fore. Both possibilities have something to say, but it is extremely important not to ignore the precession, meaning that the Arabic 28 mansions system cannot possibly take as its starting-point 0°Aries tropical. This would be much too abstract. The whole lunar mansion system is so strongly connected to the stars that we have to take the precessional movement into account.

So now that we have an acceptable starting-point and a good idea about the number of mansions and the length of the mansions, it is time to discuss the amount of information available in each tradition. The Vedic system is clearly the most reliable as it has retained a wealth of information on the lunar mansions connected to a clear mythology, whereas there is hardly anything concrete to be found in the Arabic mansions; this appears to comprise mainly evidently corrupted indications on elections and magic which would provide too feeble a foundation on which to generate new principles. I was unable to find sufficient information regarding the Chinese system so it will be left aside as it is not clear to me how effective it is.

The conclusion can only be that the Arabic system can be forgotten for the time being without losing anything too valuable, and that it would be more profitable to connect Western classical astrology with the Vedic lunar mansions. This has to be done under very rigid conditions as we are not going to do any Vedic astrology – it is just the information that is going to be extracted. On the basis of fixed stars connected to a mansion, the myths from the Vedic theme will be associated with and translated into the related Western myth. This turns out be very easy and it clarifies the central mythical principle ruling a mansion along with a lot of practical information given in the Vedic tradition.

In this process the Vedic mansions will be renamed to underline the mythical core. The mansion 'Danishta' for example will be called the Mansion of the Dolphin which will be much clearer in the context of the Western classical analysis of the chart. The role of the Dolphin in antique mythology is much the same as its role in the Vedic tradition and the two perspectives combined give a surprisingly clear picture of exactly what the mansion means and what its effects on the life are. It should be clearly understood that this is not syncretism – combining unrelated things from various sources – but synthesis, making a connection between two traditions based on a shared background principle: the core mythology connected to the stars ruling the mansions.

In this way a dynamic relationship is created between both traditions, enriching the understanding on both sides. Wisdom does not come from India, neither does it come from the West or from Arabia, but it is further developed by a synthetic meeting based on an understanding of principles, and not by simply copying information. In translating the system, important Vedic elements will be left out; for example, the Vedic planetary mansion rulers will not be used. To check if the promise of a mansion will be realised in life, the rest of the chart will be analysed in the standard traditional way. The concept of karma will also be omitted, as it does not function well in a Western spiritual context.

Furthermore, it is only the Moon's position in the mansion that will be taken into account and not all the planets. This is for simplicity's sake but it is also what the ancient sources tell us to do and it seems very logical. Other positions, especially the Ascendant, may be interesting to experiment with in the long run, but it is always wise to discourage an expansion of methods. The whole thing should be approached with discipline and a discerning and cautious mind. In this way a reduced model is created, profiting optimally from the Vedic wealth of information but remaining totally Western. Vedic astrology functions here only as an information source, but by making this connection other things will become clear about the Vedic system which are not found in that tradition. So it is fruitful for both sides.

All 27 lunar mansions are explained in the scheme that follows. First the Western mythological name of the mansion is given, then the degrees in the **sidereal** zodiac and then the traditional Vedic name. These sidereal degrees can be roughly and quickly recalculated for the tropical zodiac by adding 7 degrees and going backward one sign. This is true for our current period of time but as it depends on precession it should be recalculated for other periods. Most astrology programmes offer a quick switch facility from tropical to sidereal zodiac, which is very practical. For every mansion the mythological core theme is given, the Vedic keywords are explained, and the Vedic gods are mentioned where relevant. It is striking how much insight this gives into why a Vedic mansion has a certain effect, and this knowledge is not always found in the tradition itself. Every mansion has a length of 13.20 degrees and is ruled by fixed stars whose constellation indicates the mythological theme ruling the whole mansion. The Moon's position in a mansion shows the main myth of a life and it is an important part of fixed star delineation.

Number 1 – The Ram's Horns Mansion – 0.00 to 13.20 Aries sidereal – Ashwini
The stars ruling this mansion are *Sharatan* and *Mesarthim*, the Ram's Horns and Head, and it is associated with powerful thrust and energy. This explains the traditional keywords of speed, youth, pioneering, rashness, physical action and medicine as the preservation of youth. Striking also is the connection with relationships, as the central theme of youthful freshness preserved can be very positive for relationships. The central idea of fiery impulsive action in this first Ram mansion is continued in the next mansion, also ruled by Ram stars. As always the exact placement of the ruling stars in the constellation indicate an emphasis on a specific part, in this case the thrust of the horns. In the Vedic myths associated with this mansion, the unbearable brightness of the Sun god Vivaswat is an important theme, fitting well with the abundance of fiery power in this first part of the mansion cycle. It also refers to the exaltation of the Sun in Aries, and exaltation always means exaggeration. It is the preservation of the first youthful energy that explains the keyword medicine in this mansion.

Number 2 – The Mansion of the Golden Fleece – 13.20 to 26.40 Aries sidereal – Bharani
The mythical Ram has two related meanings, both of which tell the story of a long and dedicated journey to the divine essence, or the essentially good, during which many battles are fought and many victims made. Through the air and on the Ram's back, brother and sister Phryxus and Helle flee from their bad step-mother Ino, the material desire nature, but Helle – the feminine more earthly part of the soul – falls off into the sea, the Hellespont. Phryxus succeeds in reaching his destination and he sacrifices the Ram, which gives him peace. This Hide is also known as the Golden Fleece, symbol of the divine realised in the world, and it was the goal of Jason's quest with the Argonauts.

The traditional keywords point in the same direction, that this mansion is associated with a dedicated fanatical soldier who will not be held back and who will do everything in his power to find the truth. The truth is the Golden Fleece and the risks of the quest are shown by Helle's fall and the long-winding complex adventures of the Argonauts. Three vague stars in the constellation of Aries according to the Vedic knowledge are said to have the form of a vagina and they rule this mansion that is also associated with the intense impassioned processes of death, birth and sexuality. The ruling stars are found on the hind part of the Ram, which is a clear indication of these central themes. In this mansion the god of death Yama, son of sun god Vivaswat rules, pointing to the sacrificed Ram and the close connection with the previous Aries mansion.

Number 3 – The Mansion of the Knife – 16.40 Aries to 10.00 Taurus sidereal – Krittika

This is the mansion of the Pleiades or the Weeping Sisters, an unhappy nebula of seven stars indicating disappointments and things that go wrong. The seven stars are similar to the seven planets who like wardens lock us up in the prison of material reality. In this way they cut us off from our origin behind the planets, where we long to be. The Pleiades are chased by Orion the gross hunter who is a symbol for matter separating us from the ideal world above. This central theme of cutting off explains the traditional Vedic keywords of fire, knives, sharpness and forcefulness. There is a strong element of material grossness here. This mansion is said to give ambition, decisive action, destructiveness and persistency, and several sides of the mythical story may manifest alternately. Another theme of the myth is the seduction of other people's partners, a variation of the central theme of cutting off and disappointments. Problems in the family are also associated with the Pleiades. The seven Weeping Sisters, who allowed themselves to be seduced, are the mirror image of the lofty seven stars in the Greater Bear traditionally seen as seven sages. The Pleiad sisters once were the wives of these sages but after their seduction, they fell away from the divine pole, which underlines the cutting off from the divine wisdom and the disappointments involved. The Vedic tradition sees the image of a knife in the Pleiades; in this mansion the fire god rules.

Number 4 – The Mansion of the Bull's Eye – 10.00 to 23.20 Taurus sidereal – Rohini

The star ruling this mansion is the intensely red Bull's Eye, known as *Aldebaran*. The Bull is a symbol of matter and the bull's eye is the left eye staring at earth, fixated on material forms. Therefore the central theme in this mansion is great material success, but also other forms of material expression like the arts and a strong sensuality. Aldebaran's colour is the red of passion. The essence is going *through* matter and not getting stuck in all the successes. The image is like the bull-fighter who dances with the bull and kills it before it can kill him. The same thing is seen in ancient Minoan imagery of people jumping over a bull, expressing the control of matter. The material success promised here will of course only be realised if the rest of the chart allows it. The most appropriate picture for this mansion, also called the Red One, is a steaming, wild bull. In the Vedic tradition Rohini is Soma's wife, Soma is the lunar god, quite appropriate for this Taurus mansion.

Number 5 – The Mansion of the Amazon – 23.20 Taurus to 6.40 Gemini sidereal – Mrigashira

This mansion is ruled by three stars in the gross hunter Orion, one of which is *Bellatrix* of the second magnitude, also known as the female warrior. The traditional keywords are closely related to the story of brutish Orion who was created from an ox-hide and who has no connection at all with higher things. This mansion gives doubts, as Orion is naïve with no fixed principles; he is not too intelligent despite his great successes in hunting. But there is a literal connection with hunting, nature, animals, the land, the countryside and sharpshooting. The central theme is limitation to the natural environment. The relentless hunting of Orion comes back in the associated Vedic story about Brahma who desired his own daughter. She flew from him to the stars in the shape of an antelope but Brahma then changed into a deer to chase her, after which Shiva cut off the deer's head and this head was put among the stars. For this reason this mansion is also associated with strong sexual lust; Orion is not only a hunter of animals. The ruler star *Bellatrix* is placed on the left shoulder of the hunter and is also known as 'he who destroys swiftly'. The Moon god rules this mansion, illustrating its transitory purely natural character.

Number 6 – The Mansion of the Hunter – 6.40 to 20 Gemini sidereal – Ardra

This mansion is also ruled by the Orion stars, notably the bright first magnitude *Betelgeuse*. The story of Orion who overestimates his powers and is punished is retold in the associated Vedic myth. Ardra is the demon Taraka who after many trials was given invincibility. Unwisely Taraka then decided to attack the gods, who eventually killed him. This is exactly the same as in the Western myth, where Orion boasts loudly after many successes that he is able to hunt down any animal, whereupon the gods send the Scorpion to kill him. Another version of the story is Orion pursuing Diana for which he was punished by her brother Apollo because Diana is the pure virgin goddess, again a transgression of limitations. Keywords in this mansion are about animals, hunting, strong sexuality, hardness, mercilessly chasing commercial success, and stubborn destructibility (the successful brute) – persisting without any awareness as to when to stop. This mansion is ruled by Rudra, the storm god.

Number 7 – The Mansion of the Brothers – 20 Gemini to 3.20 Cancer sidereal – Punarvasu

This is the mansion ruled by *Castor* and *Pollux*, the mortal and immortal twins representing the two parts of the human soul. One part wants to be active in the world, the other part wants to return to its divine origin. The traditional Vedic description is not very concrete but the theme of the division into two intimately connected parts is obvious. This mansion is said to give the combination of an adventurous pragmatic spirit with a thirst for knowledge, a kind of Indiana Jones motive. It has a double, ambivalent nature with two counterparts in a tense relationship. The combination of knowledge and action is mirrored in the fact that *Castor* is a Mercury star and *Pollux* a Mars star. This is also a mansion of great success as *Pollux* is one of the six royal stars, but this will only be realised if the rest of the chart permits it. The cosmic mother goddess, Aditti, rules this mansion as *Castor* and *Pollux* are symbolically the first division born directly from original unity.

Number 8 – The Mansion of the Servant – 3.20 to 16.40 Cancer sidereal – Pushya

The *Aselli* in the constellation of Cancer rule this mansion, much associated with serving. The traditional Vedic keywords are feeding, servitude and regeneration. The *Aselli* are in Christian symbolism the ox and the ass in the stable (in fact the cave: the human heart centre) present at Jesus' birth, so they will follow the Messiah – which could also make them fanatical followers. The Crib itself is the extremely malefic *Praesepe*. It is an empty crib and there is no master to be followed, but this mansion is controlled by the *Aselli* not by *Praesepe* so it does not have a dark nature overall. But of course the choice of the master served is decisive for its effect in the world. This mansion is ruled by Brihaspati, the god of wisdom, repeating the idea of following the right master.

Number 9 – The Mansion of the Hydra – 16.40 to 30 Cancer sidereal – Ashlesha

This is the mansion of pure snake power, connected to the image of the many-headed poisonous monster, the symbol of the uncontrollable desire nature. The keywords are clear about this: drugs, pornography, manipulation, crime, politics, hypnosis, secret service, spies and reptiles. There is a direct tapping into the essence of the desire nature and the Vedic keywords give deep insights into the psychology of desire. This mansion gives the power of persuasion, a sensual aura, a powerful sexuality, an exuberant life-style, a tendency to controversial behaviour but also a philosophical attitude. The Hydra is not only pure desire nature but also the life energy itself. This mansion offers direct access to this electrifying power and the myth of Hercules shows what has to be done. He cuts off all the Hydra heads, prevents their growing back by fire (spiritual warfare) and puts a heavy stone (moral rules) on the last immortal head. The direct access to the snake power in this mansion gives an understanding of the psychology of desire, which is the source of power, so there is also the possibility it will be abused. That is why Hercules is so radical. This house is ruled by Sarpa, the snake king.

Number 10 – The Mansion of the Lion's Heart – 00.00 to13.20 Leo sidereal – Magha

Regulus is the ruling star here, and fiery ambition and lust for power are the main themes in this mansion. *Regulus* is the royal star among the royals and all keywords have to do with dignity, protocol, tradition, leadership, and everything that gives status. Further descriptions can be summarized as proud, royal, respectable and imperious. There is a strong connection with one's forbears as this mansion's pride is based on the idea of continuing a respectable tradition as a channel of original truth. It is like the British taste for tradition based on pride of historical achievements rather than on a real love of the past. In the Vedic system it is the Pitris, the forbears, who rule this mansion.

Number 11 – The Mansion of the Lion's Back – 13.20 to 26.40 Leo sidereal – Purva Phalguni

This the second mansion ruled by stars in Leo, here we have *Zosma*, the Lion's Back and *Theta Leonis* also called the Chertan's Cord or the Lion's ribs. The name can be translated as 'the first reddish one'. The traditional keywords are pride, naive sincerity, independence, relaxing and enjoying life. In these keywords several aspects of Leo come to the fore. No one rides on the back of a lion, therefore independence is an example. There is a strong emphasis on marriage, love and sexuality, as this is the proud master of the house who returns to his home where he is the king. In this mansion the god Bagha rules, giving happiness in love.

Number 12 – The Mansion of the Lion's Tail – 26.40 Leo to 10.00 Virgo sidereal – Uttara Phalguni

The third mansion ruled by Leo stars has *Denebola*, the Lion's Tail. The mansion's Vedic name can be translated as 'the second reddish one', showing the strong similarity with the previous mansion. The traditional descriptions remain very Leo-like, ambition, pride, dignity, positions of honour, leadership, courage and generosity, and just as in the previous mansion relaxing and enjoying life, independence and a sincere directness. Marriage, love and sexuality are important themes too. This mansion is ruled by Aryaman, the god of friendliness.

Number 13 – The Mansion of the Hands – 10.00 to 23.20 Virgo sidereal – Hasta

This mansion is ruled by stars in the Crow of which *Algorab* is the brightest. Its main theme is also associated with the Cup the bird did not fill. This shows up very strongly in the keywords of pottery, ceramics and manual skills. The Cup is symbolically the Grail, retaining the connection with the spiritual origin, and the Crow is the bird who forgot this origin as he did not fill the Cup at the well as Apollo ordered him to do. The Crow preferred to spend his time eating nice ripe figs and on returning to Apollo he lied to the sun god that a snake had barred his way and he had been unable to complete his task. The other keywords clearly reflect this: swindlers, pick-pockets, pretenders, conjurers, sticky-fingered dexterous people. Hasta, the mansion's Vedic name, means hand, and hand–reading is another of the occupations mentioned for this mansion. An eye for detail, flexibility, dexterity and a relativistic sense of humour describe this mansion, which is ruled by the Vedic god Surya.

Number 14 – The House of the Virgin – 22.30 Virgo to 6.40 Libra sidereal – Chitra

The ruling star in this mansion is *Spica*, the star that fixes the starting-point of the sidereal zodiac which is the degree in exact opposition to itself. The traditional Vedic descriptions are a bit unclear but they all mirror the positive nature of this main star in the constellation Virgo. The keywords are: artistic talents, medicine, pioneering, defending the weak and the poor, and inventions. Vishvakarma is the god of this mansion and he can be seen as the architect of material illusions, so there is a strong connection with the essential reality behind the material veil, explaining the artistic tendencies and the radical idealism. Also inventions can be understood in this way, if you know how the material world manifests you can use this knowledge to create new things.

This all fits in well with the main theme of Virgo; purification and selection in order to realise the essence behind the material veil. *Spica* is the virgin's Wheat Ear, the end result and concentration point of the harvesting process. It is also strongly associated with Mary through whom the divine is born in the world. In Greek mythology this role is fulfilled by Astraea, daughter of the purely material Titans, opponents of the gods, who nevertheless chooses the side of the gods, which is exactly the same theme.

Number 15 – The Mansion of the Crusader – 6.40 to 6.20 Libra sidereal – Swati

The constellation ruling this house is Boötes, the Guardian of the Bear, with its main star *Arcturus*. The traditional keywords all have associations with wind, air, breath, spirit, and Swati means 'sword' indicating concrete action and battle. It is said in the descriptions of this mansion that it gives control over the instinctive nature and this fits in well with Boötes as the guardian of the bear, a very violent and fierce animal. The image is given of a decisive political strategist socially engaged who believes in progress and equality, a bit of a social democrat. Concrete results are important in this mansion, and these results may be financial, so it is not all idealism.

Boötes is pictured as well armed and in his bear hunt he enters a temple, which points to a kind of crusading energy, violent action for some holy aim. It is a tense mixture of earthly violence and divine inspiration, with a central theme of guiding the action in the correct way by higher inspiration. This is mirrored in Vedic mythology by the wind god Vayu who rules this mansion and who has two sons: the extremely violent Bhima and the spiritual Hanuman. The strong association with air and breathing points to the spiritual side of the crusade, where inspiration is found for a holy war, and this gives direction and control over the instinctive nature. Everything that has to do with air is an abstraction from the instincts, which is why it has such an important role in many meditation techniques. This mirrors the Bear/Boar theme (action/contemplation or temporal/spiritual authority) associated with Boötes. In the chart of Bruce Lee the Moon is placed in this mansion, very much illustrating its essence.

Number 16 – The Mansion of the Claws – 20 Libra to 3.20 Scorpio sidereal – Vishakha

This is the mansion ruled by Libra's *North* and *South Scales*, also to be seen as the Scorpion's Claws, as in ancient times Libra was a part of Scorpio. The Claws are associated with avenging justice, the preparedness to do whatever is necessary and just. The *South Scale* is the cosmic Dirty

Harry or Attila the Hun, the Scourge of God coming down to punish the morally corrupted. The main theme in this mansion is extreme goal-orientedness; whatever is necessary to achieve the Aim is done, and everything blocking the way is swept aside effectively and decisively. It is bend or break. Everything is done obsessively; this mansion is not exactly diplomatic or democratic, opposition is simply eliminated. You could call this the Mansion of the Long March, as it does not matter how long it takes, the aim will be achieved as the aim is just. Indra, the killer of demons, is one of the rulers of this mansion in Vedic mythology.

Number 17 – The Mansion of the Lotus – 3.20 to 16.40 Scorpio sidereal – Anuradha
This is the second mansion ruled by Scorpio and the main stars here are *Graffias* and *Isidis* in the head and the claw. The traditional Vedic descriptions are surprisingly positive: hospitality, friendship, sharing of things, which seems a little inappropriate for a sinister constellation like Scorpio, the beast that mercilessly kills Orion, the cosmic hulk. But this positive side is a logical result of the killing of gross matter in the form of the Hunter because if you get rid of Orion, the unity behind matter can be experienced. This unity is one of the keywords for this mansion of the Lotus, the beautiful flower that roots in the mud. It is a perfect parallel with the image of the royal eagle as the transformed ghastly scorpion, once lurking in dark holes, now soaring through the heavens.

Number 18 – The Mansion of the Scorpion's Heart – 16.40 to 30.00 Scorpio sidereal – Jyeshta
Intensely red *Antares*, the Scorpion's Heart and the ultimate death star, rules this mansion. The keywords all point to a strong energy and a combative spirit, according well with the essentially martial nature of the Scorpion's Heart. The Scorpion is the beast sent by the gods to sting to death material Orion, the mythical Charles Bronson, and is therefore associated with the acquiring of deep insights into occult and hidden matters. The final aim lies behind the material veil. The central theme is the killing of some powerful arrogant 'material' enemy in the shape of a person or an idea. This is the third mansion ruled by Scorpio; the role of the protective and responsible leader of the family is also underlined here. This mansion is also ruled by Indra, the killer of demons.

Number 19 – The Mansion of the Sting – 0.00 to 13.20 Sagittarius sidereal – Mula

This fourth Scorpio mansion puts a strong emphasis on the Scorpion's sting, but here there is not so much a battle with others as the sting being directed against the person himself. The beast stings itself to death because this mansion presents many disappointing experiences that require a lot of energy and optimism in order to be mastered (the self-made man). The goddess in this mansion is Nirriti, better-known as the dark death goddess Kali, pointing to disintegration. The strong disintegrating tendency will lead to a radical detachment, according well with the sting killing you again and again. In a certain sense you play the role of Orion in this mansion.

Number 20 - The Mansion of the Archer's Bow - 13.20 to 26.40 Sagittarius sidereal – Purva Ashada

This mansion is ruled by a couple of stars in the Archer's Bow, the Archer being Chiron in astrology. The traditional keywords have to do with water, maritime matters, writing and weapons, and they point to a strong power of persuasion, great optimism, radical elimination of obstacles and spiritual independence. This all accords well Chiron as the wise teacher of many heroes, and the bow of course stands for passionately spreading ideas and knowledge.

The emphasis on water seems strange but this relates to Chiron's double nature. As a centaur he is only half human – his hind part is a horse and is often shown with pronounced sexual organs. This horse part is the desire nature and the central theme of the Centaur is the painful tension between the powerful instincts and conscious abstract knowledge. Water is the symbol of desire and the activities on water mirror this part of Chiron's nature, it shows he relates to his instinctive part. The passionate spreading of knowledge is fed by the driving force of the desire nature, but as the myth shows, the instinctive part may get the upper-hand. As a consequence all the power of persuasion and the fiery pursuit of ideals may be led in the wrong direction and get off the track. The name of this mansion translates as the Invincible One. The water gods Varuna and Apa rule here.

Number 21 – The Mansion of the Horse – 26.40 Sagittarius to 10.00 Capricorn sidereal – Uttara Ashada

This is the second mansion falling under Chiron the Archer but the stars ruling here are found on his body rather than on his bow, indicating a different emphasis. The traditional keywords are horses, ambition, fighting power, drive, and the transfer of visions and insights. This mansion is called the Second Invincible One, showing the strong relation with the previous Mansion of the Bow. It is also associated with new ideas but with a stronger emphasis on the body and not only the bow itself. So there is a more realistic attitude, the fiery drive is less overwhelming. Also in this mansion the pursuit of ideals is strong and there is always the danger that the animal side of the centaur takes over too much and idealism descends into a merciless fanaticism. This mansion is ruled by the gods of willpower and uprightness, the Vishvadevas.

Number 22 – The Mansion of the Eagle – 10.00 to 23.20 Capricorn sidereal – Shravana

This mansion is ruled by the constellation of the Eagle. This is Jupiter taking Ganymede to the spiritual heights of Olympus. Another image of the eagle is the vulture sticking his head into dead bodies, but his neck is bald so he remains free of the rotting dirt of the earth. Both images point to a strong drive to search for the Truth, to spiritual aspiration and ambition. The Vedic keywords mirror this theme as the mansion produces sincere teachers and dedicated searchers for truth who use language intensively to spread their knowledge, also in the role of consultants. The symbol in this mansion is an ear, because knowledge was always transferred orally in the tradition; only much later was it written down. This mansion is ruled by Saraswati, the goddess of wisdom.

Number 23 – The Mansion of the Dolphin – 23.20 Capricorn to 6.40 Aquarius sidereal – Dhanishta

Four stars in the constellation of the Dolphin rule this mansion and the keywords music, poetry, courage, medicine, beneficence, wealth and generosity are directly connected to the Dolphin's mythical story. This story describes how the poet Arion of Lesbos, who had gathered great riches on his way home on a ship, was threatened by the ship's crew because they wanted to steal his possessions. As a last favour he asked to be allowed the singing of a lamentation and this request was granted. As he started to sing he threw himself overboard unexpectedly and was saved by a dolphin that was attracted by his music.

The symbolism of the dolphin is the key to the meaning of this story, because it is strongly associated with the South Node; it is Arion's music that attracts the dolphin, so through his music he leaves the bonds of the material world behind. The South Node represents the exit gate of life and the entrance into the higher spiritual worlds. In the traditional Vedic descriptions, themes like universal love, compassion and mystical openness are very much underlined therefore. But it might be the other side of this mansion that comes to the fore, like obsessively gathering possessions and money. This depends on the rest of the chart. In ancient times Capricorn, in which a part of this mansion falls, was also called the Dolphin. In this mansion the gods of wealth rule, the earthly Vasus.

Number 24 – The Mansion of the Cup-bearer – 6.40 to 20.00 Aquarius sidereal – Shatabisha

This mansion is controlled by Aquarius, the constellation of the Cup-bearer who pours out the sweet waters of desire conquered. This explains the strong connection with aviation and space travel; we can go upward to great heights if the waters of desires have been tamed, but this is also seen more literally in the eagle of Jupiter taking Ganymede up to Olympus to serve the wine at the feast of the gods. Keywords are hunting, rude language, and research into illnesses difficult to heal. The descriptions also give us principles like truthfulness, eccentricity, stubbornness but also helpfulness, gentleness and being traditionally religious. The central point in this is the practice and development of a more genuinely human attitude. The symbolism is connected with the taming and distilling of raw sea-water, illustrating the transformation of desire into drinkable sweet water which is kept in the cup.

In the picture in the heavens we see the waters from the cup streaming into the mouth of the Southern Fish – *Fomalhaut* – pointing to mystical enlightenment and redemption, as this is the star of the birth of Christ. The symbolism is that developing humanity precedes the spiritual; first the salt water of desire has to be distilled and purified and made sweet, and this is what the Cup-bearer does. It also explains the rigidity and the love of hunting. By following traditional rules a sense of humanity begins to develop. (In hunting, for example, ancient rules express respect for the animal and the control of aggressive impulses – something which is often misunderstood). The essence of this mansion is acting humanely, so if existing rules do not support this they are ignored. Research into diseases that are difficult to heal also fits in with the general image of humanity, as does traditional religion and gentleness. The theme of hiding and secrets is strong in this mansion, explained by the need to protect the precious refined sweet waters from pollution in the environment. In this house Varuna, the god of the waters of life rules.

Number 25 – The Mansion of the Fall – 20.00 Aquarius to 3.20 Pisces sidereal – Purba Bhradapada

This mansion is ruled by stars in Pegasus, the Flying Horse on which Bellerophon tried to reach Olympus on his own initiative. The gods were not amused and sent down a horsefly to sting Pegasus, and its rider was thrown off and fell to earth, where he spent the rest of his life lonely and blind. The Vedic keywords are negative: death, drugs, terrorism, black magic, dementia, decay... the core issue being the refusal to accept higher guidance. Magic, drugs and terrorism are all expressions of this essence on different levels, they are all ways to force entrance into the Olympic world. This is the mansion of hubris, spiritual arrogance defying the gods, followed by a fall. In all the descriptions a stubborn attitude is the central theme combined with the guilty realisation that laws and boundaries have not been respected. Pegasus is the desire to leave the bonds of material life behind but here it takes on negative forced forms. One of the ruling stars in this mansion is *Scheat*, Pegasus' Hoof sticking in the mud.

Number 26 – The Mansion of the Wing - 3.20 to 16.40 Pisces sidereal – Uttara Bhradapada

This is the second mansion controlled by Pegasus stars, but is traditionally seen as the light, mirror-image of the first Pegasus mansion. Guidance is accepted here and the Vedic keywords are very positive and spiritual: yoga, temples, meditation, erudition, beneficence, devotion, tantra and things connected to the end of life. This positive side is indicated by the fact that this mansion is co-ruled by a star in Andromeda, *Alpheratz*, with a very positive meaning. It is the soul opening itself to higher guidance and being saved from material bondage. The hero Perseus – who rescues Andromeda, the damsel in distress, from the Seamonster – rides on Pegasus demonstrating the central theme of saving.

The star in Pegasus ruling this mansion is placed on the wing tip pointing to the lighter side of the whole story. The descriptions suggest virtue, charm, willingness to sacrifice, readiness to help and almost paranormal sensitivity, equality and writing talents. But it should be made clear that the opposite side of obstinate self-destructive fanaticism is by no means absent here, and may also manifest. If you only take this mansion as positive and spiritual you will go wrong, as it is the framework of the chart which determines how this is going to work out. This mansion and the Mansion of the Fall share a common Pegasus theme with a different emphasis. Ahir Budhanya, The Snake of the Depth rules here; the essential cosmic energy, the spirituality and the paranormal sensitivity. In Western terms we can say that we can cast a glance on to Olympus in this mansion.

Number 27 – The Mansion of the Fishes – 16.40 to 30.00 Pisces sidereal – Revati

This last mansion in the cycle is ruled by the Fishes swimming in opposite directions yet tied together by a mysterious ribbon. The two fishes are the symbols of the two luminaries the Sun and Moon, the basic cosmic polarities connected here by the ribbon, pointing again to the symbolism of the nodal axis and the final phase of the cycle. The Fishes represent the divine because a fish never sleeps and can move around in the desire waters unharmed. In this last mansion, and the last constellation of the zodiacal cycle, grace descends after sacrifice. It is the phase of conclusion and the definitive solution. This explains the traditional Vedic keywords associated with the measurement of time; it is time itself as one of the conditions of earthly life ending here. So one of the essences of the Mansion of the Fishes is the gate to another higher world; escaping the limiting conditions of matter and time.

The further Vedic descriptions mention helpfulness, fixed ideas, love of travel (this mansion is symbolically the nodal axis, so the ultimate journey) and optimism (the higher better worlds become visible). Also the theme of feeding is strong as this mansion is seen as preceding manifestation, as the womb of the Sun; the nodal axis which the Fishes symbolise is the gate into and out of material life. On another level there is a clear association with marriage as the nodal axis is the conjunction of the Sun and Moon's orbits, and there is the ribbon tying together the two Fishes which can also be regarded as solar-masculine and lunar-feminine. In more down-to-earth terms, buses, trains, road-construction and maintenance engineers connect to this mansion because it has to do with keeping open roads and connections, illustrated on a cosmic level by the essential road and gate of the nodal axis. In this mansion Pushan, the god of safe journeys and feeding rules.

So by combining traditional Vedic with ancient Western mythology a deeper understanding of the mansion is possible, which can easily be integrated in Western classical chart delineation. This can be achieved without needing to understand any Vedic techniques; Vedic astrology is used only as a rich source of symbolism to illustrate the effects the lunar mansions may have on the life. The main point in the mansion analysis is the position of the Moon, the symbol of the soul connecting the spirit to a material form, but the Ascendant is also worth looking at.

It is however not a good idea to systematically analyse all the positions of planets or cusps in lunar mansions, although a mansion occupied by four planets may provide some important information. Limit yourself; in astrology less is certainly more. The most important thing is only to look at the lunar mansions after you have assessed the whole chart. It should be the last step in the delineation process and you will judge it in the frame-work of the whole chart. This is necessary to get an idea of how everything is going to work out. If we have a mansion promising wealth but this is contradicted by the financial significators in the chart, you will have to adapt your judgement of the mansion. However its mythical theme will always remain the core business of the life.

In this unified scheme the many-layeredness of the mythical stories stands out as a central point. The myth works not only on a concrete level but on psychological, moral and spiritual levels. This reminds us of the traditional *lectio divina* of biblical stories, discerning four inter-connected levels of meanings of which the mystical-spiritual meaning is the highest.

To illustrate this we could question why a snake sheds it skin. A snake is the ultimate symbol of desire, which amounts to the same thing as duality. The danger is that the snake gets stuck in this desire nature, excluding all further development. So in order to save itself from the material powers it manifests so extremely, it has to shed its skin so it can keep moving. Skin is Saturn, the planet of rigid forms always tending to become petrified. A change of form is necessary and this applies on all levels, material, psychological and spiritual. This is an example of the multi-layered symbolic thinking we need to understand the mythology. In the Mansion of the Fishes this is very clear; the various keywords derive in different ways from the same nodal axis symbolism, so that this mansion could be prominent in the chart of a train-driver (keeping the road open) but also in the chart of an astrologer (measurement of time).

6
CASE STUDIES

An Explanation of Dignities
To be able to follow the case studies in this chapter you need to know the classical system of dignities. There are two kinds of dignities describing two kinds of power. The first is essential dignity, the second is accidental dignity (more below). The degree of essential dignity is assessed by a planet's position in a sign. Mars in Aries is in its own sign and therefore has a lot of essential dignity. But Mars is also very strong in Capricorn where it has its exaltation and this is also essential dignity.

There are also negative counterparts of a planet in its own sign or in exaltation, and these are called 'detriment' and 'fall' respectively. In other words, when the planet is in the sign opposite to its rulership or exaltation. If a planet is placed in such a negative dignity, it cannot do much good and is 'essentially debilitated'. An example is Mars in Libra, opposite to its own sign, so in detriment. This is a difficult Mars which will cause trouble in some way. If Mars is placed in Cancer in opposition to its exaltation sign Capricorn, it also has no dignity (being in its fall) and will also work out in a negative way.

All planets have signs in which they are either very strong or very weak according to the logical pattern given below:

Sun: Strong in its own sign Leo, exalted in Aries.
Weak in detriment in Aquarius opposite Leo, in fall in Libra.

Moon: Strong in its own sign Cancer and exalted in Taurus.
Weak in detriment in Capricorn, in fall in Scorpio.

Mercury: Strong in its own signs Gemini and Virgo.
Weak in detriment in Sagittarius, in fall and detriment in Pisces. Virgo is Mercury's sign and exaltation, so it is extremely strong there.

Venus: Strong in its own signs Taurus and Libra, in exaltation in Pisces.
Weak: in detriment in Aries and Scorpio, in fall in Virgo.

Mars: Strong in its own signs Aries and Scorpio, exalted in Capricorn.
Weak in detriment in Libra and Taurus, in fall in Cancer.

Jupiter: Strong in its own signs Sagittarius and Pisces, exalted in Cancer.
Weak in detriment in Gemini and Virgo, in fall in Capricorn.

Saturn: Strong in its own signs Aquarius and Capricorn, exalted in Libra.
Weak in detriment in Leo and Cancer, in fall in Aries.

In this scheme only classical rulerships apply. Jupiter rules Pisces, Mars rules Scorpio and Saturn rules Aquarius. The outer planets have no role in this pattern, which is rigidly logical and easy to remember. Some astrologers do not use the term 'in detriment', they prefer 'in exile'. However detriment seems to describe better what this state means, the positive power a planet may have is absent, it is severely damaged. The normally positive planet Jupiter is quite nasty when it is in detriment.

Placement in its own sign, exaltation, detriment and fall are the most important dignities, describing the main differences in planet power. There are three other smaller positive dignities, of which the elemental attributions are the most important. A planet placed in a sign of which the elemental nature accords well with its own nature has some power, although definitely not as much as a planet in own sign or in exaltation. If a planet is placed in the right element this is called 'in triplicity' in classical astrology. Triplicity is simply another word for element.

It is easy to check whether a planet is placed in its triplicity. The first step is to determine whether we have a day chart or a night chart. If the Sun is above the horizon in the houses 7 to 12 it is day chart. If it is under the horizon in the houses 1 to 6 it is a night chart. If this is clear we apply the following the scheme:

Day Charts (Diurnal)

Sun, Venus, Mars and Saturn may get extra essential dignity by placement in a fitting sign.

Essential dignity by triplicity: Sun in fire signs, Saturn in air signs, Mars in water signs, Venus in earth signs.

Night Charts (Nocturnal)

Jupiter, the Moon, Mars and Mercury may get extra essential dignity by placement in a fitting sign.

Essential dignity by triplicity: Jupiter in fire signs, Mercury in air signs, Mars in water signs, the Moon in earth signs.

There is also another system giving each element three planets instead of two. Some classical astrologers claim that this system is better because it is older. In practice this point cannot be proven and the two-ruler system is as ancient as the three-ruler system. In all branches of astrology the two-ruler system is effective.

Besides triplicities there are also the minor dignities 'term' (*termini*: boundaries) and 'face' or decanate. These give a planet a small degree of extra power but not much. The terms are assessed on the basis of five planet zones into which every sign can be divided, in each zone one planet is placed in its 'term'. Faces work in the same way but they divide the signs in three zones of ten degrees each. These minor dignities give much less power that the other dignities but they will sometimes be important. In the scheme below an overview of all the five essential dignities is given.

Using the Table of Essential Dignities on the following page: From left to right this scheme gives for each sign the planets 'having dignity' there. The first column next to the sign symbols gives the sign rulers, the second column the exaltation rulers and under 'Triplic' the triplicity rulers are mentioned (first the ruler in a day chart, then the ruler in a night chart). Under 'terms' the term rulers are mentioned, five zones in each sign, and the last column the faces or decanate rulers having authority over zones of 10 degrees. The column 'detr' gives the planets in detriment per sign and 'fall' the planets in fall. The specific degree

A Table of the Essential Dignities of the PLANETS according to Ptolemy

Sign	Houses of the Planets	Exaltation	Triplicity of Planets		The Terms of the Planets					The Faces of the Planets			Detriment	Fall
			D	N										
♈	♂ D	☉ 19	☉	♃	♃ 6	♀ 14	☿ 21	♂ 26	♄ 30	♂ 10	☉ 20	♀ 30	♀	♄
♉	♀ N	☽ 3	♀	☽	♀ 8	☿ 15	♃ 22	♄ 26	♂ 30	☿ 10	☽ 20	♄ 30	♂	
♊	☿ D	☊ 3	♄	☿	☿ 7	♃ 13	♀ 21	♄ 25	♂ 30	♃ 10	♂ 20	☉ 30	♃	
♋	☽ D/N	♃ 15	♂	♂	♂ 6	♃ 13	☿ 20	♀ 27	♄ 30	♀ 10	☿ 20	☽ 30	♄	♂
♌	☉ D/N		☉	♃	♄ 6	☿ 13	♀ 19	♃ 25	♂ 30	♄ 10	♃ 20	♂ 30	♄	
♍	☿ N	☿ 15	♀	☽	☿ 7	♀ 13	♃ 18	♄ 24	♂ 30	☉ 10	♀ 20	☿ 30	♃	♀
♎	♀ D	♄ 21	♄	☿	♄ 6	♀ 11	♃ 19	☿ 24	♂ 30	☽ 10	♄ 20	♃ 30	♂	☉
♏	♂ N		♂	♂	♂ 6	♃ 14	♀ 21	☿ 27	♄ 30	♂ 10	☉ 20	♀ 30	♀	☽
♐	♃ D	☋ 3	☉	♃	♃ 8	♀ 14	☿ 19	♄ 25	♂ 30	☿ 10	☽ 20	♄ 30	☿	
♑	♄ N	♂ 28	♀	☽	♀ 6	☿ 12	♃ 19	♂ 25	♄ 30	♃ 10	♂ 20	☉ 30	☽	♃
♒	♄ D		♄	☿	♄ 6	☿ 12	♀ 20	♃ 25	♂ 30	♀ 10	☿ 20	☽ 30	☉	
♓	♃ N	♀ 27	♂	♂	♀ 8	♃ 14	☿ 20	♂ 26	♄ 30	♄ 10	♃ 20	♂ 30	☿	☿

numbers mentioned in the exaltation column indicate the place in the sign where the planet is extra exalted. From the right to the left the rulers get weaker, the sign ruler is very much more important than the ruler of a term or a face.

As an example, we can take Mercury in the ninth degree of Taurus in a diurnal chart. How much dignity does Mercury get there? The sign ruler of Taurus is Venus and the exaltation ruler is the Moon; this means that Taurus is a sign ruled by Venus and that the Moon is exalted there. Thus Venus and the Moon have lots of power there to work in a positive way. Mercury does not, and it will get no dignity through rulership or exaltation. The Lord of the earth triplicity is Venus in this diurnal chart, so Mercury does not get any essential dignity through triplicity either. But Mercury does have some dignity by term. The planet is placed in the second term of Taurus between 8 and 15 degrees and in this term Mercury rules so he is in the right place by term. The first decanate of Taurus, the first 10 degree zone of the sign, is also ruled by Mercury, so it also gets some strength through face. We then say that Mercury has term and face dignity. It's not much, but it is better than nothing at all and much better than debilitation by fall or detriment.

Another term to be explained is 'peregrine'. A planet is peregrine when it has no dignity at all, positive nor negative. It is not placed in its own sign or in exaltation, triplicity, term, face, detriment or fall. Peregrine means drifting; it is not bad, it is not good, it just has no direction. That is why it tends to be challenging because things that have no clear direction go astray quite easily. It is often said that a planet is in detriment or fall **and** peregrine because it has no positive dignity. This is wrong, a planet in a bad state is downright bad, a drifting planet drifts and this is not the same thing. It cannot be neutral and bad at the same time.

We also need to consider the benefics and malefics. The benefics are Jupiter and Venus and these planets tend to have an effect which is pleasant for us. But this is only true if they have some essential dignity; their benefic nature is diminished as they lose dignity. Jupiter in detriment in Virgo for example cannot be called benefic any more, it is an 'accidental' malefic and it will not work out well. Saturn and Mars are malefics by nature and tend to have unpleasant effects. However, if the malefics have essential dignity, they lose much of their malefic character and may even work out better than expected. The other three planets are more or less neutral although the same dignity principle applies, the more essential dignity they have the more positive their effects are.

Accidental dignity
The degree of essential dignity or planetary power shows its quality, how purely and effectively it can be its own beneficial self. Venus in Libra is totally Venus and in this condition the planet can act according to its nature. The other kind of dignity is called 'accidental' and it shows something else: the force with which a planet can manifest in the world. The point is not whether this planet is working as it was meant according to its nature, it only shows how strong its influence in the world is. Accidental dignity measures quantity, essential dignity measures quality. We can use the simple scheme below to assess the degree of accidental dignity.

Strong: placement in an angular house, in the 11th house, fast movement (not for Saturn), direct movement, no narrow aspects with malefics, joy (see below), conjunction with the favourable fixed stars *Spica* and *Regulus*.

Moderate: placement in houses 2, 3, 5 or 9

Weak: conjunction or opposition with the Sun (combust), retrograding, placement in the malefic houses 6, 8 or 12, very slow movement (not for Saturn), narrow aspects with malefics, besiegement (placement between aspects with two malefics), in opposition with the house it joys in, on the malefic fixed star *Algol*.

The Moon is weak when waning and strong when waxing, and it is weakened in the via combusta, the 'burnt road' (the zone from 15 Libra to 15 Scorpio). The North Node expands and strengthens and a conjunction with the North Node is generally positive, however when something like the cause of an illness conjuncts this expansive force this is not favourable. The South Node will diminish things and inhibit, and is mostly negative.

Joy is an accidental dignity derived from placement in a 'good' house, a house where the planet feels at home by nature: Mercury in the first house, the Moon in the third house, Venus in the fifth house, Mars in the sixth house, the Sun in the ninth house, Jupiter in the eleventh house and Saturn in the twelfth house. A planet in its joy feels okay and therefore has some more force to manifest itself in the world. A planet in opposition with its house of joy does not feel okay and so it is weakened.

A very damaging debilitation is combustion, a conjunction with the Sun. An orb between a planet and the Sun in conjunction that is between 17'30" seconds and 8°30' is called combustion, which harms the planet and impedes its ability to act. An orb between 8°30' and 17°30' is termed 'under the Sun's beams', which is also difficult but not as bad by far as combustion. Combustion can also take place by an opposition with the Sun, with the same orb as when conjunct. However, there is a special case called 'cazimi', in which a planet precisely conjunct the Sun is extremely powerful – a cazimi planet cannot be stopped. The orb for cazimi is 17'30" minutes of arc, so we do not see this too often.

There are also the accidental dignities of *hayz* and *halb*, referring to the correct position a planet has in a chart that makes the planet stronger. Halb means in the correct half of the chart. The diurnal planets Saturn, Sun and Jupiter should be above the horizon in diurnal charts and below the horizon in nocturnal charts, and vice versa for the nocturnal planets Moon, Venus and Mars. To be in hayz, which means making the planet accidentally stronger than if it is only halb, the diurnal masculine planets have to placed not only in the correct part of the chart but also in a masculine sign. The nocturnal feminine planets Venus and the Moon should be in halb and in feminine signs to be in hayz. (Air-Fire signs are masculine, Earth-Water signs feminine). Mars is masculine and nocturnal, a Mercury rising before the Sun is diurnal otherwise nocturnal. Hayz/halb is only one of many accidental dignities and its importance should not be exaggerated.

Saturn, Jupiter and Mars will be accidentally stronger if they rise before the Sun (oriental position), while the Moon, Venus and Mercury are stronger rising after the Sun (occidental position), and they become weaker by being in the reversed positions. Gaining in north latitude (that is with increasing visibility in the sky) will make a planet stronger; increasing south latitude weaker. This makes sense, as accidental dignity has to do with the power to manifest in the world.

Receptions

Receptions are of crucial importance in astrology; they show what effects the planets have on each other and whether they harm or help each other. To assess these connections we need the table of essential dignities. An example will show how this works. Suppose we are assessing the effects of Mercury in Aries in the life. The most important receptions Mercury makes from Aries will guide the analysis of the chart further. The general rule in analysing receptions is that a planet in a sign will have a positive effect on its dispositors and a negative effect on the planets in fall and detriment in this sign. So Mercury in Aries has a negative influence on Venus (which has its detriment in Aries) and Saturn (which has its fall in Aries). It works positively on Mars (sign ruler of Aries) and the Sun (which has its exaltation in Aries). Receptions also work through the weaker triplicity, term and face dispositors, but these receptions will obviously be weaker.

Through the network of receptions we can map all these connections between the relevant significators systematically, and we should always carry out such an analysis before proceeding further.

24 Case Studies

Frida Kahlo – The Weeping Sister

The life of this Mexican artist could be called dramatic; her fate seemed to be fear, loneliness, extreme illness and improbably horrible accidents. This can be seen clearly in the positions of malefic fixed stars on many important points in the chart. What immediately strikes the eye is the dominating Moon in the tenth house on *Alcyone* the main star in the Pleiades, the Weeping Sisters or the Nebula of Tears. *Alcyone* with the Pleiades is one of the most malefic stars in the heavens, and the texts have little that is good to say about it: blindness, disease, fevers, extreme lust... it will not exactly make you happy or peaceful. The fact that there are seven Pleiades indicates that their effect is like that of the seven planets in a symbolic way, they draw you into the material life on earth and cut you off from the better, higher worlds behind the planets.

This gives plenty of trouble, misery and disappointments; more concretely shown by the Pleiades' mythical story. It is the cosmic hulk

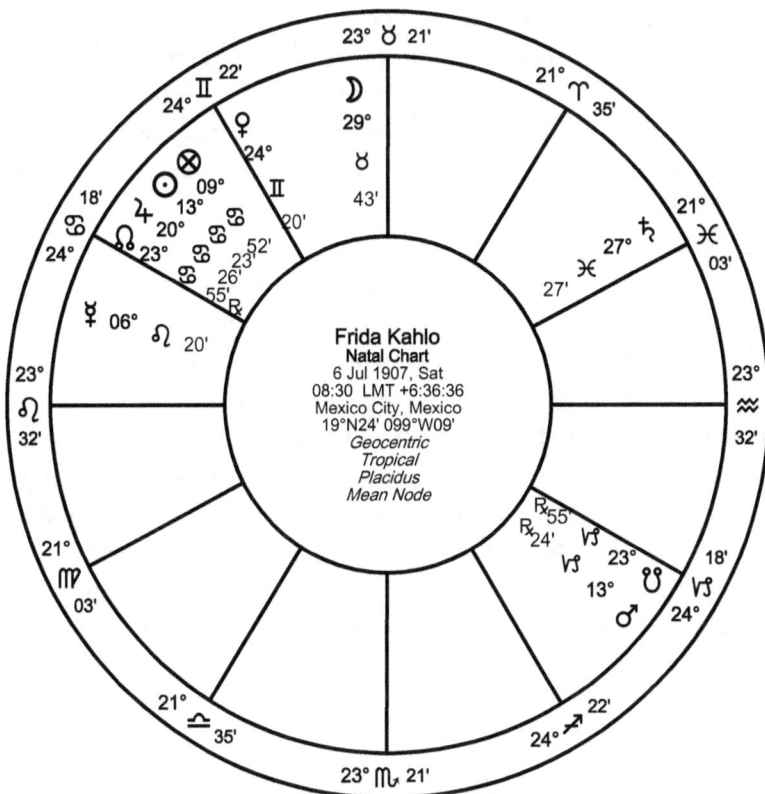

Orion, a symbol of sheer material force who chases them. He is a hunter of animals but also of women, which is why one of the keywords for this star is extreme lust. The Pleiades are the companions of the Moon goddess Diana, a pure virgin who carefully kept herself aloof from men. She indicates the purity the Pleiades strive for and which is violated by Orion. This story is mirrored by the planetary nature of *Alcyone* and the Pleiades: a combination of the Moon and Mars.

In Kahlo's chart the Pleiades' energy manifests through the Moon, one of the luminaries in elevation occupying the highest dominating place, so this Moon will greatly affect the life. The Moon is also Lord 12, the ruler of the house of loneliness, self-destruction, addiction and misery, and this does not make things any better. The only positive point is that the Moon has a lot of essential dignity being in its exaltation in Taurus. It therefore has a lot of quality, it functions well and is a compensation for all the misery. The stream of negative emotions and experiences can be expressed through the Moon in a more positive way and this was the motivation Kahlo explicitly mentioned for her artistic endeavours: emotional stabilisation. She is known as a surrealistic artist, and this fits in well with the Moon with its fluid forms. Surrealism is very watery and lunar; it turns its back on the rigid Saturnian forms of reality. The Moon also shows Kahlo's fame as an independent feminist. The Pleiades are the companions of the virgin goddess Diana who will not have anything to do with men. Typically, the two sides of the mythical story manifested in Kahlo's life, on the one hand she was the independent feminist servant of Diana, and on the other she was Orion, sexually active with men and women. So several parts of a story, several roles in a myth, can show themselves in a life; the myth is more like a script offering various possibilities to be played out. The whole picture of misery and misfortune is underlined by the star right on the MC, extremely malefic *Algol* associated with losing your head, chaos and crisis. Algol is Medusa's Head cut off by Perseus, and it will cause extreme trouble also when activated in progression or dominating a solar return chart from an angle, for example.

This central Moon is in narrow sextile with Saturn Lord 6, further emphasizing the theme of illness and misfortune. Saturn is placed on *Scheat*, Pegasus' Hoof, associated in the old texts with murder, suicide, extreme misery and death by drowning. The central issue of the Pegasus story is the refusal to accept any guidance, with a deep fall as the consequence of this obstinacy. This is the third star position indicating more than moderate problems. It manifested when at 18 years old Kahlo was involved in a bus accident, in which she was pierced through by a steel tube. The nodal axis with the South Node right on the sixth cusp of illness also indicates this improbably horrible accident almost as a literal picture: the pipe is like the nodal axis going straight through her body. If the nodes are closely conjunct a planet or cusp they will have a clear effect in the life, much less than if they are just floating around somewhere in a house. It is only conjunctions with the nodes that count, no other aspects. To a certain extent, the nodes are comparable to fixed stars.

Stars on the nodes are, however, of less interest, but if the node conjuncts a planet or a cusp on a star, this star is naturally part of the picture. In Kahlo's chart this is the case, where the cusp of the sixth house of illness falls on the star of fate *Terebellum*. The expansive strengthening North Node is found on the other side on the twelfth cusp on *Procyon*, the very bright main star of the fierce Lesser Dog, with a Mercury/Mars nature. It's not a pleasant combination to have exactly on the cusp of the house of silly things we do to harm ourselves. Jupiter Lord 5 of creativity is nearby in narrow aspect with the MC, and is on royal and successful *Pollux*, contributing a lot to her fame as an artist.

In the fifth house of creativity we see a strong exalted Mars on *Vega*, a bright star belonging to the elite of about 20 first magnitude stars. It is the main star of the Lyre and much associated with the arts. Opposing Mars is the Sun, Lord 1, representing Kahlo most personally, and it is on the main star of the Greater Dog, fierce *Sirius*. This indicates many conflicts with men and with authorities, not a peaceful position. Her relationships were as stormy as the rest of her life. Finally, Mercury is on malefic *Praesepe* in the twelfth house of misery, and the same Mercury is on the MC on *Algol* by antiscion, so this chart has a poisoned cocktail of *Algol*, *Praesepe* and *Alcyone* that you don't see too often. Mercury rules the eleventh house of legs and is in narrow square with the Arabian Part of Illness, Asc + Mars – Saturn (in diurnal charts, turn for nocturnal charts) pointing to Kahlo's obsession with her right leg, lamed by poliomyelitis.

The lunar mansion is the Mansion of the Knife with the Pleiades as its ruling stars. This mansion's theme is separation, cutting off, and battle; keywords are unfaithfulness, social engagement and struggle. We can see this clearly in her turbulent love life and politically in her communist sympathies.

Adolf Hitler – The Crushed Crab

Whether someone is morally good or not is something astrology cannot give 100% clarity about, but you can read indications in the chart that increase the chances of extreme moral corruption. This is, for example, shown by many planets in fall or detriment, very difficult fixed stars on the angles or the luminaries, and a weak ninth house. If we have no such things and many planets are strong with no bad fixed stars activated, it is less probable that someone will act immorally. It remains a mystery of the soul whether someone will really turn his back on the light and

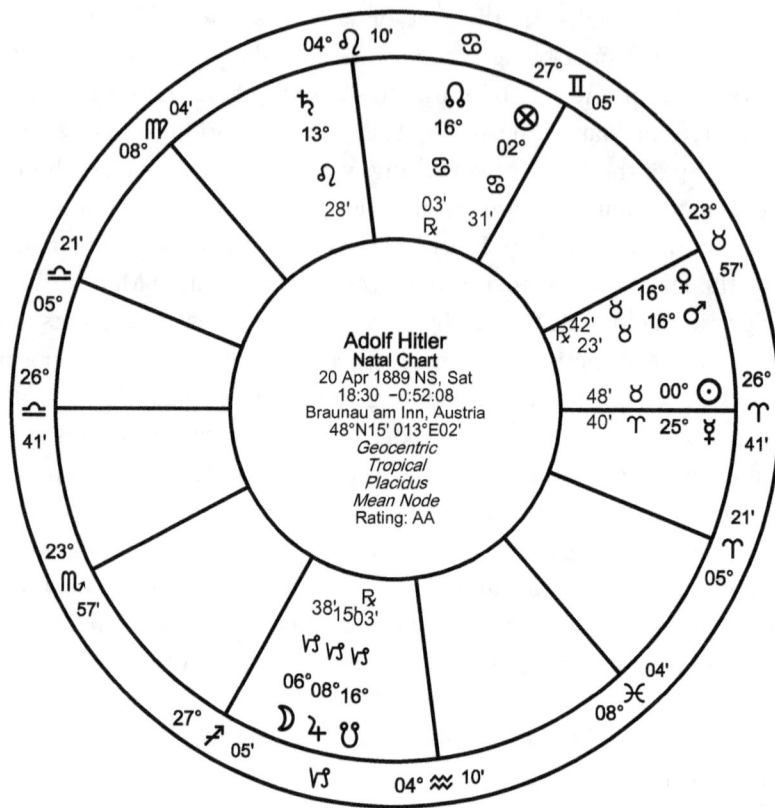

embrace the darkness, but at least we can shed some light on this matter by involving the fixed stars.

In Hitler's chart the position of Mercury is immediately noticeable; it is Lord 9 and is on the Descendant, so it will manifest strongly in his life. This person will be talking a lot about visions and philosophical-political ideas to the background of the cardinal fast-moving fire of the Ram, under control of the dispositor, Mars. This is an indication that it will not be too pleasant to listen to him. Mars in detriment in Taurus shows its worst sides, but there is a certain charisma and an ability to hold a crowd with a strong Venus close by. The Descendant is on the *Vertex* nebula in Andromeda so this connects Mercury/Lord 9 with the destructive Seamonster coming to devour the soul and create chaos. Most stars in Andromeda have a positive effect and often give connections with the arts, but *Vertex* is a nebula in the face of the Princess, pointing to blindness. So it will go wrong. *Vertex* has a Mars/Moon nature.

The tender soul, open to higher spheres by which it could escape the bonds of matter, is devoured and the Seamonster's chaos will have the upper-hand. This is an important mythical theme as so much in this chart, with four planets in the seventh house, is directed towards other people. Mercury itself is very close to *Al Pherg* in the constellation of Pisces, a star of fate associated with the Head of Typhon, one the fearful dark opponents of the gods who battles unflaggingly to put out the Olympic light. This primordial monster with a body consisting completely of snakes is said to have an especially terrifying voice, so both *Vertex* and *Al Pherg* are clearly in play; *Vertex* closer to the Descendant, *Al Pherg* closer to Mercury.

In the seventh house the Sun, Lord 10 of career, is placed on the star *Mesarthim*, an apocryphal star, although it is easy to find its meaning. It is the first Ram star, also called the Fat Ram, so not really subtle. It is a fresh, newborn Arien pushy kind of power which will not be stopped by anything or anyone. A bit higher in the seventh house there is a striking Venus/Mars conjunction. Mars is in detriment so nasty, but Venus in its own sign is positive. Two contradictory indications yet it is clear that the end result will not be very nice as Saturn in detriment in the tenth house falls by antiscion exactly on this conjunction. There is a remarkable concentration of energies in the seventh house of other people: Saturn in detriment by antiscion on Mars in detriment conjunct Venus, the peregrine Sun on the Fat Ram, dominating Mercury Lord 9 with the Descendant on *Vertex* and the Head of Typhon.

The only positive thing in the chart is the strong Venus which is in its own sign and is also the Lord of the Geniture, indicating Hitler's frustrated ambitions as a painter. It is indeed clear that Venus will not be easy to use in a positive way as it is in a narrow conjunction with both malefics in detriment, and with Saturn by antiscion. So anger, hatred, and a lack of self-control will undermine his sense of beauty and harmony. The nebula *Praesepe* is found on the MC, which according to the old texts is associated with the 'exhalation of heaped-up bodies'. Can a chart be more cruelly graphic? *Praesepe* symbolises the fragments left of the Crab after having been crushed by Hercules; also an adequate picture of Germany after the war. Duce Benito Mussolini, Hitler's Italian partner in crime, had his Sun on *Praesepe*. The star gives definite talents to cause strife and bloodshed on a large scale, but of course also on a smaller scale, depending on the power of the chart.

All this would be quite sufficient to create an indication of imminent evil, but in addition Jupiter and the Moon are found low in the chart, respectively in detriment and in fall on the star *Facies* in the Archer. *Facies* is the nebula in the Archer's face and has all the driving power of the dubious and often violent centaur race, but also combined with blindness. It is a Sun-Mars star so not exactly very nice. We have four planets in a bad condition, two planets in the middle and only one, Venus, that has some quality. But Venus is so heavily afflicted it can do nothing to save the chart. In delineating a chart, a pattern gradually builds up which points in a certain direction, and here we see more and more indications for an extremely malefic mind, a piling up of weakness, darkness, aggression and hatred.

To make the picture complete, *Izar* is on the Ascendant. This small star in the girdle of the Guardian of the Bear is always pictured with many weapons, with spears and a sickle. The Boötes theme is pure action unconnected to any form of spiritual guidance, and it is symbolic of the Bear/Boar struggle, so important in European history. The constellation is also strongly associated with hunting and crusading. It is not peace-loving. The Nazi cult of the warrior is something that easily fits this image of the soldier who no longer recognizes a higher authority. It is the Bear that got rid of the Boar and broke loose (interesting to note that Berlin is the City of the Bear). The radical desecration of everything is clearly to be seen in the myth; Boötes penetrated into the temple where the priests nearly killed him as he was not supposed to be there.

The connections of this chart with the prenatal lunation and eclipse enabled this specific person to fall to such incredible depths. There is also a strong synastry with Germany's charts, with the charts of this historical period, and even more strikingly with the chart of Munich, the city that supported his rise to power. The natal chart in combination with the relevant mundane charts determines what a person can achieve, and shows the limitations of what human beings are able to do on the basis of individual willpower and effort only. As in so many cases the lunar mansion crowns the work, it is the Mansion of the Archer's Bow, associated with radical visions and teachings, the illusion of invincibility and the merciless elimination of every obstacle standing in the way. The Archer is Chiron the teacher, and all the semi-occult theories in Nazism are brought in, and the mansion's ruling stars are on his bow, therefore we have this radical attitude. It will try to realise what it believes: *Triumph der Wille* (Triumph of the Will.)

Bill Gates – The Lesser Dog
Microsoft tycoon Bill Gates' chart has a star on the Ascendant which on its own says a lot about his life. It is powerful *Procyon*, the main star in the Lesser Dog constellation. *Procyon* occupies seventh place in the list of stars ranked by magnitude, so this is a very important point in the chart. The lower the number of magnitude, the brighter the star is and the stronger its power of manifestation in the world. As usual, a star on an angle describes rather accurately one of the main themes in the life, so it is both a convincing way to check the effect of a star, and also a useful technique for rectifying a chart.

Both the Dogs, the lesser and the greater, are known for their fierce fighting spirit, their capacity to bite hard and to persist. The Greater Dog, with *Sirius* as its main star, can be described as a brute who often openly intimidates and violently pushes through, while the lesser Dog is a more dexterous and flexible little beast. The difference between the Dogs is also expressed by their planetary natures. For *Sirius* it is expansive Jupiter with Mars, for *Procyon* it is Mars with Mercury. The Lesser Dog is the smart little animal dexterous enough to beat larger opponents, and you can say this is a theme in Bill Gates' life. As a young dog he outstripped the large established computer manufacturers.

The Dogs are the guardians of the soul in the myth and this shows that they have a lot of fighting-power but they do not have the capacity to be good leaders – they are too aggressive for that. There has to be something else, a person or an ideal guiding the Dog energy otherwise it will become too fierce and get involved in fights too often. This will certainly be a problem for Bill Gates as the Moon, also Lord 1, (that is Gates himself), is on the star *Algenib* in the constellation of Pegasus. The core issue in the myth of the Flying Horse is that its rider Bellerophon decided to fly to Olympus without being invited or permitted to do so. For Gates, there is considerable danger that he will be much too self-willed and will push too far with dire consequences.

Microsoft was involved in many judicial procedures because it abused its monopoly position and settlements had to be made with several competitors. These settlements cost Microsoft a lot of money, and also

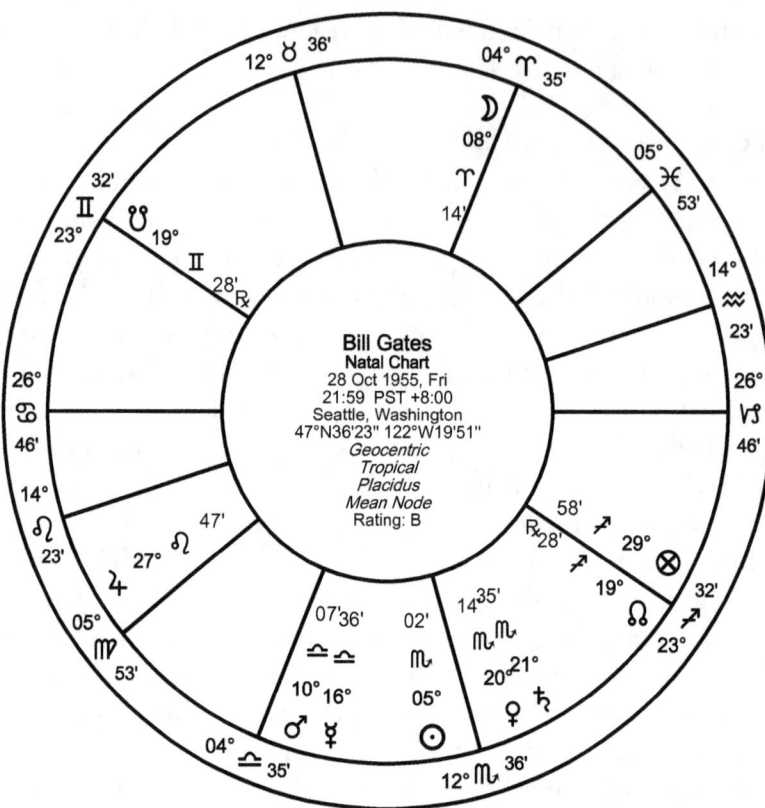

got it in trouble with the European Union. Of course, Microsoft is not exactly the same as the person Bill Gates, but he is the main architect of this strategy, mirroring the *Procyon* and *Algenib* themes. The Moon in the tenth house as the general significator of the common people and the lesser luminary is an important indication for success and smart marketing. Gates understands what the people want but there will be a lot of tension and struggle because of the opposition with Mars/Lord 10 which is in a bad condition.

The ruler of the second house, the Sun, does not immediately make clear that Gates is one of the richest men in the world. It does not have much essential dignity, neither is it very strong accidentally, placed in Scorpio in the fourth house. You would expect some more striking financial significators but this will become clearer if we look a bit further and take into account the fixed stars. The natural significator of wealth, Jupiter, has some good essential dignity by triplicity and is found in the second house of money on the most royal star of them all, *Regulus*. As if this is not enough the Sun, the ruler of the second house, conjuncts by antiscion the Part of the Sun (Asc + Sun – Moon), also called the Part of Abundance.

The most powerful royal stars like *Regulus* have a three to four degree orb, which means that the weaker stars found near *Regulus* will be outshone by it. So Jupiter is not on *Alphard* at 26.40 Leo, not on *Adhafera* 26.57 Leo, not on *Algieba* at 27.17 Leo, but simply on the big boss *Regulus*. There are times to exert Virgo-like precision but it is better to leave your planets in Virgo at home if you approach *Regulus*. Technical precision is sometimes valuable, but it is certainly not a solution to everything, as too much technical detail prevents an overview. If you say that Jupiter is on *Algieba* because this is the star closest to it purely in degrees, you cannot explain Gates' excessive wealth. Good classical astrology can only be developed if you are prepared to test techniques and rules in practice and if necessary to adapt or even reject them.

This strong generous Jupiter also points at Gates' philanthropic activities. After his retirement from Microsoft he, among other things, used his wealth to support educational projects in developing countries. Jupiter is aptly Lord 9 of higher knowledge in Gates' chart and it is Lord 6 of misfortunes which the Great Benefic in good condition is eager to overcome. Jupiter on *Regulus* is the key position in this chart and it is in a strong synastry aspect with the prenatal lunation and eclipse, embedding Gates' chart in a positive way in during his lifetime. Without this embedding we would not have heard of him; it is this cosmic energy working through him that gave him success.

In Gates' chart business success is clearly shown and this is underlined by the Arabian Parts. The Part of Vocation (MC + Moon – Sun), the job your soul wants to do in the world, is right on cusp 3 under disposition of Mercury. Bill Gates wants to do something practical that is involved with information and communication. His Part of Fame (Asc + Sun – Jupiter in nocturnal charts, reverse in diurnal charts) is exactly on cusp 4, showing what he is known for: the *home* computer. Finally, the lunar mansion is the Mansion of the Wing controlled partly by stars in Pegasus, partly by stars in Andromeda. It is connected with a strong self-will but also with charity and spirituality, mirroring both his business and his later philanthropic activities.

Clint Eastwood – The Claws of Justice

Clint Eastwood started his career as an actor in Westerns, mainly playing very cool roles. He always used violence for a more or less justified cause – an image he definitively established as police officer Harry Callahan in the *Dirty Harry* series. Callahan does not respect the police rules of conduct too much, he has his own methods, and these methods are quite direct, rough, and in many cases downright illegal. But Callahan never turns into a bad guy because he always works for justice. He simply does what needs to be done; the victims of crime will be avenged, the murderers will be punished. Clint Eastwood is not only a successful and popular actor, he is also a film director and was for some time active as an independent politician in California. His success is clearly indicated by a couple of prominent royal fixed stars, and without such powerful stars fame is not easy to achieve, whatever your talents may be. Apart from prominent royal stars and/or first magnitude elite stars, you also need a clear synastry with pre-natal charts to achieve great fame, and Clint Eastwood has both.

The best and most instructive way to approach a chart is to look at what stands out in the chart and start delineation without referring to any other information you may have about the person. Otherwise it's tempting to start looking for a particular characteristic that you know existed. It's like a prediction after the event which is always successful because you know what happened. In astrology we should be able to see how the life will be without that knowledge, not in concrete details but in general outlines. Only after having made the first steps of delineation can the general picture be coloured in using information gained from other sources. Such information is indeed of crucial importance for good astrology, but only as added spice to fill out the analysis after the initial work is done.

What stands out in Eastwood's chart is Mercury, Lord 8 of death, retrograding on the Descendant (referring to other people); it is on *Algol*, the ultimate malefic star that spreads death and destruction. Without knowing anything about his life, this indicates an important theme which will manifest; it could also be a good position for a merciless and violent Mafia boss. At this point we join the astrological analysis to the information about the life and *then* we see this Mercury is also giving us a good picture of Dirty Harry's methods. Maybe it is better that Eastwood

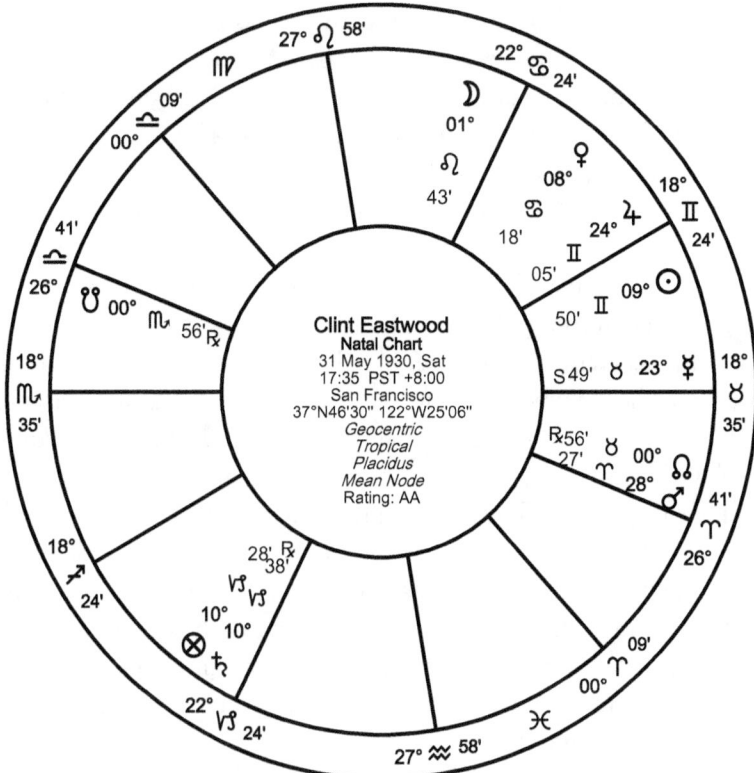

lives out this energy on the film screen and not in reality, as his chart promises enormous success. On the MC, the main point for the career, is royal *Regulus*, the Heart of the Lion, with a Mars/Jupiter nature. And as if this is not enough the other royal star of great success and wealth, martially red *Aldebaran*, is conjunct the Sun, Lord 10. *Aldebaran* is one the few stars in the heavens with a pure Mars nature and this is most appropriate for an actor who often played such violent roles. Together with the angular Mercury/Lord 8 on *Algol*, these two royal stars give more than a flavour of violence to the chart; it literally *breathes* violence. Fortunately, Mars itself is essentially strong, and is also Lord of the Geniture, so his great talent, on cusp 6, is used for correcting sixth house misery, that is misery afflicted on you by other people or life in general.

Eastwood's great talent is shown by Mars in a narrow trine with the MC, and this compensates for the accidental weakness in the falling sixth house, as does the fact that Mars is in the correct house, in its joy. The planet is also Lord 5 of creativity and on the star *Mirach* in Andromeda, one of the few stars with a pure Venus nature. Here we see an artistic feeling for beautiful pictures and forms, but Venus itself is not very strong; Eastwood is not a painter, he expresses his aesthetic taste as a martial action hero on film. The fact that Mars has its strengthening joy in the sixth house is easy to explain. In the case of sixth-house hard luck you need some bold action to correct the situation; this may be a surgical knife or Dirty Harry's king-sized .44 Magnum. Mars is simply in the right place in the sixth house, therefore in its joy.

Is it by accident that the serial killer in *Dirty Harry* Part 1 calls himself Scorpio? Maybe not, as it is Eastwood's ascending sign, but more important is that the ascending degree is on the *North Scale* bringing into play the mythical theme of the weighing of souls, of justice and restoring the balance. Together with the *South Scale* four degrees further in Scorpio, this is the Libra constellation also known as the Scorpion's Claws, illustrating the often harsh nature of the corrective action of justice. Scorpio is the vicious beast that mercilessly killed Orion with his poison because the Hunter had been bragging he could catch every animal and beat every opponent. Orion forgot that the gods are the bosses and so he was eliminated. Eastwood as Dirty Harry is this avenging angel. Both Claws/Scales, North and South, are connected to this theme and although the *South Scale* clearly is the most malefic of the star pair, Eastwood's chart is so violent that the *North Scale* will also be expressed in a rather vicious way.

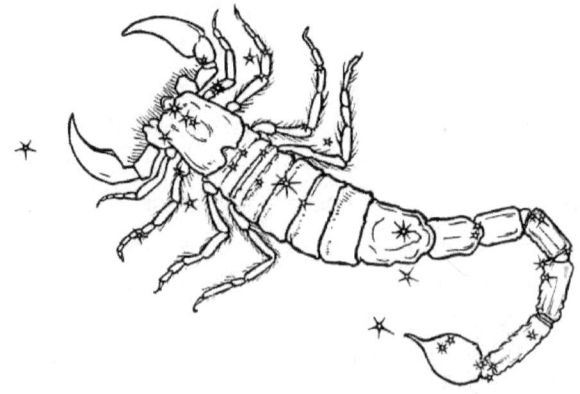

This mythical image is one of the main keys to his success, and this is the satisfaction you feel when Dirty Harry finds and kills a murderer. Ultimate justice is done; this is the essence of the Scales. As it is stated in the Bible and other holy books, no one will escape when the Day of Judgement comes. This is what resonates in our souls if we see Harry Callahan fire his .44 magnum erasing the scum. All myths show an aspect of the divine. Of course, Eastwood mainly expresses these themes on the screen and not in reality, but this distinction is not as sharp as it sometimes seems. In stories the mythical themes are often shown in a purer form than in life and in more than one sense a story is also reality and vice versa. There is even astrological evidence for this, for if we use a fictitious time mentioned in a film to make a chart for this film, this chart often turns out to describe the story in detail – so a story is not as fictitious as it seems and there are different levels of reality.

Eastwood's Moon is in the Mansion of the Servants, ruled by the two Asses, the Aselli ridden on by the gods in their battle with the Titans. The asses are the subdued forces of chaos and resonate with the servant's theme. Traditional keywords are safety and stability, creating places where people can rest and be nurtured. Certainly this is appropriate for Eastwood as is the whole theme of battle with the Titans. The gods use the dark Aselli forces to beat their opponents. It will be clear that such a martial chart as Eastwood's will not indicate a successful hotel manager, for example, for that he would need a much stronger lunar/watery influence in the chart.

Margaret Thatcher – Atilla the Hun

The fact that this chart has three planets in fall and detriment, three planets peregrine and only one planet with a small essential dignity by term, shows that it is not necessary to have a lot of essential dignity in your chart to be successful. What counts, apart from powerful fixed stars, is accidental dignity, especially planets on angles, which shows power of manifestation in the world. It is not always the thorough understanding connected to essential dignity which brings people to high positions. A lot of essential dignity in a chart does decrease the chance of malefic or immoral behaviour but again there is no guarantee, for example, several Nazi-leaders had planets with good essential dignity. What essential

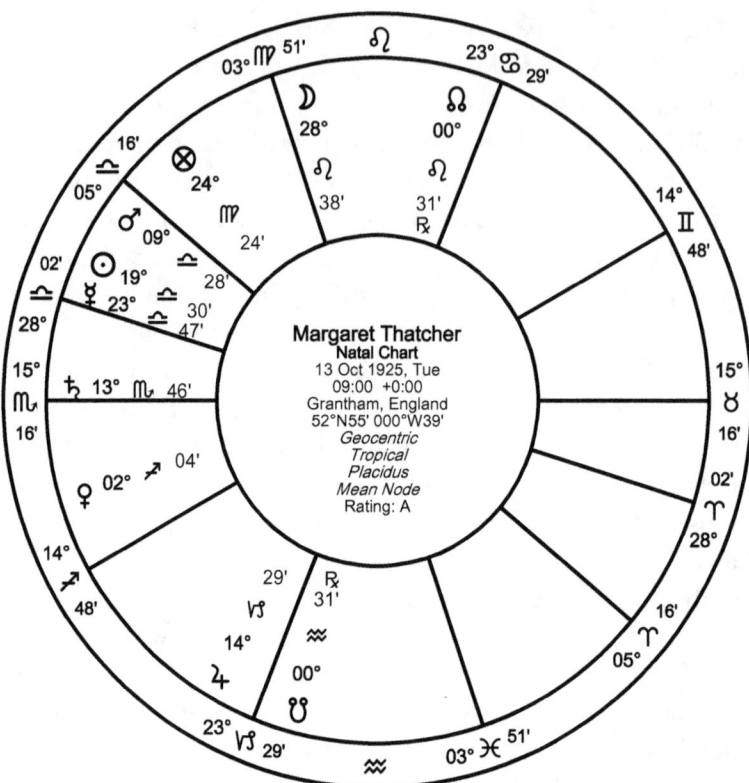

dignity does show is an ability to handle certain fields of activity well because you really understand them. If you have an essentially strong planet you know how it ticks, although this certainly is not necessary to exert influence on the world – as this chart proves.

In the Iron Lady's natal chart the nickname is immediately clear, the dominating planet in her life on the Ascendant is a peregrine Saturn. Peregrination indicates a lack of the right direction. Although it will not act in a purely malefic way, the planet will tend to show its less pleasant sides, certainly if it is a malefic by nature as in this case. For Saturn this points to hardness, mercilessness, rigidity, coldness, a lack of emotional concern. It could be corrected by a strong mutual reception or an aspect with a planet that has a lot of essential strength, but in this chart Saturn is in strong mutual reception with a planet that can only worsen things; a vicious Mars in detriment in Libra. This connection will serve to increase the hardness of Saturn, the martial iron will harden the

Saturnian rigidity into steel. Two planets in reception are connected in a way comparable to a certain extent to a narrow aspect, but if they are going to give each other some real support they should have some good essential dignity, otherwise they have nothing to offer and may even harm each other.

This is the case here. The iron of Mars hardens Saturn into ferro-concrete and the fixed stars involved will not make things any easier. The Ascendant with Saturn is on the extremely powerful *South Scale*, the Scorpion's South Claw, the most malefic of the Claws. It is connected to merciless corrective action, and as it is called 'the Insufficient Price' it will push things all the way and even beyond. The Scales' theme is the same as in Clint Eastwood's chart but the flavour is different. Wherever we look in this chart we find no essential dignity to counterbalance the dominating harshness. We are really looking at Atilla the Hun here; she will not be stopped, her claw will grab you and she will squeeze till you cry for mercy and most probably longer than that.

Mars in such a strong mutual reception with this rock-hard Saturn is Lord 1 and this malefic in detriment in the worst possible condition is on *Vindemiatrix*, a most unpleasant fixed star in the constellation of Virgo. This is the Sorcerer's Apprentice, it gives an over-estimation of your abilities, and points to someone who has the illusion that she can do something for which she does not have the knowledge. The star tends to let loose powers over which the person has no control, harming the environment strongly, although this is not seen and not recognized by the person themselves, for *Vindemiatrix* gives blindness too. She cannot be convinced of the harmful nature of her actions whatever the reactions in the environment may be. *Vindemiatrix* will show its worst sides as Mars the planet on it is in detriment.

This combination of the two malefics in bad condition and these difficult fixed stars is rather frightening. Moreover, the lesser luminary the Moon and the general significator of the people, is on super royal *Regulus* giving her the throne, so there is no getting around her. Often the texts say that *Regulus* will give you the throne but will also take it away again, but this is certainly not always so. It depends on the precise position of the star, the power of the rest of the chart and on the choices of the person. In general the Lion's Heart requires an internal distancing from the intolerant Leo ambition. If you are less attached to power and success, it is less probable you will fall from your throne because you can see what is happening around you and to you.

Although the Moon is in a weaker falling house, there is a direct connection by square with Mercury, Lord 10 of career, which is placed in the weakening twelfth house. This weak Lord 10 makes its way out through the powerful Moon on the Lions' Heart; a narrow aspect or strong reception can liberate a planet in a weak house provided that the liberating planet has some power, as in this case the *Regulus*-Moon. It is as if this planet puts his arm around the shoulder of his weaker brother and takes him with him on his adventures. It is striking that Mercury in the twelfth house is the only planet in the whole chart with some essential dignity. It is not a deep understanding that the Iron Lady builds on, it is more a fixed determination to eliminate her opponents.

Mercury Lord 10 is also on a powerful star of the first magnitude, both *Arcturus* and royal *Spica* are at 23.11 and 22.48 degrees respectively at the end of Libra. A choice must be made as to which of the two stars works clearest through Mercury/Lord 10. *Spica's* planetary nature is Venus/Mars, *Arcturus'* nature is Mars/Jupiter, so Mercury does not fit one better than the other. *Spica* is nearer the zodiac but Mercury on 23.47 Libra is closer in longitude to *Arcturus*, which will have the strongest effect on Lord 10. *Arcturus* is the Guardian of the Bear, connected to crusading, bold action and decisiveness. The Guardian can unleash the power of the bear if she chooses to. The Iron Lady's lunar mansion is that of the Lion's Heart, strongly associated with a lust for power, authority and ambition.

Diana, Princess of Wales – *Spica* Par Excellence

In Diana's chart it is the MC on royal *Spica* that immediately strikes the eye; this royal star will have a major influence on her public life. *Spica* as the main star in Virgo and the Wheat Ear is something quite different from the ambitious throne star *Regulus*, yet its protective influence can still take you to a higher position than could be expected. *Spica* describes well what happened to a girl who was chosen to be the future Queen of England. We all know how this ended and although *Spica* in a dominating position is protective, it does not mean everything will turn out well. Our celestial art is based on the reading and balancing of often

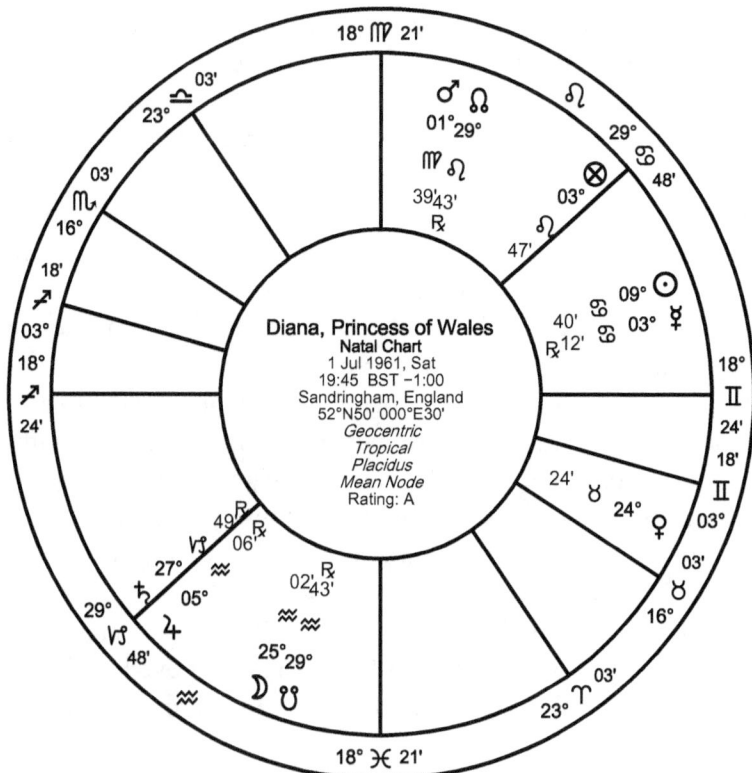

opposing indications in the chart and cannot be reduced to simply one factor or technique.

But it is clear that *Spica* has given Diana her angel-like image. *Spica* as the Wheat Ear is the concentration and harvesting point of the constellation, the focus of the Virgoan purification activities. Here the chaff is separated from the wheat, keeping only the purified essence. In Greek and Christian mythology the story of the virgin is about a human being choosing the side of the gods. It is Mary as the immaculate holy Mother of God, or Astraea a Titan's daughter who refuses to support the earth giants in their battle against the Olympic light and goes over to the gods. This is someone who self-confidently makes the choice for inner purity and is seen as the Queen of Hearts protecting the weak and the sick. This was in direct contrast to the stiffness of the rest of the royal family.

But then another, darker, tone becomes apparent. Venus, Lord 10 of career, is placed on supermalefic *Algol*, death and disaster. Medusa will affect the career too. On one side is an almost Mary-like image while on the other side is raw desire, the inhuman energy of the Gorgon working through Venus as the MC ruler. This also makes her almost irresistibly attractive. Venus in a good condition in its own sign, Taurus, as Lord 10 and Lord 5 is more than able to play this role of Medusa – not only a monster but also a seductive beautiful woman. It is the pure intense glamour of the desire nature we see here. Diana certainly liked this appreciation by other people. Venus is conjunct the Part of Fortune by antiscion in the eighth house of others; her deepest wish is to please and to seduce so that others will appreciate her.

The lunar mansion is the Mansion of the Dolphin. The key themes in this mansion are gathering wealth, but also courage, charity and music. It is the story of Arion the poet who on his way home on a ship was threatened by its crew, who wanted to steal his money. He asked to be allowed to sing as a last favour but jumped overboard unexpectedly and was saved by a dolphin, a symbol of the gate to the next world. Many of these themes like courage, wealth and charity, mirror Diana's life and also seem to indicate her ultimate fate of 'jumping overboard'. Arion prefers to leave the ship before the crew steals his money; this is fate not a conscious decision.

Her marriage to the Crown Prince is shown by the Sun, general significator of kings, conjuncting and combusting Lord 7 of relationships. By antiscion the Sun is exactly on the Descendant too, strongly underlining the connection of the royal Sun with the marriage, but this is also an opposition with the Ascendant, Diana herself. The main significator of relationships is Mercury Lord 7 afflicted by combustion and retrogradation and in narrow sextile with a nasty peregrine Mars in Virgo – not exactly an indication for a stable marriage with a solar figure. The Arabian Part of Marriage opposes the Sun, again causing trouble with some solar guy. The Part's formula is Asc + cusp 7 – Venus. The Arabian parts come into play most clearly by narrow aspects with planets, and these aspects will activate the parts. Without an aspect the parts remain silent; it is the force of the planet which brings the part to earth, to life.

All in all, it is not a good idea for her to get involved with the Sun. Saturn men would have been a better choice, so no aristocrats! Saturn is Diana's Lord of the Geniture, the strongest planet and her anchor in life, but as the chart shows, solar men will come and only after having very bad experience(s) with the Sun does the possibility of consciously choosing the best option, Saturn, arise. Lord 7 and the seventh house show what kind of partners we will meet 'automatically' and also the themes playing a role in the relationship. The best option for a good marriage is in many cases not given by the seventh house but by the Lord of the Geniture, the stabilising energy in the chart.

On Diana's Ascendant, her most personal point, we find the star *Sabik*, one of the many stars in the constellation of Ophiuchus, the Snake-Bearer. The snake is a profound and meaningful animal symbol, which can be seen as the pure dualistic life/desire energy itself and it is clear that there is a very dark aspect to it too. It is the snake that seduces Adam and Eve into taking a bite from the apple by which they lose their primordial divine unity and become vulnerable to suffering. This snake energy through the the constellation Ophiuchus directly connects to Diana's life. *Rasalhaque* is the Head of the Snake-bearer and *Sinistra*, *Yed Prior* and *Yed Posterior* are the hands that touch the beast, and are the most dangerous points with a very bad press. The concentration point is *Unukalhai*, the main star and the Snake's Heart associated with poisoning, accidents, violence and immoral behaviour. So every star in the Snake and its Bearer has to do with this dualistic life energy which may change into pure desire, leading you astray with dire consequences. Therefore we have awful keywords for *Yed Prior* and *Sinistra*, the hands in direct contact with the snake. *Sabik* on the left knee of the Snake-Bearer and on Diana's Ascendant is not very encouraging either: success in evil deeds, wastefulness, lost energy and perverted morals. The dubious snake energy, hard to control, certainly did play a role in Diana's life; she was not only the sweet Queen of Hearts. Snake energy may be harmonized by practising medicine to balance bad energies, or by skinning, changing and innovating yourself in some way on some level so that you don't get stuck in harmful old patterns or 'skins'. Another helpful image is the serpent-charmer guiding the serpent energy subtly and elegantly. This is the reason that serpent-charmers exist at all, to show the people how to do this. Note Lord 8 in the chart, indicating the circumstances of death, is on the *South Node*, symbolically the entrance of a tunnel.

Marie Curie – The Hydra's Poison Arrow

The concentration of three planets in the tenth house is immediately obvious in this chart. Saturn, Venus and Mars are conjunct within four degrees, and if there is a star nearby its mythical story will have played a major role in the life. And yes, the three planets are together on *Bungula*, a first magnitude star in the Centaur constellation – specifically on its less pleasant left leg. Centaurs were always described as a wild race of dangerous half-beasts but there were two among them who were civilized and more or less in control of their animal half, these were Chiron and Pholus. Chiron is found in the heavens as the zodiacal constellation Sagittarius, while the constellation Centaur is Pholus, whose myth resembles Chiron's story. Pholus died by accident when he was wounded by an arrow loaded with Hydra poison shot by his friend Hercules to kill a group of other centaurs who attacked them.

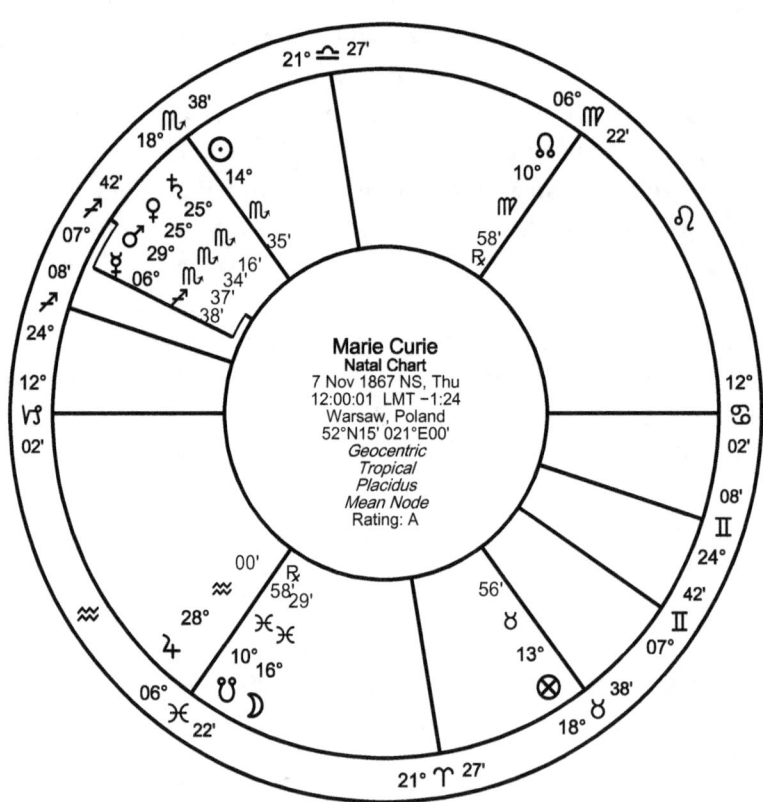

Pholus picked up the poisoned arrow because he was curious as to how such a small thing could kill so easily. This was fatal as he wounded himself and died of the same vicious poison meant for the enemy – a classic case of 'curiosity killed the cat'. This is almost literally Marie Curie's story. She received two Nobel prizes and was a pioneer in research on radioactivity but this was also the cause of her death. She came too close to radio-activity and as a result developed fatal leukemia. Radio-activity fascinated her; she wondered how something that was invisible could be so lethal. Hers is the story of Pholus; symbolically she picked up the radio-active arrow and died.

The radio-active decay process, of which radiation is a side-effect, is essentially a return from an overly densified and heavy state of matter to normal stable conditions. It is matter itself changing into energy and this is the principle on which nuclear energy generation is based. Therefore this process is symbolised by Saturn. It is the Saturnian material form that is in play here, underlined by the fact that the stable final state of radio-active decay is always lead, the metal attributed to Saturn. It is like bringing back order in dangerous conditions of over-activity, returning from chaos to structure. This is the signature of uranium and other radio-active substances.

It is also appropriate, since radio-activity is lethally dangerous, that it is symbolised by Saturn, the Great Malefic, and it will also be clear on the basis of this signature why it is used to treat chaotic growth processes like cancer. In Marie Curie's chart, Saturn is clearly in play conjuncting Venus, Lord 9 of higher knowledge, conjunct and disposed by a strong Mars, Lord 10 of career. Mars is the general significator of chemical processes and energy, certainly in a fluid water sign like Scorpio. Nearby is Mercury, the planet of research and science, on royal and martial *Antares*, the star of death and the end of cycles. This is more than appropriate for the nature of her research and for her own fate.

But Marie Curie has won **two** Nobel prizes which is an extraordinary achievement, so we would expect to find still more star power. Indeed the Sun, trining the other luminary the Moon, is on the MC within the usual 5-degree orb and on the royal *South Scale*, a strong position for a glorious career. Both Claws or *Scales* are active in the chart, the non-royal *North Scale* is right on the MC. This gives a strong emphasis on the grace/justice theme, corrective action to restore the balance which may work out on any level of meaning. The strange thing about Lucida Lancis, the *South Scale*, is that it has become weaker and weaker in magnitude through the ages but is still royal and stronger than the other Scale despite this visible fact. This again shows that essence is not literally what you see in matter.

So in Madame Curie's chart there are two royal stars on important points and three planets on first magnitude stars. To make this picture of great success complete, first magnitude elite star *Vega*, the Falling Vulture in the Lyre, is on the Ascendant. It is strongly associated with art but also with teaching, its essence is spreading the knowledge of how it is 'up there' down here on earth. The vulture is traditionally seen as a symbol of purity, as it feeds on corpses but nothing sticks to its bald neck. Marie Curie is always praised for her sober and modest sincerity to which her dry and cold melancholic temperament will no doubt also have attributed strongly. The precision and thoroughness associated with the melancholic temperament are of course very useful for a scientist.

There are five planets concentrated in the upper half of the chart and near the MC giving a clear focus, but her soul is somewhere else. The Part of Fortune, which shows her soul desire, is near the IC in opposition to the Sun on the MC on the royal star that gives her so much success, but it seems she does not care about all these worldly prizes. The role of Jupiter as Lord 12 of self-destruction also stands out; it squares the three-planet conjunction in the tenth house indicating the harm she did to herself. The killing planet or anareta is Mercury Lord 8, and although Saturn symbolises the radio-active process in general, radiation specifically is Mercury as it goes unseen and penetrates everywhere, also making hidden things visible. Mercury in detriment is on royal death star *Antares* and it is also the Lord of Illness. It was certainly the way she died that contributed to her immortal fame.

Silvio Berlusconi – The Sorcerer's Apprentice
Media tycoon and politician Silvio Berlusconi dominated Italian politics for many years and the first thing we notice in his chart is the Sun-Mercury conjunction on the Ascendant. Having the Sun right on the most individual point in the chart is not a bad starting-point for success, but it is a Sun in fall so he does not know how to be a good leader.

Case Studies

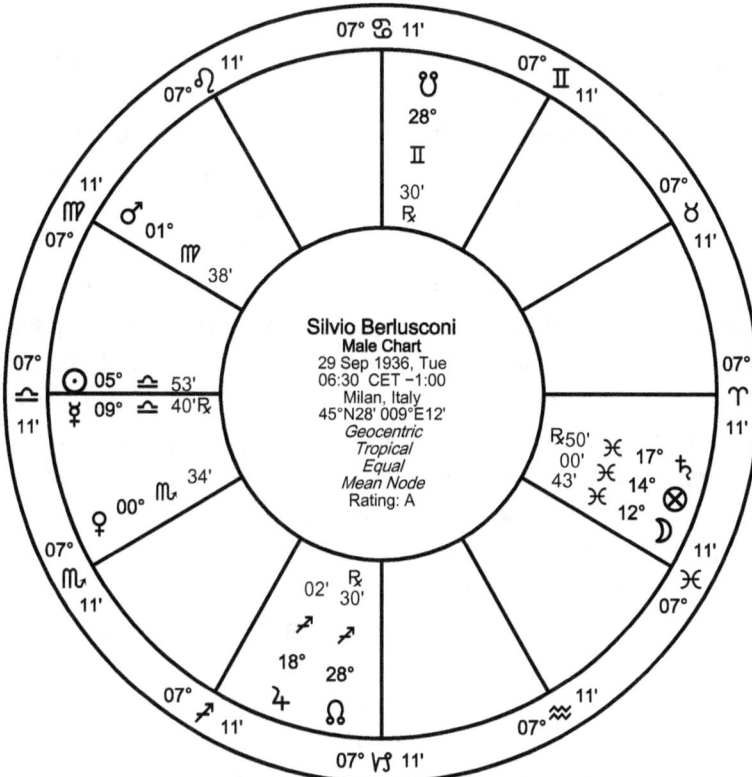

This is not a wise king who knows how to be the centre of the system, how to balance the contrary forces in the kingdom; this Sun in its fall will show up the worst sides of the solar energy. More intriguing than this very public solar force is Mercury so nearby. The Trickster planet is effectively hidden from sight by being combust. Nevertheless, Mercury has a lot of influence in the chart as it is on the Ascendant and directly connected to Berlusconi's most individual point.

The more we study this Mercury, the darker the picture becomes. The planet has no essential dignity, it is peregrine and will consequently tend to get off the track, already a mercurial characteristic, and show its more negative sides. It is also retrograde, indicating it is not in harmony with the environment and that it will act in unexpected ways because it moves counter to the normal direction. Even more important is the fact that Mercury also rules the twelfth house of secrets and operations behind the scenes – essentially the twelfth house is about breaking rules and transgressing norms. Berlusconi will be able to do many things unseen. Mercury is far too influential here and as it is protected by the powerful Sun; he can do it all because he is the king.

As if it is not enough that the Trickster planet is the twelfth house ruler as well as combust, retrograde and peregrine, it is also on the star *Vindemiatrix*. This star is part of the constellation Virgo, normally seen as having quite positive effects in a life. But *Vindemiatrix* is a very negative special case. Like every Virgo star it is linked with harvesting but on *Vindemiatrix* it is premature harvesting with dire consequences. The star is associated with the story of Amphelos who fell and broke his neck gathering grapes. Amphelos is the son of a satyr and a nymph so a product of two very lustful natural beings. *Vindemiatrix* is also the Sorcerers' Apprentice, associated with theft and arrogance, with overestimation of one's capacity. It is someone who unleashes powers he can't control, harming his environment in this way.

Mercury's position in the chart describes in fact a large part of Berlusconi's everyday life as well as on a psychological level. But there is still more, as on the sixth house cusp there is a conjunction of the Moon and the Part of Fortune on a star in the first magnitude elite corps, *Achernar*. This star represents the Mouth of the River Eridanus and is connected with positive things like religion, spirituality and beneficence. The star is one of the few with a pure Jupiter nature and Jupiter is in very good condition in the chart, aspecting the Moon/PoF conjunction. This all sounds like positive compensation for the bad Mercury on the Ascendant, but we can say that this wasn't the case. This makes clear that all sides of the myth are important, diverse parts and episodes of the story show themselves in the life. It is too simple to classify in terms of only being positive or negative.

The myth of the River is also the story of Phaeton, who although having been warned several times, took the Sun's solar chariot thinking he could steer it through the heavens. But he could not control the horses and they all came crashing down in flames, scorching the land with solar fire. We see a strong element of usurpation here, taking a leader's role and a throne you are not entitled to, or for which you don't have the capacities, and this will harm the kingdom severely. In many cases this has to do with political, ideological or spiritual ideas. This is the dark side of *Achernar*, as the success and power it gives will scorch the land because you don't have the knowledge to lead it in the right direction, and many will suffer from your overestimation. It is the combination of *Vindemiatrix* and *Achernar* here that gives the lack of self-criticism despite the obvious failures.

The Moon/PoF conjunction is on the weakening sixth house cusp but the Moon Lord 10 of career is in trine with the MC and so will work more powerfully than could be expected from a sixth house position. Of course, the Moon, the general significator of the common people on the servants' sixth house cusp, shows that Berlusconi is a man of the people. His Part of Fortune (also the Part of the Moon) is with them, and he reaches them through his TV channels, because he knows what they want. Despite all the less savoury matters he is involved in, he is still very popular and this has to do with generously feeding the people through the media. *Achernar* is an overflowing Jupiter star in the Mouth of the River. Berlusconi's whole career is described by these two stars, *Vindemiatrix* and *Achernar*, showing the power they have in the life.

His wealth cannot be seen in the second house of possessions; neither the house itself nor its ruler are exceptionally strong. It is however not only the second house and its ruler that can show wealth – it is the context of the whole chart that counts. A strong chart in general gives more wealth and this Sun on the Ascendant will certainly manifest strongly in the life. The Sun is the ruler of the eleventh house, which indicates how you are rewarded. Moreover, the prenatal eclipse and lunation emphasize this strong Jupiter in domicile, general significator of wealth, very clearly. It is impossible to understand a chart without also looking at this mundane embedding by prenatal charts. Jupiter is the strongest planet in his chart, the Lord of the Geniture, showing his talent. The Great Benefic, trining the Moon/PoF conjunction is the general significator of politics and it is placed in the third house of routine communications. This also shows where his wealth is coming from.

Jupiter itself is on a star with a dubious reputation. *Sabik*, the left Knee of the Snake-bearer, is said to give perverted morals and bring success in evil deeds. If you bear the snake, beware you are not bitten. Berlusconi's Moon is in the Mansion of the Cup-bearer, and its keywords apart from coarse language are hidden things and many secrets. And also the occult. Berlusconi was a member of the corrupted freemason's lodge

Propaganda-2. This fact serves well to illustrate the effect of the Cup-bearer's Mansion in a life which may have its darker sides, as this life so filled with secrets surely indicates.

Alan Leo – Tradition in Detriment

Only by looking at the Ascendant would it have been clear that this person would do something important with something old. On the Ascendant we find Saturn, the planet of old things and of astrology, on the most powerful royal star in the heavens, *Regulus*, the Heart of the Lion. This position determined the main part of Alan Leo's life, and we could actually stop here and still have a good idea of what he achieved overall. It is also immediately clear that this person will not accept the old things dominating his life in a traditional form; Saturn is in its detriment in the sign of Leo, the heavenly house governed by the Sun. The Sun is the ruler of the first house, Leo himself, so he wants to determine how old things will be passed on.

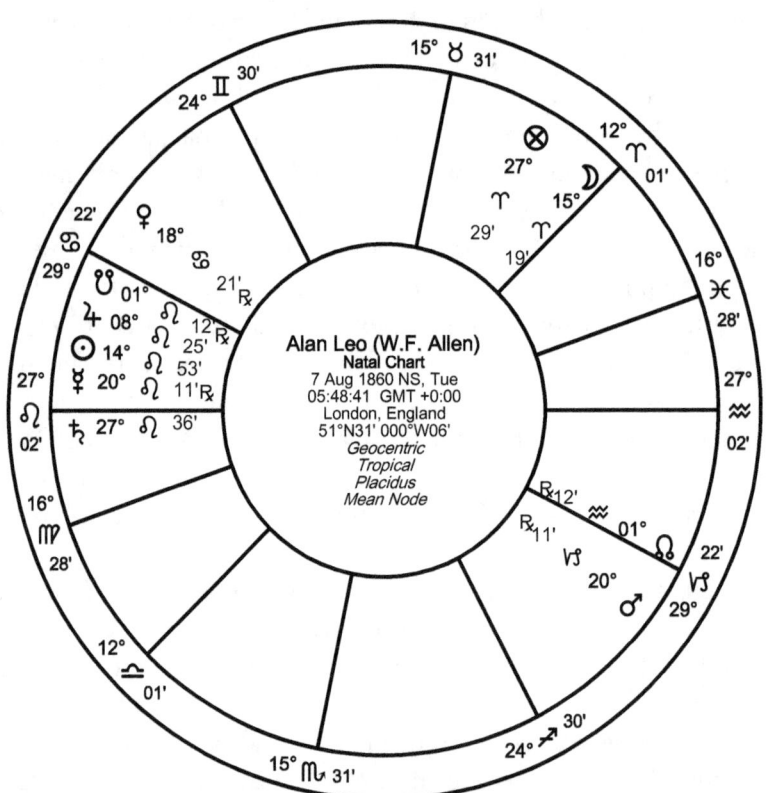

Astrology often pays homage to this man because he was one of the main architects of the renaissance of astrology at the end of the 19th century and yes, he certainly has this power with Saturn on mighty *Regulus*. Moreover, this all-pervasive Saturn is in the term and face of Mars which in its turn is in the sign of Saturn. So there is a reception of medium strength between Mars and Saturn showing that his Saturn activities were connected to everything symbolised by Mars in the chart. The ninth house of astrology and the fourth house of the root of things are ruled by a retrograde Mars indicating going back to the past. Mars has a lot of dignity in its exaltation in Capricorn, and his soul's desire, the Part of Fortune, is in the ninth house disposed by Mars. His soul thirsts for higher knowledge.

His engagement with spiritual matters is certainly sincere. The point is that Mars Lord 9 has little to say in this mutual reception with Saturn – it cannot keep this Saturn firmly under control. In a reception the powers of disposition should always be weighed and Saturn is the stronger in this case. Mars in the last part of Leo only disposes of Saturn by relatively weak term and face rulership whereas Saturn is the ruler of the sign Mars is placed in. So the Great Malefic in its worst possible condition will rather influence Mars in a negative way; Mars does not have the disposition power to correct Saturn. To formulate this more plainly: his ardent desire to come closer to God was outweighed by the conviction that you cannot do this through traditional spiritual ideas and practices.

Leo has a very ambiguous relationship with Saturn on his Ascendant on *Regulus*. It is his big unavoidable trump in the world but as Leo himself says, the Sun as Lord 1 in the twelfth house 'hates/harms' Saturn through negative reception, and this Saturn, as we have seen, is in a bad condition. It is clear that Leo is going to have the upper hand over tradition, and in his own sign he will be guided by his personal ideas and it is he who will decide what will happen to this Saturn in detriment in his power. Alan Leo was one of the driving forces in regenerating astrology at the end of the nineteenth century, which he did by creating a whole new form, clearing away a large part of the traditional astrological methods. Nowadays this form of astrology is called modern astrology, existing side by side with traditional astrology, which itself has been regenerated in the two last decades of the 20th century.

It is fascinating to realise that Alan Leo also introduced Sun-sign astrology, which is not found in the traditional method. It is a literal effect of his Sun Lord 1 dominating Saturn. The Sun/Lord 1 is placed in the twelfth house but it is hardly weakened by this as it is in narrow square with the MC and right on the MC by antiscion. An antiscion points to something hidden or indirect, the ambition to be the theosophical re-inventor of astrology is not exactly the straightest path to a great career. Through antiscial position and the square with the MC, the Sun will be able to manifest in the world, and of course Alan Leo did this, although it was not exactly mainstream.

Nevertheless, the twelfth house themes remain very clear; the Sun is not only placed in the house of secrets, it also trines the Moon Lord 12. This indicates the paranormal and magical elements in theosophy and theosophical astrology that he espoused like the invocation of planetary spirits, and the astrological research done by looking into crystal balls. It is well known that the interpretation of Neptune as a dissolving and blurring energy was also based on Leo's observation of Neptune in his crystal ball appearing as a foggy patch. Leo was an enthusiastic member of the Theosophical Society and the Society's tendencies towards the paranormal are no secret.

Venus Lord 10 of career is in a strengthening narrow sextile with the MC and on *Castor*, the mortal Twin, who has a more earthly orientation than his immortal brother *Pollux*, and whose planetary nature is purely Mercurial – appropriate for Leo's activities as a proficient networker, translator, publisher and popular author. A Gemini star always introduces a strong element of doubleness of a high/low relation and Leo was indeed interested in astrology but was also the first to effectively commercialise it in the form of duplicated standard chart delineation texts. His example has been followed up until the current time and there are now many computer programs producing chart interpretations and even predictions.

It is Leo's lunar mansion which gives you one of those moments of the pure joy of astrology. The Moon is in the last mansion of the Fishes. According to tradition it can be associated with people who study time in some way because this is the final mansion, literally marking where time ends and where the gate to the next world opens.

Louis Sixteenth of France – the Slaughtered Lion

As the court astrologer of the French kings you would have frowned on seeing this chart of the newborn prince, who was set to become the next king of France. In view of the changing times in which a king could not be sure of his throne or even his life, this chart is at the very least disquieting. The conjunction of the Sun Lord 12 and Jupiter Lord 4 of tradition, dynasty and family on *Regulus* immediately draws our attention. This is a strong conjunction in itself but it is severely weakened by the placement in the twelfth house of misery, loneliness and self-destruction, with no way out as there is no aspect nor a mutual reception with a strong planet. This weakness is underlined by a retrograde Mercury Lord 1 and Lord 10, about to lose all its dignity by moving further backward out of the sign of its domicile and exaltation.

Here is a strong theme of falling from and losing a high position with the story of the Nemean Lion in the central role. In the myth it is the

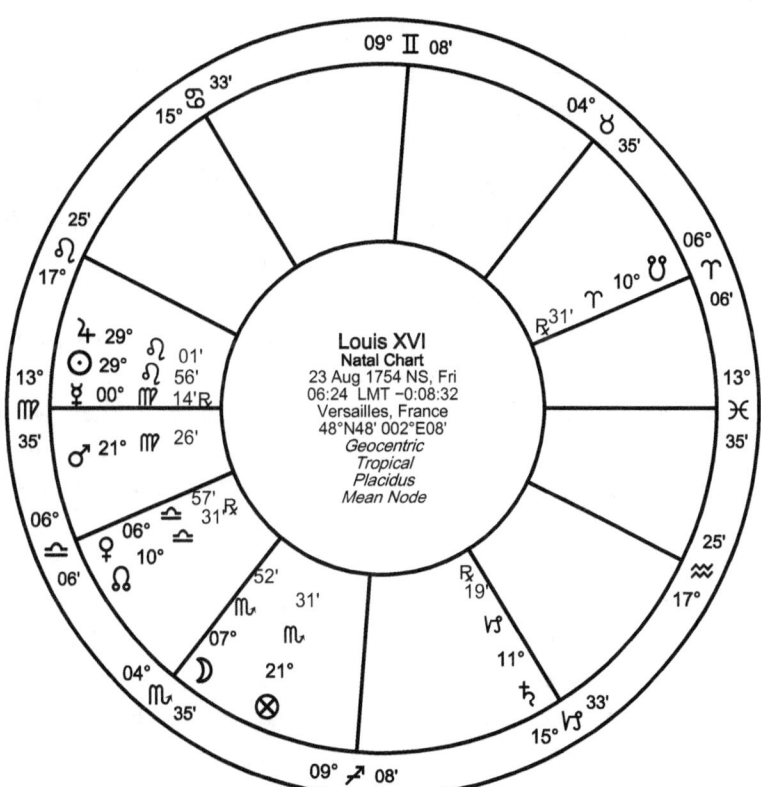

hero Hercules who kills the Nemean Lion and strips the beast of its skin, which he will wear around his shoulders as a sign that he owns the Leo power and not the other way around. The Nemean Lion is a symbol for raw, often overly strong ambition, and an intense lust for power, to be sacrificed by the hero to lead these energies in the right direction. Louis the Sixteenth certainly did try to do this but it could not prevent the disasters of the French Revolution; this fate is shown by the emphasis on the isolating twelfth house.

It is clear from other fixed star positions that this *Regulus* story of the slaughtered Lion could become most relevant and acute. The MC/IC axis falls within the usual orb for royal stars on the *Aldebaran/Antares* axis that once marked the spring/autumn equinoxes, and still carries this meaning. So an old thing will die to make place for something new, and as *Antares*, the star of autumn, is on the IC it is the dynasty that will end; the ancient French kingdom is completing its last phase. *Antares* is the Heart of the Scorpion, the sinister poisonous beast which may become an eagle in a transformed shape. This illustrates what to do in the case of *Antares* problems – release what is dying as it will be taken away from you anyhow. But giving up is difficult because Scorpio is the sign of fixed desire (fixed Water sign in the zodiac).

So the king has to give up the dynasty and the tradition on which his authority is based? This is a lot to ask – will he be able to do this? Louis' temperament is not purely choleric, he is not a fiery hothead who will get on the barricades without a second thought. Naturally, Mars in the first house in a poor condition will not have made him easy-going, yet despite this he did see the necessity of reforming and did indeed try to implement reforms. The big problem was his isolation – there was no support from the nobility, the judicial authorities or the clergy; it was the conservative opposition that blocked the gradual reform he tried to realise.

This dramatic situation is shown by the powerless Jupiter-Sun conjunction in the isolating twelfth house, without any help from elsewhere in the chart. This is underlined by Mercury Lord 1 and 10 about to retrograde out of its own sign deeper into the twelfth house and into combustion; he cannot win as he will lose so much power. Even if you try do the right thing inspired by your myth, and Louis tried, your fate as shown by the chart is often stronger. There are no magical, psychological, or even mythical strategies which will make you the master of your fate. Knowledge of your chart will enable you to make optimal choices in a situation, but you cannot get around the stars that rule you. If an evil wind blows you cannot change the wind, but you can try to take cover till the storm calms down.

Louis took steps to sacrifice a part of his absolute power. Doing this he lived the Leo myth in a positive way (as an able astrologer would have recommended), but this did not save the day. He was certainly no blind fool as some kings were; he was very much aware that in England, Charles the First, who was quite a hot-head, had been decapitated during the Civil War, and this made Louis cautious and prone to allow changes to temper the revolutionary forces. It was to no avail. Everybody knows him as the last French king who was killed in a dramatic and humiliating way by revolutionary extremists. It is the myth of the Lion being played out in real life.

Just look at how far the directives from above rule the life. Louis ended his life under the guillotine, a public execution as if he was not a king but some ordinary criminal. The way you die is shown in the chart by the ruler of the eighth house or a planet placed in that house, the 'anareta'. On the cusp of the eighth house there is the malefic South Node; in Vedic mythology the nodal axis represents the separated head and tail of the snake Vasuki. Mars, the knife, is Lord 8 by antiscion exactly on cusp 8 in opposition to Venus within two degrees, Venus is anatomically the throat and rules the second house also referring to the throat. This is more than appropriate for one of the most famous executions in history.

Curro Romero – To Kill the Bull
We would expect a planet on a star in the constellation Taurus in the chart of one of Spain's most famous bull-fighters. The *corrida*, the traditional bull-fight in Spain, gives an exact picture of the essence of the myth of the Bull. The ritual has its roots deep in time and it shows the right way of handling matter, of how to play with the bull. It is not a good idea just to stand in its way as it will simply trample you. It's better to play and dance along with it, exhaust it and then kill it. There are many forms to show this mythical play enacted, for example the ancient pictures showing a man jumping over the bull and during his jump he

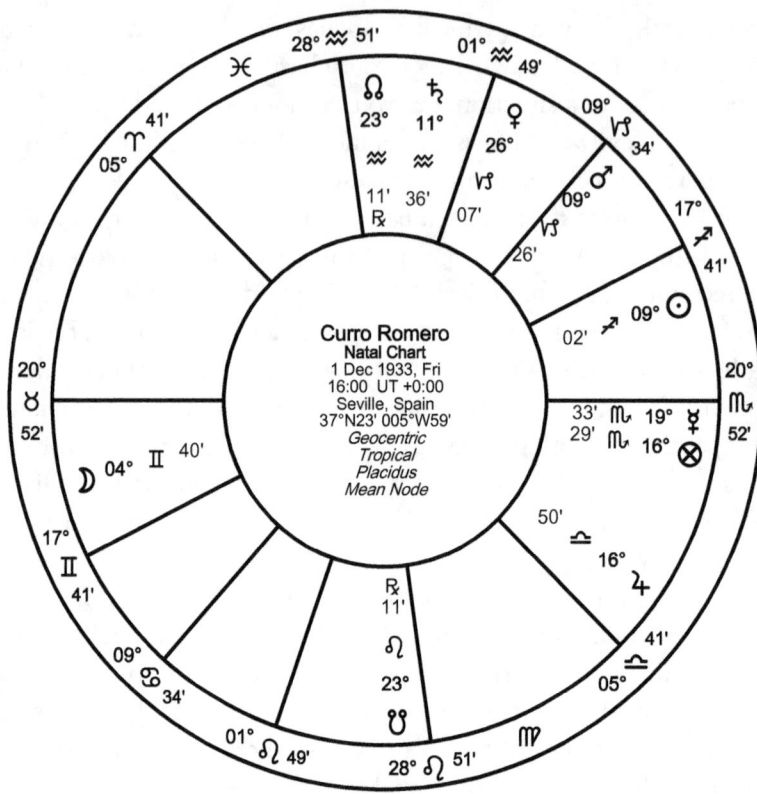

is coloured black to indicate material life as a passing phase of darkness. There are variations of the bull-fight in Portugal in which the fighters only jump over the bull but don't kill it in the end. But whatever form it takes, it is always meant as a ritual-symbolic manual on how to handle matter. The message is that the bull of matter is necessary and fun but it has to be killed in the end; the attachment to it has to be severed to make you happy. In Romero's chart we don't have a luminary or the MC on the famous royal star in Taurus, the Moon is four degrees away from *Aldebaran*, the Bull's Eye, and that is a bit too wide to count even for a luminary on a royal star. This is more than compensated however by the lunar Mansion the Moon is found in, which is ruled by *Aldebaran*.

The Moon is also on the main star in the Hyades, a nebulous star group belonging to the constellation of Taurus. The Hyades are a specific intensification of the whole Taurean theme that indicates misfortune and disappointment because we live in a material world. The Hyades, the seven half-sisters of the Pleaides, are a part of Taurus and refer to the seven seals of the planets imprisoning us on earth in matter and cutting us off from the higher worlds. Myths like those of the Bull can show us how to handle this material prison until the moment comes when those seals are broken. It is not for nothing that the bull-fighter wears the 'suit of colours', which symbolise the planetary forces he controls.

The Hyades are a nebulous star group, a signature for blindness which arises because we have become trapped in matter. This very material Moon on the Hyades has however a powerful opponent in the chart, the Sun combusting it through opposition, the higher solar consciousness on the martial and royal death star *Antares*. This solar power is going to be victorious over the Taurean-lunar instinctiveness because the Moon is applying to this combusting opposition. This is the essence of the whole corrida, divine Sun kills material Moon. The other planetary positions in the chart can be seen as supporting this main opposition of the two luminaries. Mercury conjuncts the Part of Fortune on an angle on the Scales, the harsh Claws of Justice and Mercy. So the desire of the soul, the Part of Fortune, is on the Insufficient Price, the merciless *South Scale* of Justice. It wants to kill the corrupting bull of matter so that the correct balance is restored.

This position on the Scales or the Claws is underlined by the antiscion of Saturn falling on the Descendant. Saturn is Lord 10, and very strong in its own sign, so he will do something traditional as his profession. Saturn is the general significator of death and it is conjunct two weak stars in Capricorn, *Armus* and *Dorsum*, the Heart and the Back of the Sea-goat. Here the light is weak in Capricorn, which can be seen as the zodiacal South Node or, as it was called in ancient days the Delphin, the exit of life. When Typhon, death, appears, the earthy goat transforms into a divine fish. So it is all about playing with death here, with Typhon manifesting as the bull. Romero's talent, Saturn, on these Capricorn stars exactly shows where the blow is dealt, as the bull-fighter finally thrusts the sword through the neck into the bull's heart to kill the beast. A bull that wins, as very occasionally happens, is not put into the corrida again because it knows all the tricks. Matter is very smart, despite its apparent dull heaviness.

The chart shows the capacity to handle large animals; a strongly dignified Mars is Lord 12 of animals 'larger than a goat', placed on the cusp of the ninth house of ritual. Mars is also the ruler of the eighth house of death seen from the twelfth of large animals, giving us the death of large animals. The Descendant emphasized by the PoF/Mercury in conjunction with the antiscion of Saturn, is also the eighth cusp taken from the twelfth, so killing large animals is important. It is clear that Romero will be the boss over the large animals, and this is shown by the disposition Lord 10 of profession has over Mars Lord 12. There are many indications for success here with the royal *South Scale*, the mansion of the Bull's eye which often gives success, and many angular planets. The MC strengthens this as it is on the main star in the Eagle, *Altair*, a star of an appropriate Jupiter/Mars nature belonging to the elite of first magnitude stars.

The emphasis on religion in the chart is striking: *Altair* on the MC, Saturn the planet of wisdom being so strong, Lord 9 in the tenth house, and the strong Mars on the ninth cusp. It shows that the corrida is an important ritual, not a European rodeo. This essence is brought out so elegantly by the Sun as the general significator of the spirit, and traditionally the symbol of the presence of God in His creation, in opposition with the Moon, the symbol of our transient material world. This all falls on the star axis *Antares/Aldebaran* representing death/new life. The Arabian Part of Vocation, the MC's own Part of Fortune (MC + Moon – Sun, so your ideal job) is on *Pollux*, the immortal of the Twins, who is not only a fighter and man of action, but also a tamer of large animals.

Salvador Dali – Desperate Perseus

The chart of the most famous surrealist artist in the world clearly shows how strong a planet on an angle will manifest in the life. In this case it is the Moon on the MC, and the lesser luminary is also the ruler of the first house; not a bad combination for success as it shows Dali himself on top. The Moon not only represents popularity – almost everybody will have a Dali poster somewhere in the house – it is also an appropriate significator for surrealism with its flowing forms and dreamy landscapes. As an artistic movement, surrealism strove to convey the unconscious and the uncontrollable nature of man, although Dali had definitely a style of his own within the surrealistic school.

The dominating Moon on the MC is on the star *Difda*, placed in

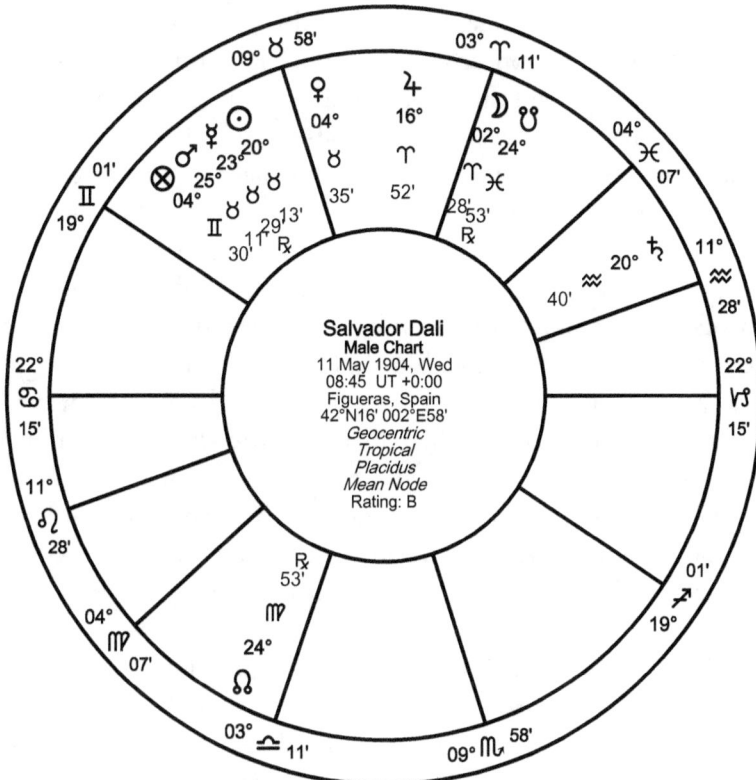

the Tail of the Seamonster of chaos, sent by furious Poseidon to devour Princess Andromeda, the symbol of the soul. This is one of the most important mythical themes in Dali's life and he produced his art balancing on the sharp edge of madness. The constellation Andromeda can be associated with the arts as all its stars have an outspoken Venus nature. Through these Venus qualities the Princess, who is the soul, tries to escape from the threatening Whale, a picture of the chaos of raw desire. This is exactly what Dali was concerned with. His art is a flight from madness, an escape from chaos, a theme which is further emphasized by other planetary positions in the chart. Mars Lord 10 of career and Lord 5 of creativity are in detriment conjunct Mercury Lord 12 of misery and self-destruction on the dark 'losing your head' star *Algol*, so there is a lot of confusion.

Fortunately, there is a very benefic factor in the chart; a strong Saturn in Aquarius is Lord 7, meaning it is a partner who provides him with more stability and keeps him grounded. This is his famous wife Gala. In the conjunction on *Algol* we see again a different aspect of the Gorgon Medusa and the whole Andromeda-Perseus story, the same Perseus who chopped off Medusa's Head also saved Princess Andromeda. Perseus used Medusa's repulsive head with hair-like snakes to petrify the Seamonster, but Medusa can also appear in a beautiful, seductive form. This is certainly connected to Dali's artistic activities; it points to veiling ugliness by giving it an attractive aesthetically seductive form. Both sides of Medusa can be seen here, the beauty and the madness, which are essentially the same thing in Dali's *Algol* mind.

Dali's imagery is fantastic and mad, a disquieting distortion that mirrors the raw destructive desire of which Medusa is the symbol. According to some versions of the myth, Medusa had made love with Poseidon in the temple of Athena and was punished for this transgression with the snake-hair. This refers again to the loss of thinking and rational control, as Athena is the ultimate goddess of clear thinking and rationality, born as she is from Zeus' head. Feminist interpretations of this story sometimes miss the point here; the story has nothing to do with the position of women in history or society then or now. The essential task is becoming the hero Perseus, for women and men alike, and cutting off the head of the desire monster that destroys the clarity of your thinking. Dali's art is an expression of this mythical battle against chaos and very often it looks more as if he is losing.

The rest of the chart is an instrument to effectively play this mythical role, and this convergence of energies is often seen in charts of successful people. The planet of the arts, Venus, is strong in its own sign and triplicity in the tenth house without any affliction. This is of course positive and gives a strong aesthetic talent, but in itself would not have been enough to explain his enormous success. You need powerful fixed stars, angular planets and a good synastry with the prenatal lunation and eclipse for this. This Moon on the MC mentioned above, so important for his popularity, is on the expansive Jupiter-like North Node by antiscion and in mutual reception with the Greater Luminary, the Sun, also strong in the positive eleventh house of the fruits of your labour. This Sun is peregrine but accidentally moderately strong, and the connection by reception of the two luminaries certainly adds to his success.

The Ascendant falls on the royal fixed star *Pollux*, the immortal

Twin, and as a royal star it will bring great success. It is a martial star, a fighter and a soldier, a tamer of horses and a man of action. This is something Dali needed because the rest of the chart does not really point to effective persistent action – it is rather laid-back and he is also phlegmatic by temperament. At the same time there is the theme of duality which is associated with the Gemini stars; something idealistic combined with something earthy. In Dali's case this is very true, there is much speculation about the dubious ways he sometimes made money; he was not the archetypically poor artist making brilliant work without a penny to pay the rent. He was commercially smart, and this can be seen in the reception of the Sun Lord 2 with the strong Moon on the MC and Jupiter, the general significator of wealth in the tenth house; not bad for money.

We can't help but notice that all seven classical planets are above the horizon, indicating visibility in the world. Compare this with Nicolai Tesla's chart further on. Such a direct interpretation using the section of the chart which is most emphasized gives you a good first impression of where the activity is going. Someone with most planets at the right western side will be involved a lot with other people, for example, whereas someone with all planets below the horizon will literally not be seen.

Mick Jagger – The Gorgon

We would expect to see some raw and powerful planetary positions in the chart of someone who is almost a caricature, an archetypical rock star, and what immediately strikes us is the Sun/Jupiter conjunction on the Ascendant. This is a clear indication that this is the chart of someone who is not going to be brushed aside easily, and all the more so because the Sun is Lord 1 and the 'significator of manners' which is very strong in its own sign. So he is a natural leader who will determine his own course of life and who knows how to be a king. It is already light when he is born, so Jupiter is peregrine in this diurnal chart. Jupiter does not have triplicity dignity, which tends to show its less positive sides, and this adds excess to the behaviour. This is not a sign of discipline and control. Jupiter also Lord 9 of norms and convictions, is on the *Praesepe* nebula close to the two *Aselli* in the constellation of Cancer. This can be seen as the Heart of Crab and represents the raw thirst to taste life to the full, it

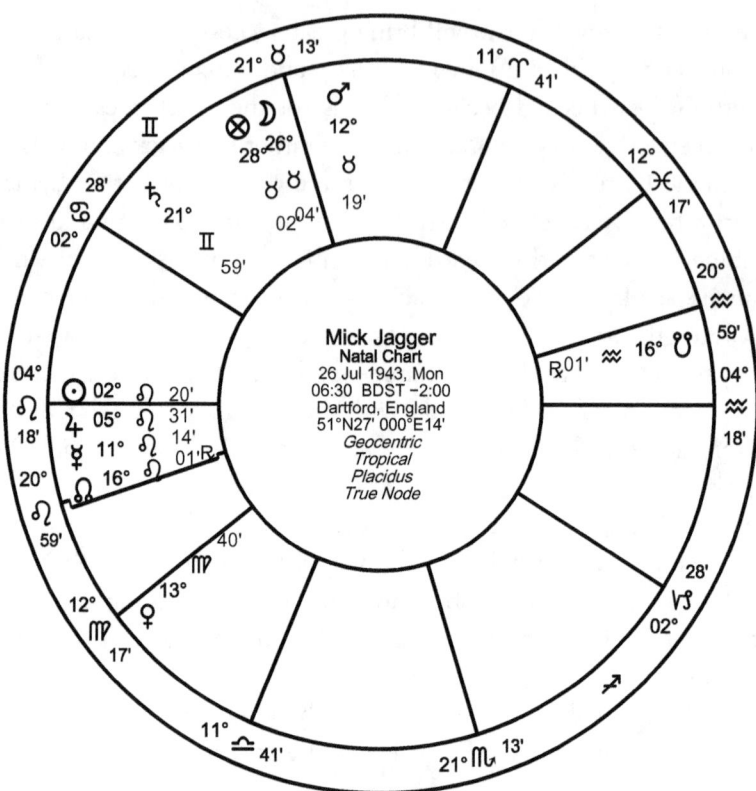

is the pure essence of the desire for life. It is also the concentration point of the water element which will not allow itself to be structured and so may create chaos. As a cold-blooded animal Cancer has no potentially divine solar centre, so it will be driven along by the oceanic streams without resisting. *Praesepe* is also called the Crib and it is empty, the saviour, the solar child-king, is not there and so the animal nature rules in the stable.

The *Aselli* or the Asses are the stars flanking the Crib and they can be associated with serving and honouring the child in the Crib. But on *Praesepe* itself there is no serving, the desires are followed without restraint. That is why this nebula can be so destructive – it tends to spread chaos, and certainly in mundane astrology its causes bloodshed. The Moon conjunct the Part of Fortune (the Moon Part) is on *Algol*. The Moon is Lord 12 of addictions, self-destruction and misery, and its antiscion is exactly on the Ascendant. So the two most malefic and destructive stars, *Algol* and *Praesepe*, representing a concentration of unbridled lust are closely cooperating through this life, and these energies are empowered by a royal Sun/Jupiter conjunction on the Ascendant. Quite a chart and quite a man!

'Sympathy for the Devil' and 'Satisfaction' can be understood well on the basis of astrology, for *Algol* is also called the Demon's Head. Even the name Rolling Stones can be seen in the chart. A stone is Saturn and should be immobile, laying still and providing stability, not rolling downhill, but this Sun-Jupiter conjunction hates Saturn by negative reception and will not accept its discipline. Jagger has no royal stars on important points but you could see these two powerful stars *Algol* and *Praesepe* as the Dark Kings; they do have a lot of power to manifest. They represent strong mythical energies and that is why Jagger became such a myth. In his magnetic attraction the myth is using his life as an instrument to manifest. *Algol* clearly shows its capacity to glamorously attract and make people lose their heads.

Mars, Lord 10 of career and Lord 5 of creativity, is on the star *Almach* in Andromeda which has a pure Venus nature and is strongly connected to artistic activities. Andromeda is the image of the soul threatened to be devoured by the Seamonster of unbridled desire, and this gives a motivation to escape through the arts. Again Perseus plays a role as the hero that saves the princess from the monster by petrifying it with Medusa's Head. This is the conquered desire nature used as a weapon against manipulation. Only a man who controls his instinctive reactions to a certain extent is really free, otherwise he is no more than a beast used by the powers that be. Mars Lord 10 is in detriment and trines the planet of the arts, Venus, also in bad condition. It is not going to be pretty, but this could hardly be expected with *Algol* and *Praesepe* so dominant.

As usual the Arabian parts offer some interesting extra information and clarifications. The Part of Fame (Asc + Jupiter – Sun in diurnal charts) is right on Jupiter on *Praesepe* close to the Ascendant. This part does not automatically make you famous, but if the potential is there it indicates what you are famous or notorious for. In the charts of famous people the energies usually converge to form a powerful pattern, and focusing is one of the reasons for fame. As astrologers we mostly delineate charts of common people and in a way this is more difficult as the grocer's chart most probably lacks the concentrated focus we see in Jagger's.

So it depends on the chart how the parts are given their exact meaning. The parts are activated most strongly by narrow aspects with planets or conjunction with cusps. Jagger's chart has the Part of Vocation on the Descendant, indicating a strong wish to perform for a public. This part indicates your ideal job, which is not necessarily the same as your talent. Talent and vocation have to be combined in some activity ideally but this cannot always be realised, we are not all happy with our jobs like Mick Jagger. Of the seven planetary parts, the Jupiter part (Asc + Jup − Part of the Sun) is on the Moon/PoF conjunction and so by antiscion on the Ascendant again. This part indicates Help from Above, success or support given for free, and has concrete as well as spiritual connotations. It is amusing to see the Part of Sexual Intercourse (Asc + Venus − Sun) in conjunction with this lustful Venus on the third house cusp of routine travel: groupies!

Madonna − On the Back of the Lion

Superstar and pop idol Madonna is in her sixties and is still going strong. The chart shows her power at first glance, as is so often indicated by angular planets. The Moon and Mercury are placed near the Ascendant and this astrologically explains her stage name − the Madonna is the maternal energy of the Moon. Traditionally the Holy Virgin is pictured standing on a crescent Moon and in ancient times was known as the Star of the Sea − symbolising that she guides seafarers and anyone involved with the sea − so our desires and this function is essentially lunar. This is exactly what Madonna does, she plays with desire and with feminine attraction. That this will be rather provocative is shown by the peregrine wavering condition of the Moon, which by nature already unstable, will produce raw and straight-forward emotions.

This conjunction of the Moon and Mercury in Virgo, a sign that is traditionally loud-voiced, is positive for the power of expression, although Mercury's retrogradation will cause some trouble. Indeed there is some discussion about the real quality of her voice and she seems to be insecure about this herself. Retrogradation is a weakening factor it is true, but there is so much compensation coming from the Moon, and Mercury's essential dignity, and the strength of the whole constellation,

Case Studies

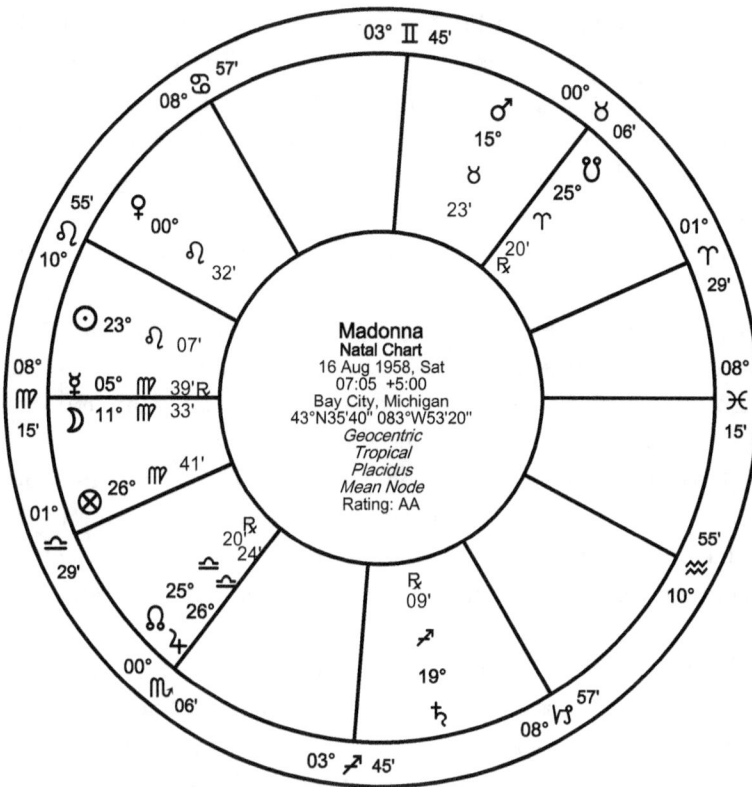

that it will not be more than a minor problem. As the Moon is the general significator of the people and Mercury signifies trade, this gives her a great insight into the development of trends which can be commercially exploited.

The Moon is also on *Zosma* the Back of the Lion. This gives the Moon a lot of ambition and independence; no one is allowed to ride a lion and the old texts underline the star's negative effects. Shamelessness, selfishness and immoral behaviour are mentioned as keywords for *Zosma*, which has a Saturn-Venus nature, and as neither of those planets have dignity in the chart, just like the Moon on it, these less pleasant sides will manifest. Madonna is certainly shameless on stage and she is definitely the boss, and in control of the whole show. Don't try to bypass her in any way, or the Lion will show its teeth.

We can also predict the effect of the Moon more clearly by looking at the lunar mansion it occupies. It is a mansion controlled by two stars in the constellation of Leo, one of which is again Zosma. In the Vedic tradition one of its names is the 'Second Red One' and other images are the fireplace, the little fig tree and the lingam and phallus. The connotations of pleasure of an erotic nature are clear and among its keywords not only musicians, entertainers and singers are mentioned, but also sometimes relationships and sex therapists. With such a success you would expect some planets or angles on royal stars and indeed the Great Benefic Jupiter is placed on the expansive North Node on royal Spica in the second house of money. This is very nice for the financial situation, all the more so as Jupiter is the general significator of wealth, although by antiscion Jupiter is in opposition with Mercury and near the Descendant. Jupiter, still carrying the benefic Spica influence in its antiscial position, is also Lord 7, and Mercury is Lord 1, so this shows tense relationships by opposition but not too dramatic because of the protective Spica energy. The Virgin's Spike is powerful and will ascertain a good outcome if it is not contradicted by other powerful positions as in the case of Princess Diana.

Madonna has been married twice, which seems very restrained considering her status as a megastar. There are a lot of superstars whose love life is extremely problematic. The Sun is in the twelfth house but it has a lot of essential dignity in its own sign and it is in narrow sextile with the strongly benefic Jupiter. This aspect with a strong factor provides an escape from the isolating twelfth house for the Sun and this is again good for relationships as Jupiter is Lord 7 and the Sun is the general significator of men. Jupiter is in a strong mutual reception by exaltation and sign with Saturn Lord 5 of pleasure, sexuality and creativity, also supporting Jupiter in its role as money significator, so sex and fun will bring money in and Saturn indicates the darker sides of the erotic show she puts on. The outspoken tendency to provocation by mixing religious symbols and sex is brought out by Mars in detriment in the ninth house of religion in narrow trine with the Moon, her Madonna-planet.

The Part of Fortune – indicating her soul's desire in the world – is on the star *Labrum*, associated with the Crow's story of abandoning your mission because the grass is greener in the next field, but also with the Grail Cup of searching for heavenly beauty in material dirt. The Grail Cup is a spiritual symbol but on a lower level is connected to feminine sexuality as it is receptive. Mythical-symbolic images work out on many levels. This also points to one of Madonna's most striking characteristics, her capacity to reinvent herself again and again; she is the ultimate shape-shifter. The PoF on *Labrum* shows she wants to go on and on to something more attractive in search of beauty, and it is disposed by Mercury, the planet of many shapes, and the ruler of the tenth house squaring the MC. With the two most changeable planets, the Moon and Mercury, Lord 1 and 10, in a mutable Mercury-disposed sign in the Ascendant, it is no wonder that we get a shape-shifter.

Edith Piaf – Fire!
Some charts are so clear, and the case of Edith Piaf is a good example. It is obvious that this person will not have a very peaceful life. The temperament is strongly choleric so this is someone who will fight, who will say what is on her mind and is determined to be heard. The condition of Mars is always extra important in a fiery temperament, as a planet structures and organises the potential of the elemental energies of the signs, passing these energies on to our earthly world. The better the condition of the planet, the better it will be able to perform its task; this is the main reason that classical astrology concentrates on the planets rather than the signs.

And what kind of Mars this is! The fire planet does not have too much essential dignity in the last degrees of Leo, face and term dignity is not strong, but it is much better than nothing at all. The part of the zodiac Mars is placed in is called feral or fierce, this connotation being given traditionally to the whole of Leo and the second part – the instinctive lower horse part – of Sagittarius. Practice confirms this idea is correct, that raw animal energies are concentrated in these parts of the zodiac, and in addition Mars is on *Regulus* the Heart of the Lion giving great success but also a scorching ambition. The killing of the Lion, the sacrifice of blinding ambition, is the right solution to the more negative characteristics and dangers *Regulus* brings along with it.

Mars' rulerships makes the picture complete. The fire planet is the ruler of the first house indicating Piaf herself, and it is Lord 5 of creativity. There is so much fire in play that there will not be much sweetness about her artistic creations. Mars is conjunct the Arabian Part of Fame (formula: Asc + Jupiter – Sun in diurnal charts, reverse the formula by night as in this case: Asc + Sun – Jupiter), indicating what

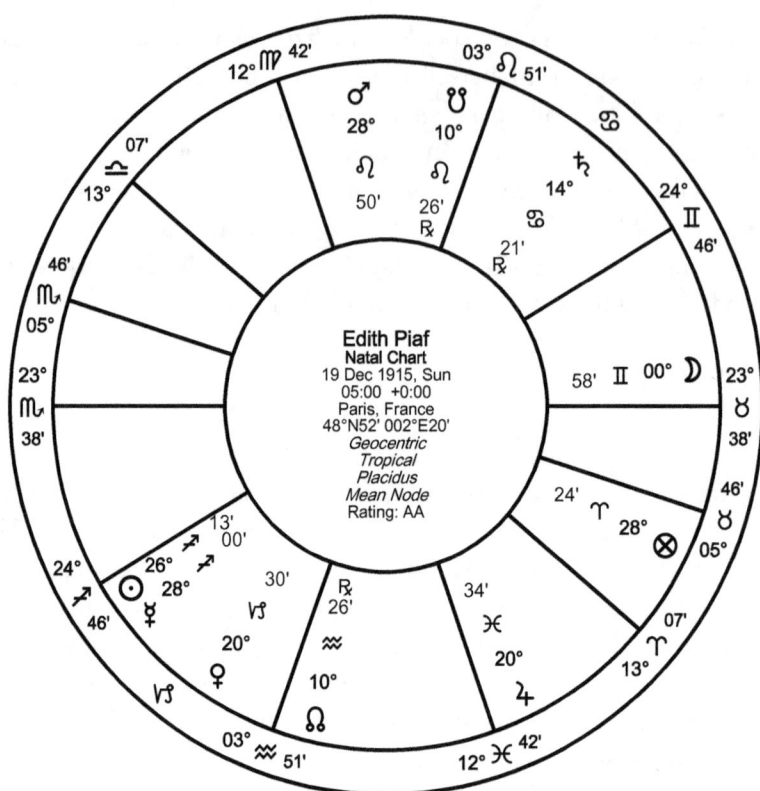

you are known for, or notorious for, and Mars is in a positive mutual reception through triplicity with this strong Jupiter in the fourth house. This connects Mars as her creativity with this benefic Jupiter in Pisces, Lord 4 of roots and tradition; the chanson is not the most modern form of music.

Piaf's best-known song is as martial and choleric as can be, 'Non je regrette rien'. Why would a choleric ever regret something? He drew his knife when it was necessary and it does not make any sense to talk it over again. This song also had its political and patriotic side as Piaf dedicated it to the soldiers of the foreign legion who had dirtied their hands during the war in Algeria. Here we see a concrete expression of Mars (soldiers) in the ninth house (foreign countries) as Lord 5 (a song) on *Regulus* (great fame), with the Part of Fame and in mutual reception with Jupiter Lord 4 indicating the roots and therefore the native country.

The importance of Mars is underlined by the position of the Part of Fortune, the desire of the soul indicating what we really and profoundly want from this earthly life. It is in the fifth house, disposed by Mars and in narrow trine with it. So she really wants to do martial fifth house stuff. As Mars is the general significator of sexuality and also rules the fifth house of all kinds of pleasures, we clearly see her reputation as a devourer of men here. To delineate sexuality in the chart the temperament should always be taken into account separately from the condition of the fifth house. A cold and dry melancholic who does not want to connect too much, will have quite a different sex life to individuals brimming with fire like Edith Piaf. The fire excess has to find its way out of the system otherwise it will get stuck and cause all kinds of problems.

As for love and relationships, a choleric person is not too harmonious a partner, and the condition of the seventh house adds to this trouble, as extremely malefic *Algol* is on Piaf's Descendant. With *Algol* things go wrong because the snake hairs of desire totally dominate rationality, symbolised by the head, and chaos is the result. As mentioned before, *Algol* is a repulsive monster but it also takes the shape of a seductive beautiful woman, which makes following your instinctive impulses so irresistibly attractive. But the reality is not nice, as chaos is always the result – as it was in Piaf's life. The only thing that could have helped is cutting off the monster's head, the painful sacrifice of the intense desire for others. It is Perseus' sword of distinction which has to be wielded here: what is really worthwhile and what should be thrown away? Also the unstable Moon, planet of change, in the seventh house on the Pleiades, the Weeping Sisters, and in the associated lunar mansion of the Knife, do not make things any better for relationships.

A further analysis of the career brings out this Mars even more strongly; it is also in narrow trine with Mercury Lord 10 combust and on the star *Acumen* associated with blindness. It is a well-known fact that performing was hell for Piaf as she was extremely nervous before going on stage despite her fiery character. Mercury, the planet of nerves and Lord 10 of public events, is weak in detriment and combust on a nebulous blinding star. So as soon as she appears in front of the footlights (Sun), her capacity to think and speak (Mercury) is seriously weakened (combust and detriment). Piaf indeed had some astrological reasons to be nervous! It is her martial combative spirit and the scorchingly ambitious *Regulus* that make her go on stage despite the nerves – the proud Heart of the Lion will not allow nervousness to humiliate him.

On the Ascendant there is another star of the first magnitude, *Agena* the right foreleg of the Centaur Pholus. Although *Agena* as the right leg has a more positive meaning than the left leg *Bungula*, the same theme of a strong tension between the instinctive life and conscious control plays an important role here. Pholus is killed by an arrow dipped in Hydra poison, a symbol of desire, and in this way becomes the victim of his more base parts. In Piaf's life and work the painful articulation of the fiery instinctive life is central; it is an attempt to rise above the emotions by expressing them in an artistic form, but there is obviously the danger in her unsettled life that the Hydra poison will get the better of her in the end.

Marilyn Monroe – The Chained Princess
Marilyn Monroe's success can be spotted right away in the eleventh house, the most positive house for her. The Sun is placed here, in conjunction with Mercury on *Aldebaran*, the sensual red Eye of the Bull and one of the absolute top-dog royal stars. A very good position to become a huge success. As the eleventh house is not the career itself but the profits received through it or the favours given by the king, it is clearly indicated here why there were so many powerful men in her life. The Sun is the general significator of kings and is tied to the eleventh house not only by placement, but also by this conjunction with Mercury Lord 11.

Mercury is very strong as it is not really combust, despite its nearness to the Sun, and as the conjunction takes place in Mercury's own sign of Gemini it makes Mercury strong enough to manifest powerfully through the combustion. Mercury in fact gets the full support of the Sun on royal *Aldebaran*, as this type of combustion can be regarded as a mutual reception – the Sun controls Mercury by its beams but Mercury also controls the Sun by disposition. This all happens in the Mercurial air sign Gemini which is 'voiced' according to the tradition and indeed she had a voice, a royal sensual *Aldebaran* voice.

In the seventh house we find the Moon and Jupiter, which are both peregrine. Neither planet is renowned for boundaries or stability, so this is not too promising for relationships. In addition the seventh house is ruled by a weak retrograde Saturn in aspect with the Moon in the seventh house – this is not going to be helpful in establishing a loving

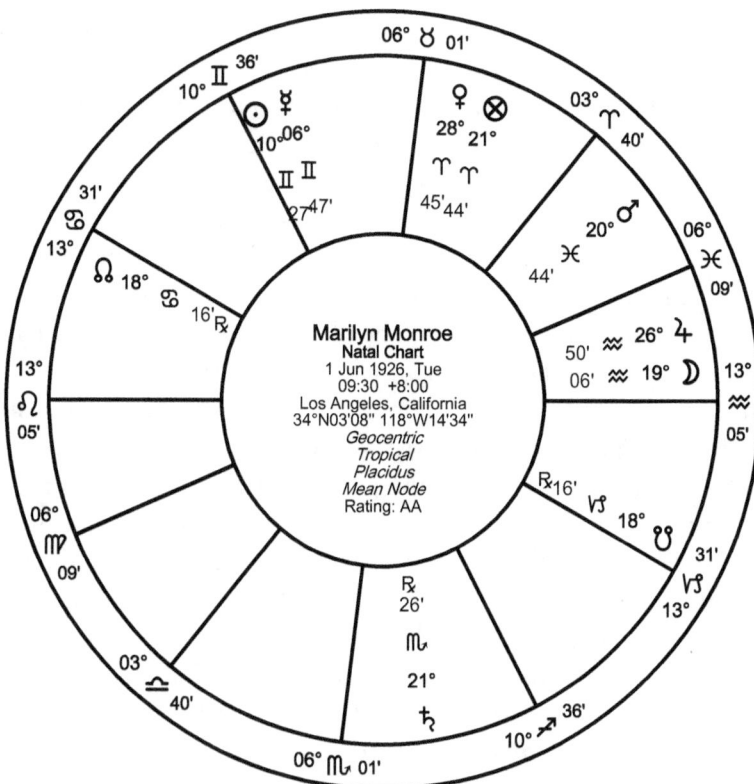

relationship. Saturn is also on the star *Unukalhai*, the Snake's Heart, and this combination will bring unpleasant experiences with dubious men. The ruler of the seventh house shows what kind of partner automatically comes into our life, as well as the themes characterising our love relationships.

Very appropriate for the ultimate sex symbol, Lord 10 of career, Venus, is in Aries in detriment. According to tradition this makes one very sexy, and it is not a Venus that will behave correctly and stay within the limitations of her role as Venus in Libra would do. The lusty aspect of Venus will come to the fore and the placement of Venus on the star *Mirach*, one of the two stars of a purely Venusian nature, will of course strengthen this seductiveness further. *Mirach* is appropriately a star in the girdle of Princess Andromeda, who was chained to a rock and threatened by the Whale sent by Poseidon to devour her.

This seamonster is symbolically the desire nature and the Princess is the soul trying to escape the hideous whale, which is why she sings so beautifully; she longs for Perseus to come and rescue her. Andromeda is the ultimate damsel in distress, an ancient and powerful theme which will resonate with many men. Who doesn't want to be Perseus? Andromeda is a pure Venus constellation and is much associated with the arts, of which the planetary symbol shows the essence: the circle of spirit on top of the cross of matter creating order and harmony in material forms. This is the essence of beauty, the divine light shining through the material form. In Monroe's case this Venus energy will be manifested more as lust than in a serious artistic way. The planet of beauty and love is in its detriment, dominated by the impulsive heat of Mars.

It is striking that Venus is right at the end of Aries and about to enter its own sign. Marilyn Monroe will certainly want to do something with her Venus! In progression the planet will be essentially strong for a long time. This does not mean that the detriment of Venus in her natal position is not valid but it does show that the natal potential will come out better as long as Venus is in Taurus by progression. In following progressions, changes of dignity by entry into a new term or into a new sign will manifest clearly in the life. The only aspect this important Venus Lord 10 makes, is a narrow sextile with Jupiter Lord 5 of pleasure, in an angle in an Air sign – very appropriate for an actress whose most famous image is the dress lifted by a stream of air from a ventilator. To show how precise Arabian parts work out, the Part of Fame (Asc + Jupiter – Sun, reverse in nocturnal charts) is exactly on this Venus, aspected by the airy erotic Jupiter!

There was also a strong, dark side to Marilyn Monroe: her addiction to pills and alcohol which is said to have finally led to her suicide. The South Node, always a point of extreme problems, vulnerability and suffering, is on cusp 6 of illness and the ruler of the sixth house is a weak peregrine Saturn, the planet of depression on the miserable Heart of the Snake. Saturn affects the emotions and the mind very much as it aspects the emotional Moon, also Lord 12 of self-destruction, placed in a Saturn sign, and Mercury is in the triplicity of Saturn. These are not exactly merry positions. Behind the blonde Venus-in-Aries image there is another rather dark reality.

In a medical-astrological perspective this Saturn influence could be harmonised by giving a homeopathic lead preparation in a high potency. Lead is the metal of Saturn. The Great Malefic is also disposed by a moderately strong Mars in its triplicity in Pisces which it also aspects. So anything associated with Mars could serve to heal the destructive influence of Saturn. Mars rules the ninth house of religion where we also find the yearning of her soul, the Part of Fortune, so spiritual development could have saved her from the despair indicated by Saturn. Again the lunar mansion is almost shocking, it is the mansion of the Delphin, associated with music and wealth, and represents the poet Arion of Lesbos who killed himself by jumping overboard to escape from the hands of his kidnappers.

Nicolai Tesla – The Spell of Saint Elmo's Fire
Nicolai Tesla developed many applications of electricity and was very much, almost incredibly, ahead of his time; what catches the eye immediately is that all the planets are below the horizon except for Jupiter, which is placed in the weakening twelfth house. So this is someone who will have a problem being noticed in the world – he is invisible, under the horizon and this invisibility is further strengthened by the weakness of Saturn Lord 10 in detriment. And this was indeed the case; with a view to his extraordinary achievements in the field of electricity, Tesla did not get the recognition he deserved at all. There are many people who achieved far less and who could not stand in his shadow, but they have become much more famous than Tesla. This illustrates the difference between essential and accidental dignity, between quality and power.

The only angular planet, the Sun, also draws attention to itself as being so near the IC it is the planet with the strongest accidental dignity, the strongest power of manifestation in the world. Of course, the IC is not the optimal placement for success, it is after all the lowest point connected with mid-night in opposition with the MC. Planets near the MC or the Ascendant are much easier to use in terms of the career; even a strong planet on the Descendant has its disadvantages despite its angularity, because it is in the house of your opponents and not really yours. The Sun on the IC, light shining at the darkest point in Tesla's chart, is nevertheless more than appropriate for someone mainly known for activities connected to electricity and lighting!

That this person is all about energy is underlined by the narrow square the Sun makes with Mars, the general significator of energy. Venus is

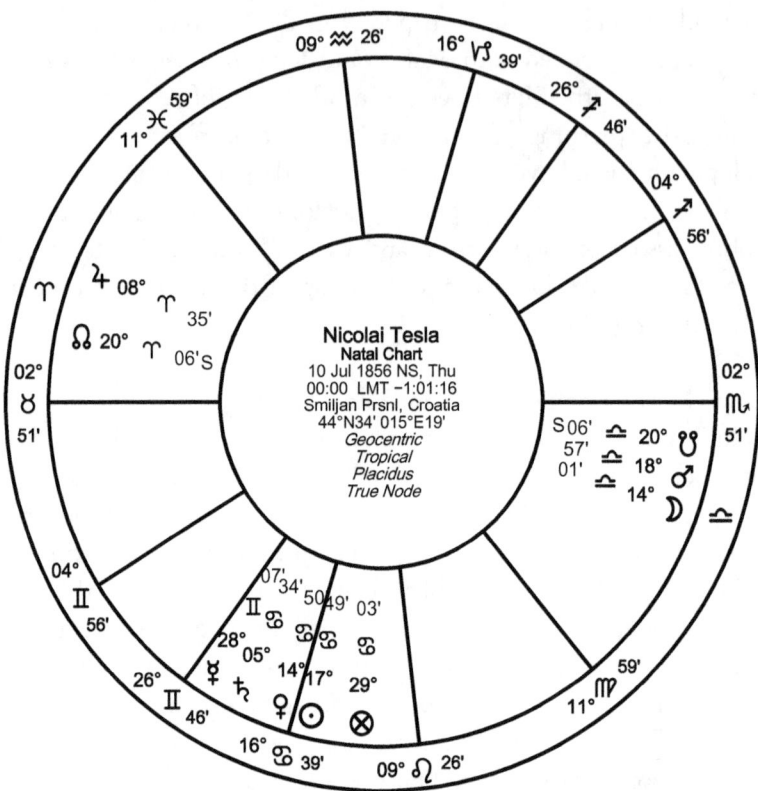

Lord 1 and so Tesla himself is also strongly involved with this square of energy and light. Lord 1 is combust so very much absorbed by the Greater Luminary. The position of Mars on the South Node is remarkable, the descending South Node strengthening the idea of energy coming down, suggested also by the Sun on the IC. Mars is weak in its detriment, having come over from its own house Aries on the other side, but it is right on *Spica*, a powerfully protective star. The Sun on the IC is also the ruler of the fifth house of creative products – and Tesla designed and built many of his innovations himself. Mercury Lord 3 on cusp 3 and strong in its own sign shows he had the technical practical talent to do so.

In a very intriguing way the Sun's placement on *Castor*, the mortal half of the renowned Twins *Castor* and *Pollux*, indicates a lot of important things in his life. In fact, this placement of the Sun on the mortal Twin is really astonishing – as happens so often if you work with the fixed stars – because the great shocking event in Tesla's life was the premature death of his brother! This brother was regarded as the real genius of the two and indeed the brother is very strong as Mercury is Lord 3 right on cusp 3, but it is about to leave the strength of its own sign and soon run into this horrible Saturn in detriment in Cancer. All his life Tesla had a feeling of guilt that he was obliged to do what his supposedly smarter dead brother had not been able to do.

A further analysis of this Sun on *Castor* brings amazing insights. *Castor* and *Pollux* are not only the mortal/immortal Twin pair they are also traditionally connected to St Elmo's fire, a light phenomenon around ship-masts or other high points appearing when a thunderbolt is about to strike, so a discharge of electricity. Thus we have discovered something quite amazing here, not only are the premature death of his brother and Tesla's electrical research 'caused' by the same myth, it's has also become clear why St Elmo's fire was traditionally regarded as a manifestation of *Castor* and *Pollux* – it is all connected to high tension between two poles.

Castor and *Pollux* are not only the protectors of sailors, giving us this association with St Elmo's fire in the masts of ships, they more generally give a picture of a polarity of complementary cosmic energy streams. In the East this is called Yin and Yang, in the West in traditional alchemy it is known as Sulphur and Mercury. Another image of this basic polarity is Caduceus, the staff with two snakes circling around it, showing the expanding and contracting powers balancing and building up the whole cosmos. This is what *Castor* and *Pollux* are essentially about, a tense polarity of opposite forces which explains their name for St Elmo's fire and the association with electricity. Without realising it, Tesla occupied himself with the essential polarity between Sulphur and Mercury, and this was the source of his genius.

So the Twins' myth has very diverse layers, very concrete but at the same time psychological and cosmological; it also refers to the combination of knowledge and action, the 'Indiana Jones' motif, very appropriate for an inventor who in a sense expresses the solar-theoretical inspiration in lunar-practical forms. It is the same dynamic tension of the two polar energy streams and it explains why one of the keywords for the Twins is ambiguity or a double nature, high and low, idealistic and very practical. This is further illustrated by the planetary nature of the two stars: for *Castor* this is pragmatic Mercury, for *Pollux* this is fiery

Mars. How concrete stars can be is shown by the fact that Tesla's brother was killed by a horse and *Castor* and *Pollux* are yes... tamers of horses. You can't beat that!

The other stars in the charts fill in this out-spoken picture. Mercury Lord 3 on cusp 3, the dying brother is on *Betelgeuze*, a very powerful success star in Orion with the strong connotation that it will not last long.... The lunar mansion is again the crown on the work – the Mansion of the Hands is associated with practicality, an eye for details and giving material form to creative ideas.

Henry the Eighth – The Eye of the Bull
The charismatic English king, Henry the Eighth, will always be known for his six marriages and the hard-hearted way he disposed of the women who could not produce an heir to the throne. The chart shows this theme clearly: Venus, the general significator of women, is in elevation in the tenth house conjunct both the Part of Fortune (the soul's desire) and the South Node (the cleaved snake). Even if we had not known anything about this person, we would have seen that extreme trouble (South Node) with women (Venus) would have been an important theme in this life (elevated position). With the biographical information this can be made more detailed, but the basic theme can be seen without this.

Although the nodes are not fixed stars, their effect is strongly associated with the symbolic-mythical background of the snake. The snake is the great symbol of the fundamental duality of life, the separation of the created from the creator, in sharp contrast with the primordial unity that preceded the state of duality. This is why we find the snake in the Garden of Eden in the Tree of the Knowledge of Good and Evil. This antithesis leads to the loss of unity, as the snake stands at the beginning of life separated from God, the source of everything. This also explains why the effects of the nodes are always seen as extreme, they represent the original life-force itself. In the tradition of the druids this is shown by the symbol of a snake producing the world egg from his mouth, so duality (snake) gives birth (egg) to the world we live in.

The North Node is the Head of the Dragon (= Snake) and it will be obvious that this is the point at which the snake of duality will manifest as unlimited ambition and an insatiable desire for the material possessions. The Tail of the Dragon is the counter-point at which things

Case Studies 167

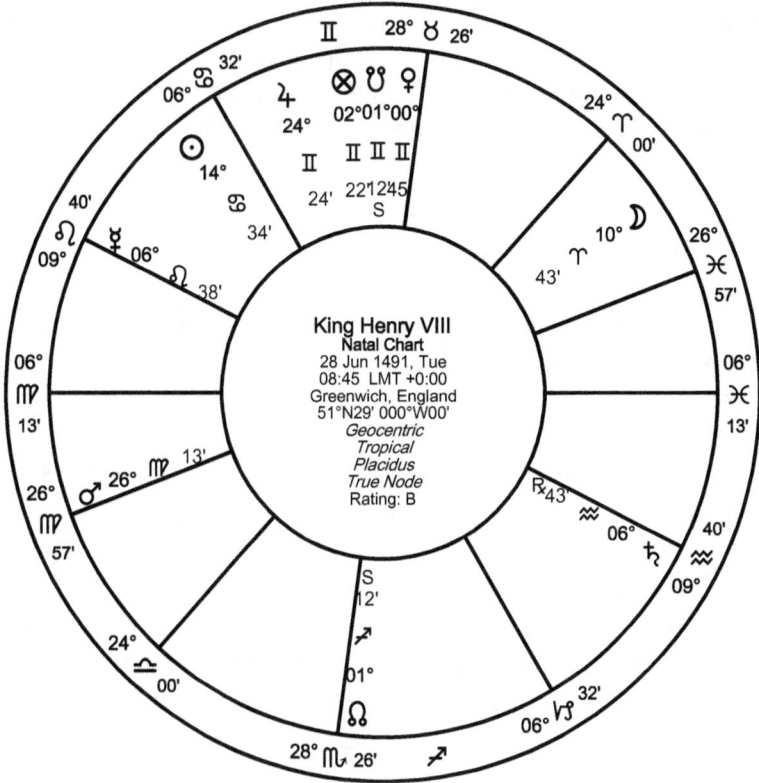

will be taken away from you in an extreme way. In Henry's chart, Venus as Lord 10 is conjunct the malefic Tail of the Dragon so in his public life he will have problems with women associated with extreme limitations. The Head of the Dragon also has a role to play in the fourth house of family, tradition and dynasty. It gives the strong urge to produce a male heir to continue the dynasty. This was the important factor in all the marriage troubles, but the South Node is emphasized more by the conjunction with Venus and this conjunction is seen very clearly in his life. The opposition between Lord 1, Henry himself, and Saturn Lord 5 of children, is another indication of problems with offspring.

The constellation on the South Node dominating the chart and the life is also placed on the powerful royal star *Aldebaran*, the red Eye of the Bull. This star is associated with the myth of princess Europa who was abducted to the Isle of Crete by Zeus, the king of the gods, disguised as a bull. This symbolism is most appropriate as Henry does the same thing

– he abducts women and they soon find themselves at the dangerous exit gate of the South Node, at which they may lose their head. A good astrologer would definitely tell women not to get too involved with this man! The fact that marriage and relationships will not be one of the smoothest parts of his life is underlined again by Lord 7, expansive Jupiter, in detriment in Gemini in narrow square with Mars Lord 9, the planet of disharmony, which harms Lord 7 by negative reception.

At the same time this aspect shows that Henry separated England from the Catholic Church of Rome, in the process creating the Church of England. The motive for this was the refusal of the Pope to grant Henry a divorce from Catherine of Aragon, a tension clearly indicated by the square between Lords 7 and 9.

The Sun, the general significator of kings, is placed between *Castor* and *Pollux*, and Henry became king at a young age when his older brother died suddenly and unexpectedly. This Gemini myth points to a double nature, a contrast between an earthly tendency to action and a more refined nature; Henry could be both coarse and a man of culture who supported the arts and sciences. He was a gifted musician and writer, indicated partly by the dominating Venus in elevation, but also and more so by Saturn Lord 5 of creativity strong in its own Air sign, Aquarius.

The MC is placed on *Prima Hyadum* the main star of the Hyades, a nebula of seven stars which look much like the Pleiades. In mythology the Hyades are the Pleiades' half-sisters and are associated with similar themes of tears and disappointment. The Hyades nursed the wine god Bacchus as an infant, but despite their good care he grew up to be an irredeemable drunk – it is all about intentions that go wrong. This almost literally corresponds with the image of Henry as the lazy old king who occupied himself mainly with his mistresses and with eating; the promising vigorous young man ended up as a fat old wreck, who would be known to history as an unscrupulous murderer.

The Hyades as well as the Pleiades consist of seven stars embedded in a nebulous cloud and this not only connects the star groups with each other but also with the symbolism of the Pole. The Pole is traditionally associated with God as it is the axis around which everything turns; the regulating principle. Close to the Pole is the constellation of the Great Bear, also consisting of seven stars and not easy to miss in the night sky.

These stars represent seven sages, and their wisdom is shown by their closeness to the God-Pole. The Pleiades and the Hyades can be seen as a fallen image of these sages as their wives (the Pleiades) were seduced and fell from their high position close to the Pole to a common place in the zodiac. This is the deeper reason why both the star groups are associated with things that go wrong and with disappointments, and is further underlined by the fact the Pleiades' and the Hyades' father is Atlas, a Titan, an Earth Giant and so an opponent of the gods.

It becomes clear here why it is a good idea to look at the lunar mansion only as the last step in the delineation of the chart; the mansions are always part of the whole pattern of the life. In Henry's case the Moon is placed in the very last mansion of the cycle, the Mansion of the Fishes, which is associated with time and roads, but it also has a spiritual inclination too. With Lord 9 in such a bad condition, spiritual development is not very probable, but there are other meanings, like the closing of a cycle. Henry was one of the historical figures that contributed to the end of the Middle Ages by splitting up the church, and endings are seen even more so in the theme of marriage, which is also strongly associated with this mansion.

Donald Trump – The Nemean Lion

Like it or not, Donald Trump is one of the most influential politicians of this decade, so we would expect to see some real heavy-duty star power in his chart. Indeed we are not disappointed; if ever there was a chart proving you can't do effective astrology without fixed stars, this is it! This is a special case, as a chart jam-packed with power like this one is seldom seen. This confirms the founding principle of astrology, that we can and will only live the life that was given to us at birth as shown by the chart. Here we have a smart guy who believes he is planning effective strategies, but in fact it is the positions of the stars and planets that determine his life, not him. Astrology shows he is not the ultimate American Dream, or Nightmare if you like, he is just living out a most promising chart.

What strikes the eye immediately is Mars conjunct the Ascendant. It is not in the twelfth house, as in traditional astrology the orb for a cusp is five degrees. So whatever this Mars stands for will play a major role in his life. In the first place it describes his behaviour, directly connected

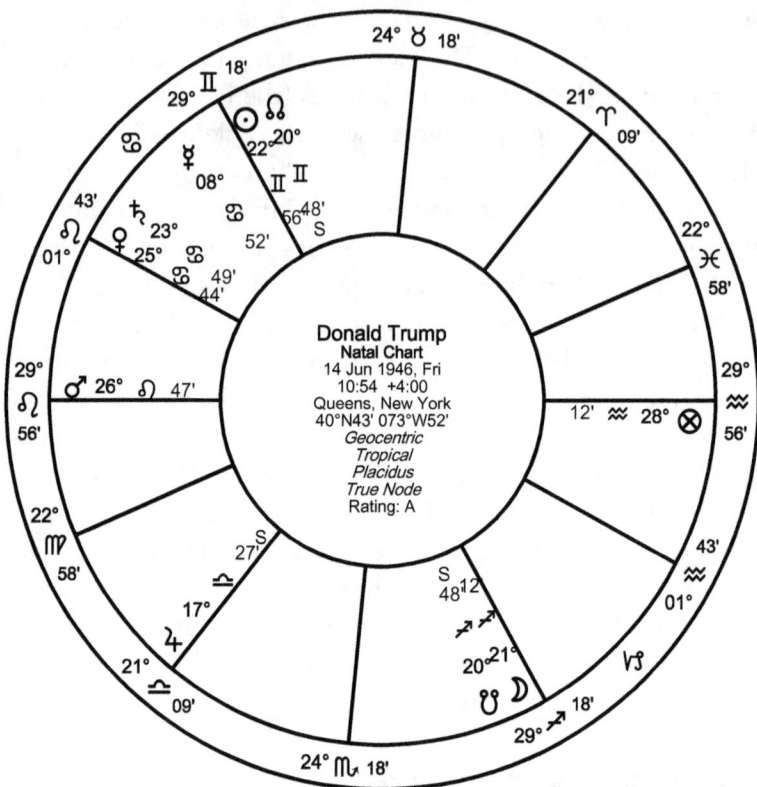

as it is to his most personal point of incarnation. This is an adequate description, as no one could accuse Donald Trump of being a particularly nice or harmonious person. Mars is extra important here because his temperament, his general line of behaviour, and his general physical build, are strongly choleric. That means fiery and all this fire comes out through this Mars. This is really a soldier we see here, someone who will always fight for some cause.

He will be a leader as Mars and the Ascendant are both on *Regulus*, the Heart of the Lion that leads to the throne. A double position on the most royal star of the royals! The ambitious and proud essence of the Leo energy that can bring so much success will manifest through Mars, indicating this is someone who will fight fiercely for domination. This is emphasized by the opposition of Mars with the Part of Fortune, his soul's desire, what he hungers for in life, and this hunger is Mars on *Regulus* dominating others by overwhelming force – "Me and America first".

This all-important Mars is the ruler of the fourth house, which also rules the father. It was from his father that Donald Trump took over the real estate business. His father also saved him more than once when he had run into financial problems, so the image of the powerful and effective businessman is only partly true.

Mars as the ruler of the fourth house is not only the father but it also stands for real estate, and on *Regulus* this is big real estate like Trump Towers. He, his father and real estate are very closely connected as is shown by this Mars. Mars also indicates a part of his wealth, but Mercury, the ruler of the second house of mobile possessions, is not in a bad state either, although this is not immediately obvious. Mercury is placed in the strong eleventh house; it is not much afflicted, which is good, but it is not really very strong, and this only comes out through the antiscion (position mirrored in the axis 0° Cancer – 0° Capricorn). Mercury's antiscion conjuncts the Sun, as Lord 1, or Trump himself, and this Sun is on the Jupiter-like powerfully expansive North Node, all placed in the tenth house of the career. This is not bad at all.

This in itself would be sufficient to give him considerable amounts of money, but there is more. The Sun-Lord 1/North Node conjunction is on the powerful fixed star *Capella*, a member of the first magnitude elite, making this Sun-Lord 1/North Node/antiscion Lord 2 conjunction even stronger. *Capella* is the main star in the Charioteer, a constellation connected to speed and also to transport and traffic, among other things. Trump has invested in transportation companies, and this shows again the very literal level at which the mythological symbolism also works out. Concrete reality around us is a level in the symbolical structure of the cosmos.

There is more to be taken into account. This Sun also opposes the Moon, so there is a Full Moon in his chart giving the Sun, as the ruler of the first house, Trump himself, a lot of power over everything the Moon stands for. At Full Moon the Moon is weak; it is the weakest point in the cycle as the Moon is completely filled with the solar light, and has no light of its own. The essential function of the Moon is to reflect the solar light and at Full Moon this function is fully developed, which means that the Moon is totally dominated by the Sun, in this case Donald Trump. The fact that this Full Moon falls on the nodal axis makes it a lunar eclipse – so the Moon is not only completely dominated by the Sun, it is also knocked out by the Sun, making its power even more complete. As the Moon is the significator of the people, this lunar eclipse is one of the key positions, explaining his populist power.

This capacity to overwhelm and blind others is repeated on the MC where we find *Algol*, the most malefic star in the heavens. This does not necessarily mean that the career will be harmed; on the contrary, as shown by many other cases, it can be a mighty foundation for great success. *Algol* as Medusa can give you seductive glamour, symbolised by the monster with snakes as hair also depicted as a beautiful woman. It is able to attract others powerfully because it is the essence of the desire nature, so Trump can put snakes on other people's heads, taking away their ability to think clearly. Even the poorer people who are directly harmed by his policies still tend to support him, blinded by this seductive glamour.

So we have a double super-royal *Regulus* on the Ascendant, powerfully seductive *Algol* on the MC, and the Sun in the eclipse is conjunct Trump's Sun/Lord 1 on first magnitude *Capella*; but there is still more. Venus, Lord 10 of the career, is placed on powerful *Procyon*, the main star of the Lesser Dog and one of the brightest stars there is. The mythical theme of the Lesser Dog is doing it your own way. This smart vicious little animal will successfully defy the powers that be, and Trump certainly did! Nearby is Saturn and the Great Malefic will influence his career by this close conjunction explaining the financial misfortunes and near-bankruptcies he was repeatedly mixed up in. Saturn is in detriment, so it cannot give the discipline and prudence it normally grants; there is a total lack of Saturn's reticence. Fools rush in where angels fear to tread. Saturn is on another royal star, *Pollux* the immortal Twin, and yes he survived it all. Trump's lunar mansion is that of the Scorpion's heart, ruled by intensely red and martial *Antares* and connected to the theme of the arrogant hunter Orion killed by the Scorpion.

In 2020 Trump hopes to be re-elected, but this seems improbable. If we look at the Firdar, the traditional rulers of longer periods in a life, there is an unfavourable change coming up. Trump was elected president in a Firdar period with the North Node as the ruler; this North Node conjuncting the Sun/Lord 1 on *Capella* overpowering the Moon of the people with his solar light. The North Node Firdar is usually a period of success and advancement in the career, however it is followed by the Saturn-like South Node, the Dragon's Tail. In Trump's chart this happened in June 2019, and this weakening South Node, that takes away success, is on the Moon that loses all its light in this eclipse. Very bad. He has landed on the wrong end of the axis. This will make itself felt from mid-2019; Don's teflon will be scraped off. His lunar return in the election month repeats this, the South Node is on the Ascendant, so this does not look too good.

Mundane cases

If possible the fixed stars are even more indispensable in mundane astrology than in natal astrology. The cases given below are only meant as illustrations of this; a systematic complete discussion of classical mundane techniques does not fall within the scope of this book. In mundane astrology, traditionally regarded as the highest form of our celestial art, fixed stars work a bit differently compared to natal astrology as it is all about collectivities. Unlike an individual person, a collective entity has no consciousness and will live the mythical theme in a very direct way making things very clear.

Katrina in New Orleans

One of the most important instruments in mundane astrology is the Aries ingress chart calculated for the country's capital, and for the precise moment the Sun enters Aries each year. An ingress can be regarded as a country's solar return, and will show, in combination with other relevant mundane charts, what will happen to this place in the year to come. Just as in natal astrology not every mundane return chart is of similar interest. Like solar returns, ingress charts may not show much worth mentioning for years, fortunately enough. But then there will suddenly be an ingress chart with *Algol* on the MC or Saturn in detriment on an angle, and this will indicate something noteworthy happening. This will also be a sign that further research of this year in the framework of other relevant mundane charts like eclipses and great conjunctions is required to get an idea of what will be happening.

A good example of this is the Aries ingress for the United States calculated for the capital Washington DC for the year 2005. One glance

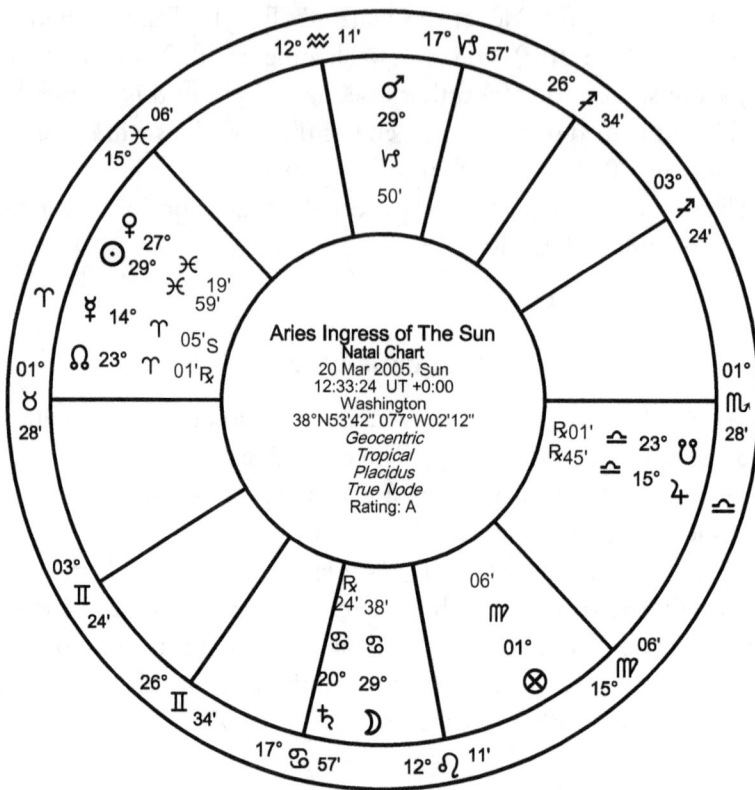

at this chart is enough to get seriously upset. Almost on the IC is a nasty retrograde Saturn in detriment in Cancer, a clear image of a fixed structure that will collapse. This will be a shock to the whole nation as Saturn has so much accidental dignity on an angle, and the collapse is emphasized by the fact that Saturn ingress-Lord 10 has fallen from his high position to the lowest point in the chart. This kind of chart always refers to really big disasters – certainly not every tornado or flood will show up on the scale of a national ingress chart.

Because of its dominant position on the IC, Saturn is sometimes called the Lord of the Year and additionally its placement on *Castor*, the dying brother, is not exactly positive. The watery nature of Cancer suggests the possibility of water being involved; if it concerned a natural disaster a flooding would be probable, but you cannot distinguish between natural and other disasters in a chart. Saturn in Cancer could be many things – it could also point to a terrorist attack. There are however some more indications of water disasters as on the Ascendant we find the curious apocryph star *Mira* in the Whale, a star not mentioned in traditional texts. It resembles *Algol* in that it is continuously dimming and flaring up again, like a permanent eclipse, which would be very malefic, and the Seamonster is much associated with watery disasters, with land being flooded. This is repeated by the star *Mirach* nearby, part of Andromeda, the Princess on the rock in the waves threatened by the Whale.

There are additional indications of flooding and further tensions shown in the ingress chart by the opposition between Mars and the Moon. Mars is placed on a small star in the Eagle, and on the MC we find *Vega* the bright main star in the Lyre. This does not seem too distressing until it is realised that the Lyre and the Eagle are also the Vultures, one flying up (Eagle) and one coming down (Lyre). This gives us quite another picture, especially as *Vega* has a darker side not clearly mentioned in the texts. Of course, these indications always have to be evaluated in the context of the evidence in the chart which is gradually building up, and part of this is Venus ingress-Lord 1 in the twelfth house of misery about to enter its detriment. This is also a threatening indication. On 29 August cyclone Katrina ripped through New Orleans causing the dykes to collapse and the city to flood.

The chart of the city of New Orleans, also called the Big Easy because of its relaxed southern atmosphere, its creative music scene and its flamboyant carnival, also shows disquieting indications. With Jupiter in Cancer in exaltation on the Ascendant it will be immediately astrologically clear how the city received its nick-name but even this nice Jupiter has its downsides in the chart. It rules the sixth house of misfortunes and narrowly squares a retrograde Saturn which is strong in exaltation but nevertheless harmed by Jupiter through negative reception. With the knowledge that dykes are needed to protect the city from the surrounding water, this aspect takes on a more threatening nature especially since Jupiter in Cancer symbolises an awful lot of fast moving water, and Saturn is weakened by being retrograde.

Venus on the MC is responsible for the musical creativity. It is on the star *Alpheratz* in Andromeda, a constellation strongly connected to the arts but its story is also bound up with the destructive Seamonster. This darker side will come to the fore more here as Venus is in its detriment and in elevation, which means it has considerable influence on the chart and on the city. It will certainly have less pleasant effects. Saturn, Lord of the Year in the 2005 US ingress chart and main cause of the trouble, is right on the Ascendant of the New Orleans' city chart, so the effects of the Saturn structure collapsing in the Cancerian water will strike especially powerfully in this place. Of course, we have the enormous advantage of hindsight, we know what has happened and where, but it is important to realise that mundane astrology was always done from the perspective of the local (court) astrologer. A New Orleans city astrologer would combine their local knowledge with the synastry between the disquieting national ingress and the city chart; it's not possible to give a prediction for the whole world and mention the places where the next earthquake or flood will strike. It is enough to check whether your country or city is safe this year. This gives you a feasible and effective astrological framework.

Secondary progressions in the city chart at the time of the flooding would also be important and we have a clear indication of something dramatic happening as there is a progressed New Moon coming up. As the Moon is Lord 1 of the city itself, the effect of this New Moon will be even more powerful than usual, and at the same time the progressed MC squares/opposes the Saturn/Jupiter square, representing the flooding potential and the breaking of the dykes. The slow, progressed Jupiter is extremely weak in Virgo and retrograding, and this is worth noting and can be added to the evidence discovered in the solar return. The solar return Ascendant is on fearful *Antares*, the star of death, Saturn natal Lord 8 in the return eighth house is right on the natal city Ascendant, and by antiscion the malefic Venus in the Whale is on the return MC.

To find the exact time in the year the disaster will strike we use lunar returns, as a lunar return is usually not too subtle; if something is going to happen it will clearly indicate the month. In this case the lunar return of 5 August covers the period of the disaster; there are four planets in the twelfth house aspecting Jupiter, the return Lord of Death on the malefic South Node, and a very harmful Mars in detriment right on the return Ascendant by antiscion. As a last part of the analysis we use transits as they cannot indicate much more than the day something happens, and only within the framework of the prediction by larger-scale factors. On 29 August transiting Venus was on the South Node on the city MC, squaring the transiting Moon as the transiting MC hits the city's Saturn.

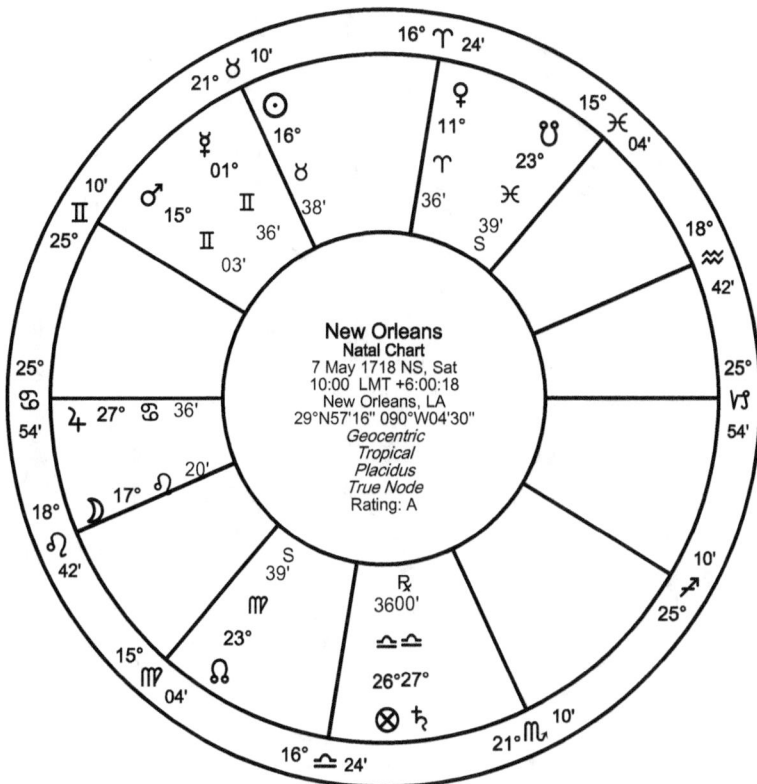

A local astrologer following the weather reports and having analysed these charts would perhaps have been able to get out of New Orleans in time. It is important to note that the basic chart in all this is the US ingress chart for 2005; without that no disaster of this scale could have happened.

A Black Election – The Crowning of King Brirendra

Nepal is one the few countries these days where the royal family consults its astrologers if some important decision is to be taken or some important event planned. This chart of the crowning of the Nepalese King Brirendra is therefore probably an election chart, but it is a very strange one. Maybe the king was deceived by his astrologers who intentionally chose a problematic chart or maybe the astrologers had no idea what they were doing. Any astrologer in possession of some real knowledge would immediately have rejected this election for a coronation as there

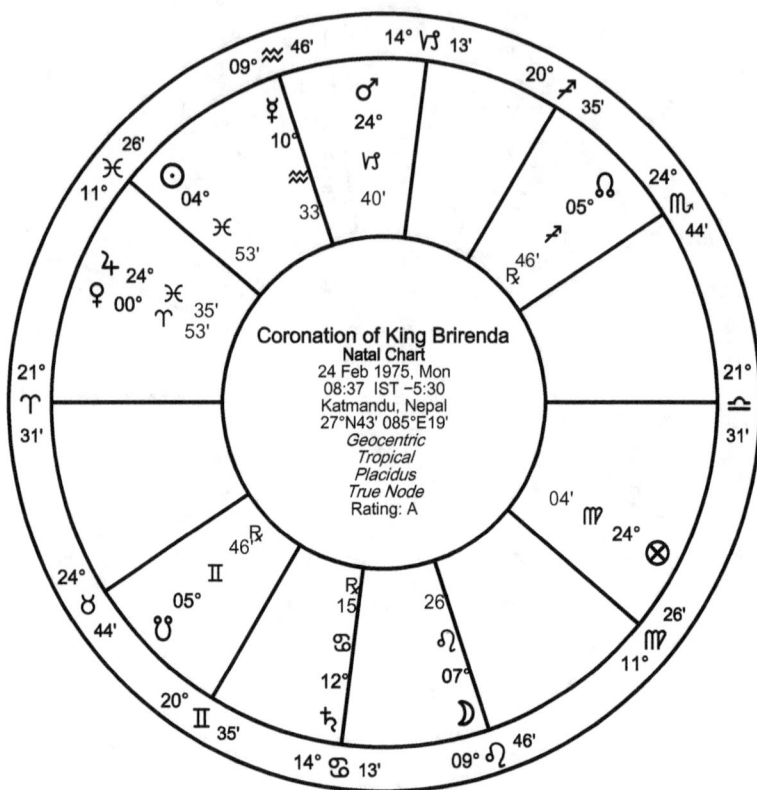

are too many obvious downsides. Yes, Mars Lord 1 is indeed strong in the tenth house, but this power is seriously undermined by its placement on *Terebellum*, a weak star of the sixth magnitude which nevertheless is connected to fateful events.

Opposite the MC, which is the most outspoken power place in the chart, is an extremely nasty Saturn Lord 10 in detriment and retrograde on the violent greater Dog-star *Sirius*; this indicates his kingship will turn against him in a vicious way, and in fact the king was slaughtered together with other members of his family by his own son. This is indicated more clearly by the Moon on the cusp of the fifth house of children on the horrible *Praesepe* cluster, the 'exhalation of piled-up corpses', which can be seen as a second *Algol*. As if this is not enough Mars through antiscion is on the strengthening North Node, but the North Node is also on *Antares*, the infamous Death Star in the house of death. Moreover, on the Ascendant we find the ghastly star *Baten Kaitos* in the constellation of the Seamonster, one of the very few stars with a pure Saturn nature and associated with chaos, violence and accidents.

Bright *Vega* is on the MC and this star is often described in a positive way, but the Lyre is also the 'Falling Grype' and it would not be the first time that the main star of the descending Vulture showed its more sinister side. Certainly in a disastrously weak chart like this election there is more opportunity for this. A vulture will come down to feed on corpses and if the whole context of the chart and the situation permit it, this can be taken literally. It shows you cannot use star interpretations in programs or texts without further testing. All these negative indications are again emphasized by the malefic nebula *Manubrium* in Sagittarius' face, placed at 16 minutes of arc from the MC. This nebula points at Sagittarius' arrow going the wrong way.

The Sun as the general significator of kingship should be strong in a coronation chart and indeed it is on bright *Deneb* the very positive main star in the Swan. But this lovely bird is hardly an image of strong government and it is more associated with artistic activities. This is not what we need, and moreover the Sun will be progressing into the weakening twelfth house soon, which is not very smart electional astrology. Jupiter is extremely strong in this chart and it does sextile Mars Lord 1 in the tenth house, but its benefic influence is much hampered by being placed in the 12th house of misery and self-destruction. The electional astrologer could have improved a lot in a very simple way, by placing the Sun in a strong position on the Ascendant, then Saturn would not have been on the IC and powerful Jupiter would have been Lord 1 with no *Baten Kaitos* on the Ascendant. This looks much better and could have been achieved simply by postponing the crowning to about an hour later.

Could this be a deliberate misuse of astrology, an election chart deliberately chosen to harm the king? It sounds improbable but the other explanation can only be that the court astrologers really didn't know what on earth they are doing. The time that fate struck can be seen clearly in the secondary progressions calculated on the basis of the elected chart. When Crown Prince Dipendra slaughtered his family on 1 June 2001 the progressed Ascendant was moving over *Algol* and the Moon was in opposition with Mars on fateful *Terebellum*. It may even be that the time of the bloodshed was chosen astrologically by the king's opponents. If the parties involved take astrology seriously enough to devise a black election, this is certainly a possibility.

The Crisis Conjunction

The chart at the root of the serious economic crisis Europe went through recently shows that you cannot use mundane astrology without the fixed stars. In this Great Conjunction chart ('GC', calculated for Brussels as Europe's political centre), which covers a period of 20 years (2000-2020), the GC degree is on *Algol*, on the cusp of the eighth house of death, endings and the other party's money. This, plus the fact that six of the seven traditional planets are placed in this malefic house, shows there will be trouble; only the Moon is found outside the eighth house. It is to be noted that there are no aspects to the outer planets in this chart: Pluto's orb with the Sun and with Mars is too wide. This, however, doesn't mean that the outer planets are not important; there are good examples in mundane astrology in which they clearly are, as long as you take them as star-like factors and not as planets at the same level as the seven classical planets.

Naturally, the GC degree will be on *Algol* everywhere in the world – it is a world-wide crisis – but only in Europe is it on cusp 8, making Europe the focal point. It's also only in Europe that the antiscion of the Great Conjunction falls right on the MC on the malefic *South Asellus* and very close to *Praesepe*. So we have a combination of the dramatic decapitation of *Algol* and the shattering chaos of the 'Heart of Cancer', quite a sinister couple. They are the two most malefic stars in the heavens. It is clear that the crisis will focus on Europe because the GC chart calculated for Washington for example only has *Algol* on the MC, which is bad but not as bad as *Algol* and *Praesepe* combined. So although the crisis started in the US, it will be not as serious there as in Europe, and China will come out best as in Peking the GC-degree on *Algol* is floating around somewhere in the third house and not on an angle. So how some country is faring economically is not really a result of policy-making, it is the other way around, policies are a result of the astrology.

The precise positions of the *Aselli* and their Crib *Praesepe* lead to some questions of a more technical nature. The MC is on 9°19' Leo, the *South Asellus* on 8°43', the *North Asellus* on 7°22' and *Praesepe* itself on 7°12', with the Saturn-Jupiter conjunction's antiscion on 7°17' Leo.

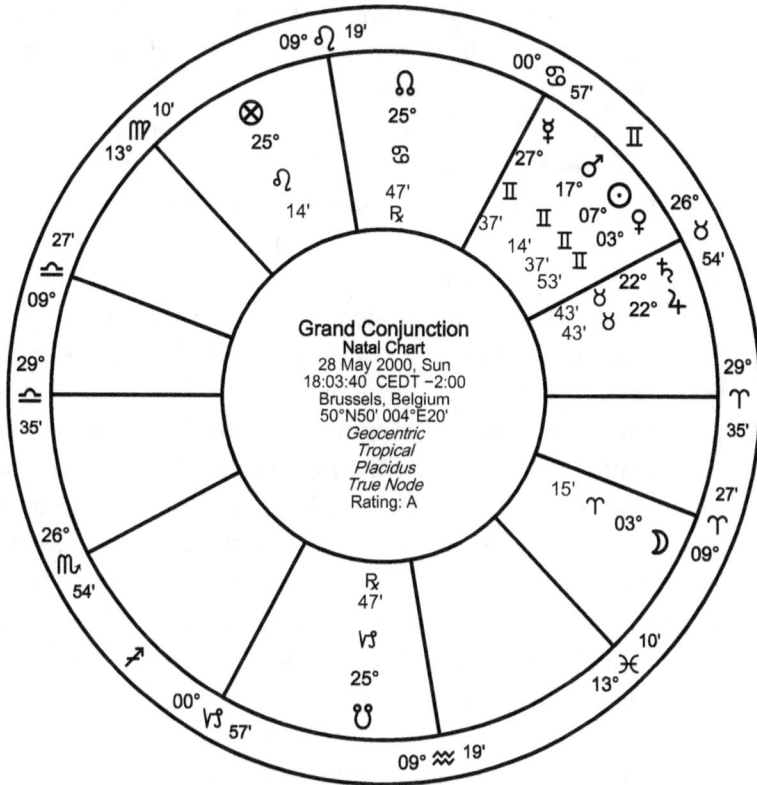

A planet's antiscial position will always bring along with it the star influence of its original position, but as a shadow point – it will not take over any star that is on its new position. So the GC's degree antiscion on the MC will be *Algol*-like but it will not be *Praesepe*-like. This does not do much however to soften the malefic effects as the GC's antiscion is conjunct the MC within the usual orb, so this is a kind of doubling of the *Algol* influence.

But which star is on the MC? If we look at it purely technically it is closest to the *South Asellus* but for a powerful and nebulous cluster like *Praesepe* an orb a bit larger than the usual 1 degree could be used, certainly as it is all happening on an angle. The solution is in this case that the whole Aselli/Crib zone in 7-9° Leo is very malefic; in Appendix A the keywords are given for the *Aselli* together, and they are not much milder than the traditional keywords for *Praesepe* itself. This whole constellation is associated with chaotic, dark powers that lead to death and fragmentation, along with distortions of truth, discord and dramatic misfortune. Their effect will be felt in the whole *Aselli* zone but the empty Crib at 7°12' is the concentration point, so the closer you come the more dramatic it will be. There are more examples of stars very close together and part of the same myth, and when this happens you can take the myth as the central story and see the individual stars more as accentuations.

The other planetary positions in the GC chart do not look very hopeful either. Lord 1 is Venus on the Hyades, the nebulous star group that will frustrate good intentions, the half-sisters of the sad Pleiades. The Hyades were Bacchus' wet-nurses and despite the energy invested in his upbringing they could not keep him away from the bottle, which is something rather appropriate for the EU in crisis. Through antiscion Venus is on the North Node, which only makes things worse as the North Node has an extreme nature and makes any factor on it, negative or positive, much more powerful. The Moon, aspecting Venus by sextile and the only planet not in the eighth house of death, is on *Difda*, a pure Saturn star in the Whale associated with 'compulsory change, misfortune and self-destruction by brute force'.

Mars is the ruler of the second house of money, peregrine and weak in the eighth house on *Rigel*, a powerful first magnitude star in Orion the Hunter. It gives success but this success will not last. *Rigel* is the left foot of the arrogant Hunter who became over-confident after too many successes and was stung to death by the Scorpion, which in this context seems also rather appropriate. Did anybody in Europe ever imagine that such a downfall and crisis would come? The Sun as Lord 10 is on *Aldebaran*, the red Bull's Eye and a star of great material success. This could be seen as one of the few positive points in the chart, although it is not very strong accidentally and as a purely martial star it does not exactly enhance harmony.

The lunar mansion is a nice finishing touch to the whole picture; it is the Mansion of the Wing, the second Pegasus mansion. The central point in the myth is the story of Bellerophon, who tried to reach Olympus on his own initiative and fell dramatically down to earth. Contrary to the first Pegasus Mansion of the Fall preceding it, besides the falling theme there's a spiritual connotation in this mansion; it has to do with leaving behind material success in favour of higher values. This does make sense but only if you know the context; the delineation of a chart is gradually built up from diverse indications until everything falls in place. But to make this happen, you also need to know what is going on in the personal life of your client or, in mundane astrology, the relevant political and economic developments unfolding in the part of the world you are considering.

The GC chart shows that between 2000 and 2020 some painful and unpleasant events will take place, especially in Europe. There are several mundane methods to determine in which years this crisis will be concentrated: we could for example analyse progressions and returns in EU charts like the Treaty of Rome. What also works is taking the GC chart as kind of natal chart for the 20-year period it covers and then checking the solar returns calculated from the GC. The first clear signs of an economic crisis manifested in 2008, and indeed in the solar return based on the 2000 Great Conjunction, the Ascendant falls exactly on the GC by antiscion on the MC connected with *Algol* and *Praesepe*, the main crisis generators as discussed above, and it has a nasty Saturn in detriment in the first house.

The Wreck of the Titanic
In studying the charts related to ships and shipwrecks it would be helpful to have an exact time for the natal chart. In some cases the time the ship was launched is known and often we will have the time of its departure before a disaster took place. These charts will certainly be interesting but it seems to be better to use a sunrise chart for the day construction of the vessel commenced. For many ships this information is available online and this strategy, suggested by John Frawley, works well enough, as the Titanic case below will show.

So our starting point for the Titanic is 5:42:20 in Belfast on 31 March 1909. This can be seen as the ship's natal chart, and if this method really works it will have to be very clear as this was a shipwreck of mythical proportions. Some stars in the Seamonster and Andromeda can be expected to play an important part alongside some powerful malefics.

Our sunrise chart is dead on target and more than a little threatening, certainly as we are dealing with a ship here. To keep it dry in the water a good strong Saturn is required, but in this chart Saturn is in detriment in

184 Fixed Stars in the Chart

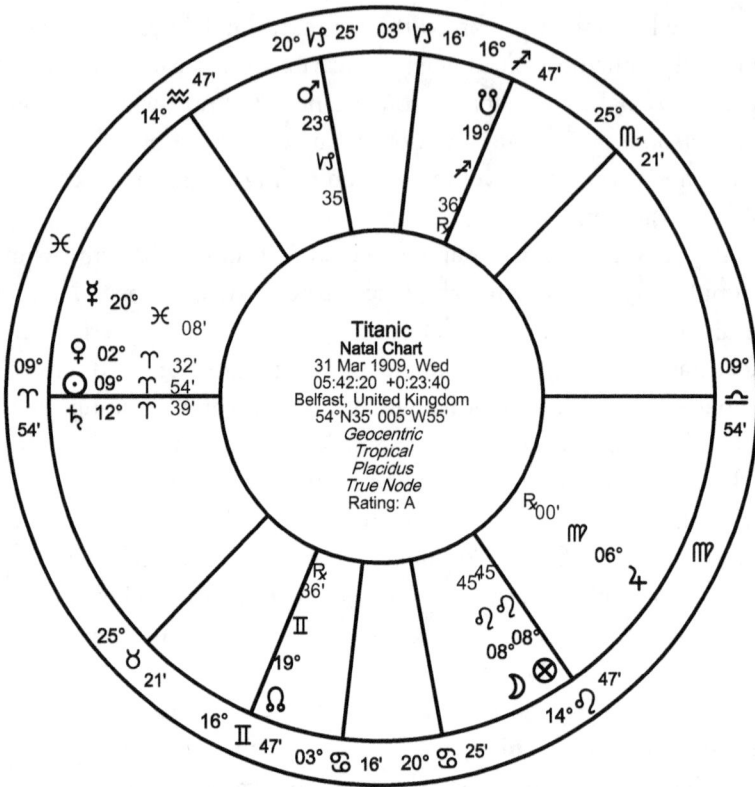

Aries, conjunct the Sun. Of course on a sunrise chart the Sun is always conjunct the Ascendant, but in this case Saturn is Lord 12 of stupid things you do to harm yourself. The notorious waterproof compartments, supposed to make the ship unsinkable, were so badly constructed that they did not work in an emergency. These inadequate compartments were meant to replace the much more expensive double skin used in shipbuilding at that time, but they're now seen as outdated. This all fits in well with Saturn, the planet of the skin and protection being in detriment, and as the ruler of the twelfth house there's an element of self-undoing.

An extremely weak Mercury in detriment in Pisces and also in fall stands out clearly in the chart. It is the ruler of the third house and falls on the Descendant by antiscion. These are the ship's life-boats of which there were simply not enough. Most victims were killed by the cold water; had there been sufficient life-boats the number of deaths would have been far fewer, so this weak and malefic Lord 3 does play an important role in the drama as its angular position indicates. Also the Descendant is on the malefic star *Vindemiatrix* associated with arrogant overestimation of one's powers and the idea you have the knowledge to do something which in reality you don't yet have – so clearly an issue with the design. Mars Lord 1 is in its exaltation; a lot was expected from this miracle of human ingenuity, but Mars is also on the fateful star *Terebellum*.

The Moon trines the Ascendant and it is on the *South Asellus*, one of the asses the gods rode in their war against the Titans – and there we have the name of the ship. This *Asellus* is part of the malefic *Praesepe* zone and is also known as the Resting Place, not something you would want to see pop up in a ship's chart. Near the Ascendant there are many stars in Andromeda, the soul-maiden who the Seamonster Cetus or the Whale is going to devour. It was the bad-tempered sea-god Poseidon who sent the Whale because Andromeda's mother Cassiopeia had been bragging that her daughter was more beautiful than Poseidon's servants. You should have heard the builders of the Titanic talking about their unsinkable baby; it was a blatant provocation of the powerful sea-god Poseidon, who would certainly have been paying close attention when Titanic captain Edward Smith said "God Himself could not sink this ship".

Saturn, also Lord 10, is on *Alpheratz*, Andromeda's Head, and on the Ascendant is *Deneb Algenubi*, a star in the the Sea-monster's Tail. Lord 7 is Venus in detriment in the twelfth house of misery on *Difda* also a star in the Tail. As Lord 7, Venus stands for the passengers, the partners or the clients of the ship, and they are in a very bad condition. This whole underlining of the Tail directly refers to the image of the Titanic's stern sticking out off the waves and the fact that the music was playing while the Seamonster was getting in. All this is indicated by the involvement of Andromeda, a constellation also strongly associated with the arts. Mythical themes may work out in a very concrete way as this example shows, and the stars have diverse levels of interpretation; it is certainly not only spiritual.

There is so much danger here, the building of the ship should be stopped immediately! The chart shouts 'misery' and the misery is appropriate and threatening for a ship. Even the solar return based on the sunrise chart is effective, so this method proves itself to be more than some creative idea. In this return chart Mars and natal Lord 1 is exactly on cusp 8 of death, its antiscion is on the IC ('down there') of the natal (sunrise) chart, and the return Ascendant is right on the sunrise (natal) cusp 8. The Moon is in elevation as return Lord 8 of Death and falls by antiscion on Saturn in the sunrise chart. The return Descendant, representing the passengers or the guests, is on mass murderer *Algol* on the antiscion of the sunrise Moon on the Resting Place. Now that is scary. Let us postpone this wonderful trip to America even though the tickets are so cheap!

Even the lunar return based on the Titanic sunrise chart just before the ship went down is outspoken. Venus, return Lord 7, sits on the Descendant on *Algol* and this is connected by antiscion again with the sunrise Moon. The lunar return Ascendant falls, just like the solar return Ascendant, on sunrise cusp 8. So yes, this technique really works; not only does the Titanic natal chart show appropriate dangerous indications, the return charts too leave little room for doubt. They have the required clarity – you don't have to try too hard to find indications of death. This opens up a whole new field of astrological research using charts without the exact timing of events, and this technique can be extended to air and space travel, for example.

It would be interesting to take a look at the natal chart of the Titanic's sister, the Olympic, and to compare the two charts. The building of the Olympic started nine months earlier at the same shipyard in Belfast. This chart certainly does not look very nice with the South Node right on the Ascendant and the malefic blindness star *Aculeus* and Saturn in detriment through antiscion conjuncting the Moon. On the Olympic's fifth trip a serious accident happened, and the passengers were saved by getting into the lifeboats. But that was all – the Olympic does not have the accumulation of misery seen in the Titanic chart. There is no excess of Seamonster so Poseidon will not interfere. After the Titanic disaster the Olympic was technically converted and improved; it served without problems for many years.

It is however striking how the third house in the Olympic chart is afflicted. Saturn in detriment in Aries is close to cusp 3 on *Difda* the Seamonster's Tail, with the Moon underlining the point by an antiscial

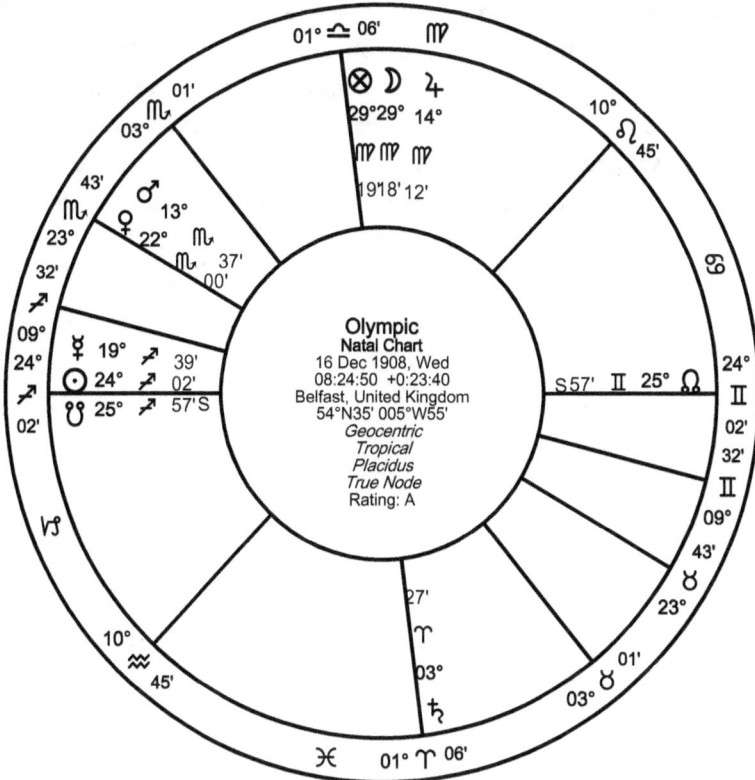

conjunction. Mars Lord 3 is itself strong in its own sign of Scorpio but it is right on the *South Scale*, the Scorpion's Claw, a powerful royal star of a malefic nature, also called the Insufficient Price. It indicates that the Olympic has a famous sister who will get into serious trouble. Even the solar return based on the Olympic natal chart for the year of the Titanic's wreck has Lord 3 Mars retrograde on *Algol* and Death Star *Antares* on cusp 3! So the death of the sister ship is clearly indicated in the Olympic's chart. This is one of those moments when we can stand in sheer awe of the cosmos. It clarifies the ultimate motivation behind astrology, again and again demonstrating 'as above so below', that humankind cannot foster the illusion that they direct their own life or history. A very humbling experience. By the way, you would not need astrology here to choose to sail on the Olympic or the Titanic, *nomen est omen* (the name is a sign)!

As in every chart we can use the Arabian parts to add information to our basic chart interpretation. For a ship, the Part of Travel over Water would be one of the most relevant. Its remarkable formula is Asc + 15° Cancer – Saturn, which can be symbolically explained as the protection and dryness offered by Saturn in the middle of the cardinal waters of Cancer. This part is on 12°14' Cancer in the Titanic sunrise chart on bright and violent *Sirius* but also conjunct – yes there he is finally – Neptune or the star-like factor Poseidon connected to dramatic flooding! The part is also in narrow square with horrible Saturn on the Ascendant representing the 'not really waterproof' compartments.

Appendix A – Keywords

This list is only meant to further clarify the effects a star has in the life. Cook-book astrology or its classical form, 'aphorism astrology' – the citation of short chart interpretation 'rules' – is always to be avoided. Keywords can only be a small part of a much larger, complete picture and although they do clarify this picture and the understanding of a star, they cannot be taken as ready-for-use texts.

This list is an adapted version of the keywords mentioned in *The Fixed Stars and Constellations in Astrology*, the 1920s book by Vivian Robson which contains a lot of interesting information but is not an effective practical method for using the stars. The book is a bit like the internet, a wealth of data but no structured knowledge. It is important not to take these keywords too literally; clearly, not every star is going to kill you, put you in prison or make you blind. It is obvious that a more symbolic interpretation is called for in most cases.

A good example of how this works could be the Southern Horn of the Bull, *Al Hecka*. The bull is sensual and wild and a horn is not the most peaceful part of its body; the south is the darker side, so keywords like accidents, debauchery and violence are really like a good solid finishing touch. In 75% of cases it is easy to see why these keywords are mentioned with the star (they may be derived from its planetary nature, the essence of the myth and the star's name). It is that other 25% that is not so obvious which is really interesting as it will stimulate further thoughts about the star and its essence.

Achernar – success in public office, beneficence, religion, danger of being usurped, overestimation of one's powers.

Acrux – religious beneficence, ceremonial, justice, magic, mystery.

Acubens – malevolence, poison, lies, crime.

Aculeus – blindness.

Acumen – blindness.

Adhafera (the Funeral Pyre) – suicide, poison, corrosive acids, liquid explosives, liquid fire, lying, stealing, crime.

Agena – position, friendship, refinement, morality, health, honour.

With Sun: mental activity, rashness, success, many friendships.

With Moon: sarcasm, bitter speech, strong passions.

With Mercury: great mental ability, sarcasm, speaking, writing, championing the masses.

With Venus: poetical, strong passions, rash friendships with women.

With Mars: legal authority, honour as speaker or writer, great mental and physical powers.

With Jupiter: intellectual success, legal or church authority, professional honour.

With Saturn: thoughtful, shrewd, association with medical men, healing powers, abrupt manner, occultism, domestic disharmony through jealousy.

Albireo (the Song of the Dying Swan) – handsome appearance, neatness, lovable disposition, beneficence in despair.

Alcyone (the Central One, the Foundation Stone) – love, eminence, blindness from fevers, smallpox and accidents to the face, see also Pleiades.

Aldebaran (the Follower) – intelligence, honour, eloquence, steadfastness, integrity, popularity, courage, ferocity, sedition, responsible position, public honours, gain of power and wealth through others, but its benefits are seldom lasting, danger of violence and sickness.

With Sun, Moon, on MC or Asc: great honour through violence with difficulties and casualties. On MC: honour, preferment, good fortune, favours from women.

With Sun: great energy, perseverance, high material honours with danger of losing them, danger from quarrels and the law, honour and riches ending in ruin and disgrace, liable to disease, fevers and violent death.

With Moon: favourable for business, honour and credit but danger of calamity, favorable for domestic, religious and public matters, danger of a violent death.

With Mercury: affects health and domestic affairs, prominence through mercurial matters, material gain, many learned friends.

With Venus: honour through literature music or art, creative abilities, favourable for health and marriage.

With Mars: great military preferment, attended by much danger, liable to accidents fevers and a violent death.

With Jupiter: great ecclesiastical honour and high military preferment.

With Saturn: great afflictions, strange mind, great wickedness, sarcasm, eloquence, good memory, studious and retiring nature, legal abilities, domestic and material success, losses through mercurial friends.

Algenib (the Wing) – notoriety, dishonour, violence, misfortune, the beggar.

With Sun: mental disturbances, fevers and ill-health, danger of accidents.

With Moon: dishonour, loss by scandal, exiled or forced to flee, ill-health, trouble through writings.

With Mercury: quick temper, mental disturbances, success in legal and other disputes.

With Venus: generous, proud, quick temper, bad morals, drink or evil habits, favourable for financial affairs.

With Mars: quick mind and body, lying, theft, danger of accidents.

With Jupiter: hypocrisy, financial success, real or pretended religious enthusiasm.

With Saturn: many enemies, success, secret help from powerful friends and influential relatives, bad morals.

Algenubi (He who rends) – bombastic, bold, cruel, heartless, brutish destructive nature, artistic appreciation, power of expression.

Algol (Piled-up Corpses, the Demon's Head) – misfortune, violence, decapitation, hanging, electrocution, mob violence, dogged violent nature, death, glamorous power of attraction and great seductive beauty.

On MC: murder, sudden death, beheading, murder, mischief, also with Sun, Moon or Jupiter: victory in wars.

With Sun: violent death, extreme sickness.

With Moon: violent death, extreme sickness.

With Mars: murder, death.

Algorab (the Crow) – destructiveness, malevolence, fiendishness, lying, scavenging.

Al Hecka (the Driver) – violence, malevolence, accidents.

With Sun: suspicious, reserved, studious, unfavourable for health (esp. lungs), aptitude for military enterprise and stratagems with danger of ambush and deceit.

With Moon: quarreling, evil habits and company, depravity.

With Mercury: hasty temper, selfishness, greed, dissipation, legal and business troubles, poor health, domestic troubles, separation from wife or children, low companions, loss of wealth, poverty.

With Venus: unfortunate, low companions, bad environment.

With Mars: evil companions, bad habits, sex troubles, afflictions of a Mars-Venus type.

With Jupiter: hypocrisy, dissipation, business losses and disgrace.

With Saturn: uncontrolled passions, drink, debauchery, perverted genius, clever writer of undesirable literature, luxurious surroundings but little wealth, isolated or confined at end of life, domestic unhappiness, accidents if also Mars is afflicting.

Alhena (the Burnt-in Mark) – eminence in art, liable to accidents afflicting the feet.

With Sun: pride, love of ease, luxury, pleasure.

With Moon: good health, honour, riches, pleasure and society, domestic benefits.

With Mercury: popularity, benefits from opposite sex, musical and artistic ability but little fame, domestic harmony, business adversely affected by pleasure and society.

With Venus: material concerns, love of dress, pleasure and flattery, artistic and musical ability.

With Mars: superficial nature, fond of pleasure, ease, luxury, ornament, display.

With Jupiter: social advancement and success, philosophical mind, love of ostentation.

With Saturn: cautious, reserve, studious, prominence in science or art, some domestic discord, sickness to children, unexpected losses but possibility of wealth, ill-health at the end of life.

Algieba (the Forehead) – many dangers, losses, violent, intemperate.

Almach – honour, eminence, artistic ability.

Alnilam – fleeting public honours.

With Sun: rash, headstrong, surly, also on MC: military preferment and gain.

With Moon: many sudden and unexpected losses and reverses, much help for friends, ill-health of family.

With Mercury: hasty, quick temper, quarrels with associates, domestic disharmony through own actions.

With Venus: trouble through love affairs, scandal, enemies among women.

With Mars: quarrels, loss by lawsuits, domestic disharmony, bad health, violent death.

With Jupiter: legal or church preferment but danger of disgrace, loss by speculation, trouble through relatives and foreign affairs.

With Saturn: courteous, domestic disharmony, leaves home early, successful but many unexpected losses, favourable for health.

Alphard (the Hydra's Heart) – wisdom, musical and artistic appreciation, knowledge of human nature, strong passions, lack of self-control, immorality, revolting deeds and sudden death by drowning, poison, asphyxiation.

On the Asc: much trouble, anxiety and loss in connection with estate and building, addicted to women and intemperance.

With Sun: power and authority but suffering from own acts and from enemies, loss of position and honour, overcome by enemies.

With Moon: lust, wantonness, profligacy, failure in projects but financial help often from a relative, ill-fortune to wife or mother, eventual disgrace and ruin, danger of death by asphyxiation.

With Mercury: trouble through writings, unfavourable for marriage, suffering through a passionate attachment that entirely changes the course of life.

With Venus: passionate attachment opposed by relatives, handsome and admired by opposite sex, favourable for gain, sorrow through love affairs if female.

With Mars: trouble and scandal through love affairs, attachment to married person, bad for child-birth, liable to miscarriage and death together with death of child, danger of serious accidents, if afflicting luminaries: danger of death by drowning and poison.

With Jupiter: strong passions, favourable for gain, attachment to widow or widower, liable to disgrace, legal trouble and judicial sentence.

With Saturn: strong passions but cool, cautious and slow to anger, secret and short love affairs of short duration, unfavourable for gain, domestic disharmony, danger of death by poison.

Alphecca – honour, dignity, poetic and artistic ability.

With Sun: active and brilliant mind, self-seeking, subject to scandal that does not affect the position.

With Moon: public honour and dignity, suffers through law, partners and neighbours, trouble through underhand dealings of enemies but eventual triumph over them, bad for love affairs, some faithful friends, greatly esteemed by Venus and Mercury people.

With Mercury: mind more active than body, somewhat indolent, benefits from friends, extravagant but saving in small things, loss by enemies.

With Venus: favourable for love affairs, benefits from friends, artistic and musical taste.

With Mars: active mind, better writer than speaker, unfavourable for gain.

With Jupiter: honour and dignity, artistic ability, benefit through ecclesiastical matters, favourable for material gain.

With Saturn: studious, popular, economical but poor, benefits from elderly friends, strong but well-controlled passions, poor health, love disappointments but marries above station, few children but harmonious ties with them.

Alpheratz – independence, freedom, love, riches, honour, keen intellect.

With Sun: honour, preferment and favours from others.

With Moon: energetic, persevering, honour, wealth, many good friends, business success.

With Mercury: active mind, benefits from judges lawyers or church men, pioneer work bringing prominence, accused of selfish motives, writes on science religion or philosophy.

With Venus: neat and tidy appearance, quiet life, good health, fond of pleasure and society, fortunate in speculation.

With Mars: sharp mind, energetic, business success through own endeavours.

With Jupiter: philosophical and religious mind, benefits from professional men, ecclesiastical honour and dignity, favourable for gain.

With Saturn: open and affable but miserly, seeks popularity, pretends to be religious for business ends, favours from clergy and lawyers, likelihood of wealth, domestic harmony, liable to diseases in the head and tumours that finally cause death.

Al Pherg (The Head of Typhon) – preparedness, steadiness, final success, determination, fatefulness, a last chance, terrible voice.

Altair (The Bird of Jove) – bold, confident, valiant, unyielding, ambitious and liberal nature, great and sudden but ephemeral wealth, position of command, makes natives guilty of bloodshed, danger from reptiles.

With Sun: public honour, notoriety, favours from superiors, many friends and some envious ones who cause trouble through writings, some ill-health and losses, danger of bites from venomous animals.

With Moon: interest in a strange and ancient discovery, disappointment and loss over property and gain, some profit and preferment, friends become enemies, trouble through company or public affairs, difficulties through or misfortune to children.

With Mercury: many difficulties, misfortune, strange experiences, disappointments on long journeys, bad for partnership, loss of a relative under strange circumstances.

With Venus: unfavourable for love affairs, strange and peculiar attractions, bad for children and gain, losses through friends.

With Mars: sharp mind, trouble through friends, society and companies but eventual gain, battle for truth.

With Jupiter: real or pretended religious zeal, hypocrisy, trouble through legal and church matters and with relatives, bad for gain, disappointment over inheritance.

With Saturn: sorrow and disappointment, mental disturbance that requires asylum or hospital treatment and probably death there, separation from family and parents, danger of accident involving inability to work or lifelong affliction.

Antares (the Rival of Mars, the Scorpion's Heart) – malevolence, destructiveness, liberality, broad-mindedness, evil presages, danger of fatality, rashness, ravenous, headstrong, self-destructive through obstinacy.

On the Asc: riches and honour, violence, sickness, benefits seldom last.

On the MC: honour, preferment good fortune.

With Sun: pretended religion, insincere, honour and riches ending in ruin and disgrace, military preferment, danger of treachery, violence committed or suffered, fevers and sickness, injuries to the right eye, violent death.

With Moon: popular, broad-minded, interested in philosophy, science or metaphysics, liable to change religious opinions, influential friends, favourable for business and domestic matters, active in local affairs, great power, honour and wealth but benefits may not prove lasting, danger of violence, sickness drowning or assassination.

With Mercury: suspicious, wrongfully accuses friends, unpopular, uses ecclesiastical influence in business, money obtained slowly and with much difficulty, danger of sickness to the native and his family, death of a relative at home or away.

With Venus: insincere, dishonest, energetic and able but selfish, unfavourable for gain and health.

With Mars: detrimental habits powerfully affecting the life, quarrels with friends and relatives, fairly favourable for gain.

With Jupiter: great religious zeal, real or pretended, ecclesiastical preferment, tendency to hypocrisy, benefits through relatives.

With Saturn: materialistic, dishonest through circumstances created by environment, religious hypocrisy, many disappointments, loss through quarrels and legal affairs, trouble through enemies, many failures, hampered by relatives, unfavourable for domestic matters, much sickness to and sorrow from children.

Arcturus (the Bear Guard, One who Rules) – riches, honour, high renown, self-determination and prosperity by navigation and voyages.

On the Asc: good fortune with many cares and anxieties through own folly.

On the MC: high office under government, great profit and reputation, if also with a luminary or Jupiter then ample fortune and great honour.

With Sun: success through slow and patient plodding, friends among clergy, favourable for gain and for dealing with the public and with lawyers.

With Moon: new friends, business success, good judgement, domestic harmony.

With Mercury: sober, industrious, popular, inclined to be religious, somewhat extravagant but well-off, help through friends, holds position of trust in large company or corporation or receives promotion under direction, favourable for health and domestic affairs.

With Venus: popular, gifts and favours from friends, some false friends of own sex.

With Mars: popular, many friends, considerable gain but does not save owing to extravagance.

With Jupiter: benefits from legal and church matters, influential position, danger of hypocrisy, gain through foreign affairs or shipping.

With Saturn: honest, selfish, inclined to be mean, shrewd in business, materialistic, favourable for gain and speculation and for domestic matters but early difficulty in married life, favourable for children but disagreement with one of them.

Armus – disagreeable, contemptable, instability, shamelessness, nagging, a troublesome and contentious nature.

Ascella – good fortune and happiness.

With Sun: good fortune, lasting happiness.

With Moon: new influential friends, valuable gifts, love of respectable women.

Aselli (the Asses) – care and responsibility, charitable and fostering, danger of violent death, serious accidents and burns.

Joint on the Asc: burning fevers, bad eyes, blindness of left eye, injuries by beasts, quarrels, slander from low women or vulgar persons, martial preferment.

Joint on the MC: disgrace and ruin often violent death.

Joint with Sun: blows, stabs, serious accidents, shooting, shipwreck, beheading, hanging, murder, violent fevers, danger of fire, disgrace and imprisonment.

Joint with Moon: inflammatory fever, pains in the head, blindness.

North Asellus (Balaam's Ass) – patience, beneficence, courage, heroic defiant leaders.

With Sun: favourable for dealing with the public and influential people, business success.

With Moon: favourable for material success, honour through public position, help from friends, favourable for gain, danger of accidents to the head, fevers, inflammatory ailments, heart weakness.

With Mercury: power and authority after many difficulties, little gain, numerous expenses, losses by writings, mortgages and bonds.

With Venus: proud, opinionated, help from an influential friend, favourable for gain.

With Mars: courageous, generous, noble, just, power and authority.

With Jupiter: great gain and influential position, favours from churchmen and gain through ecclesiastical matters, benefits from affairs.

With Saturn: somewhat self-centered and self-seeking, loss through enemies, high public office but eventual retirement with public censure, favourable for gain, unrelenting nature, domestic disharmony caused by antipathy between one of the children and the native or partner.

South Asellus (the Mare Ass, a Resting Place, the Ending)

With Sun: unfavourable for dealing with the public and influential people, trouble in business.

With Moon: ill-health, defective sight, hearing or speech, bad for business affairs, loss of friends and trouble through enemies.

With Mercury: mental affliction, much worry and disappointment, loss by fire of valuable papers, bad for success in spite of help from friends, difficulties brought about by children.

With Venus: trouble through friends, unfavourable for love and marriage, enmity of women, too fond of pleasure and society.

With Mars: energy, courage, misapplied powers, little success, public disfavour.

With Jupiter: legal and ecclesiastical troubles, hypocrisy, dishonesty, false friends danger of imprisonment.

With Saturn: untrustworthy, dishonorable, low morality, bad habits formed in early life.

Baten Kaitos (the Whale's Belly) – compulsory transportation, change or emigration, misfortune by force or accident, shipwreck but also rescue, falls and blows.

Bellatrix (Swiftly Destroying, the Female Warrior) – great military or civil honour but danger of sudden dishonour, renown, wealth, eminent friends and liability to accidents causing blindness and ruin. If prominent in a woman's chart: loquacious, shrewish, a high-pitched, hard and sharp voice.

On the MC: quarrels, hatred, fraud committed or suffered, forgery, swindling, conning and perjury.

With Sun: vacillating, changeable, indecisive in business, mechanical ability, riches and honour but final ruin, blindness by accident, disease, extreme sickness, fevers or violent death.

With Moon: luxury, lust, vain ambition, waste, ruin, blindness by accident, disease, extreme sickness, fevers or a violent death.

With Mercury: military success, favourable for friendship and social affairs.

With Venus: much suffering through love affairs owing to unrestrained feelings.

With Mars: strength, energy, success as a soldier, surgeon or metal worker, liable to accidents.

With Jupiter: philosophical and religious mind, hypocrisy, may be fanatic, legal prominence and great honour but danger of slander.

With Saturn: secluded and studious life, reserved, thoughtful, unfavourable for gain owing to lack of interest, poverty at end of life, often single, but if married the partner may die young, no children.

Betelgeuze (the Giant's Armpit) – martial honour, preferment and wealth.

On the MC: great military fortune, command, invention, ingenuity, helps in the perfection of arts and sciences.

With Sun: interest in and ability for occult and mystical subjects, acute diseases, fevers, honour and preferment ending in final ruin.

With Moon: active mind, strong will, turbulent, rebellious under restraint, military success but suffering through quarrels with superiors, likelihood of great power honour and wealth.

With Mercury: serious, studious, scientific and literary, unfavourable for gain, fame through or engravings in metals.

With Venus: somewhat retiring and reserved, great ability as a maker of fine ornaments.

With Mars: cautious, reserved, good leader and organizer, honour and preferment in military matters.

With Jupiter: serious and studious mind, shrewd and profitable business dealings, great honour in the church or law.

With Saturn: shrewd, cunning, craftily dishonest, treacherous to friends, eventful life with many ups and downs, eventual wealth but little comfort, unfavourable for domestic matters.

Bos – in conjunction with Mercury a clever and piercing intellect.

Bungula – beneficence, refinement, position of honour, friends.

With Sun: envious, self-centered, slow but fairly successful progress, many enemies, loss of inheritance.

With Moon: popular, many friends, diplomatic, secret bad habits, excessive drinking, involved in disputes but emerges successfully.

With Mercury: changeable, vacillating, fault-finding, difficult to please, good intellect, business success, trouble in domestic affairs through enemies, family sickness, disappointed ambitions.

With Venus: popular, artistic, musical abilities, benefits from friends, danger from love affairs.

With Mars: physical endurance, considerable mental power, speaker or writer, little prominence.

With Jupiter: great ecclesiastical or legal honour and preferment, ritualistic tendencies, success in foreign countries, favourable for gain.

With Saturn: studious, well read, materialistic, self-seeking, favourable for gain, accumulation of money, property and legacies though not without quarrels, favourable for marriage though some domestic disturbance, eldest child may be afflicted in early life.

Canopus – piety, conservatism, wide and comprehensive knowledge, voyages and educational work, changes evil to good.

On MC: great glory, fame and wealth, dignity and authority by the help of an old clergyman or influential person.

With Sun: domestic affliction, trouble with father or parents, financial loss, danger of accidents, burns and fevers, unfavourable end to life.

With Moon: success in martial matters as a soldier, a surgeon or a metal worker.

With Mercury: rash, headstrong, stubborn, kind-hearted, speaker or writer on unpopular subjects incurring criticism, trouble and loss through domestic matters, partners or law.

With Venus: emotional, sensitive, stubborn, strong passions, scandal by an intrigue by which reputation will suffer, public disgrace, bad for gain.

With Mars: cruel, bad-tempered, envious, jealous.

With Jupiter: great pride, religion used for business ends, voyages, honour and preferment but dishonour through public dissatisfaction.

With Saturn: discontented, occult interests, unfavourable for reputation and domestic matters, little prominence but may do good.

Capella (Little She-Goat) – honour, wealth, renown, a public position of trust and eminent friends, careful, timorous, inquisitive, very fond of knowledge and particularly of novelties.

On the MC: military, naval or ecclesiastical connections and preferment. If also with Sun, Moon or Jupiter: ample fortune and great honour.

With Sun: vacillating, changeable, too loquacious, quick speech, misunderstood and criticized, martial honour and wealth.

With Moon: inquisitive, loquacious, indiscreet speech, sarcastic, quarrelsome, many journeys and voyages, domestic disharmony, danger to sight, liable to accidents.

With Mercury: disagreeable experiences, legal action over writings and success after much difficulty.

With Venus: literary and poetical ability, unfavourable for gain.

With Mars: intellectual, learned, talents wasted on low subjects.

With Jupiter: legal or ecclesiastical connections, slander and criticism, too enthusiastic or zealous, many voyages, trouble with relatives.

With Saturn: shrewd, tidy, fond of luxury, many detrimental habits, makes much money but does not keep it, trouble from opposite sex and domestic harmony, bad health at end of life and afflicted in arms, legs or eyes, necessitating restricted movement.

Caphir (an Atonement Offering, the Submissive One) – courteous, refined and lovable character with prophetic instincts.

With Sun: involved in an intrigue, some difficulty of short duration leaving native in unpleasant position.

With Moon: popular, business worries, domestic disharmony and divorce, poor health.

With Mercury: legal troubles, criticism, many worries, business difficulties which will be overcome, ill-health, loses respect of associates.

With Venus: unfavourable for gain, much scandal from passionate love affair.

With Mars: loss through lawsuits and by fire or storm, trouble with opposite sex, marriage partner and public.

With Jupiter: trouble through legal affairs or with the church, disputes over inheritance, domestic disharmony, through intrigue and consequent scandal.

With Saturn: intelligent, studious, home troubles in early life, liable to imprisonment or execution for another's crime especially if in twelfth house, suffers through conspiracy of friends and relatives, domestic disharmony, sickly children, home broken up, death in prison.

Capulus (Perseus' Sword-hand) – blindness, defective eyesight.

Castor (A Ruler yet to Come) – distinction, keen intellect, success in law and publishing, many travels, fondness for horses, sudden fame and honour but often followed by loss of fortune and disgrace, sickness, trouble, great affliction, mischievous, prone to violence.

With Sun: prominence in occult matters, government work dealing with foreign affairs, serious accidents, blows, stabs, shooting, shipwreck, injuries to the face, blindness, disease, violent fevers, evil disposition, rape and murder committed or suffered, imprisonment, banishment, decapitation.

With Moon: timid, sensitive, lacks confidence, occult interest and psychic ability, blindness, injuries to the face, disgrace, stabs, wounds, imprisonment.

With Mercury: remarkable psychic powers entailing criticism and ridicule but eventual prominence, unfavourable for gain.

With Venus: strange and peculiar life, many extreme ups and downs, unfavourable for marriage.

With Mars: evil disposition, much travel, aimless life, many ups and downs.

With Jupiter: philosophical and occult interests, loss through law, speculation and travel, danger of judicial sentence.

With Saturn: timid, distrustful, eccentric, original mind but difficulty in expression, better writer than speaker, considerable intellectual powers, fond of detail, prejudiced against popular opinion, unfavourable for marriage, peculiar domestic conditions, early sickness of children, gain at end of life through hard work.

Castra – destructive, malevolent, uncontrollable temper.

Copula – favourable for relationships, strong passions, blindness, defective eyesight, hindrances, disappointments.

Dabih

With Sun: reserved, suspicious, mistrustful, loss through friends, responsible public position of trust and authority.

With Moon: successful in business but retires under a cloud, favourable for health, influential position but scarcely realizes ambitions, trouble through opposite sex, deserved criticism and censure.

With Mercury: reserved, suspicious, envious, self-centred, prominent position in public affairs or companies, favourable for gain, bad for domestic affairs, peculiar home conditions.

With Venus: secret love affairs, sorrow and disappointment, easily led astray, enmity of women.

With Mars: great ambition, energy, high position but danger of reversal, domestic disharmony.

With Jupiter: hypocrisy, dishonesty, high legal or ecclesiastical preferment but ultimate disgrace.

With Saturn: melancholy, studious, restless and nervous, recluse, writer, accumulates wealth in miserly fashion, often lives alone, but if married danger of separation and divorce, wrapped up in some great sorrow, long life.

Deneb Okab (the Eagle's Tail) – ability to command, liberality, success in war and beneficence.

Deneb (Adige) (the Swan's Tail) – clever intellect, ingenious nature, quick at learning.

Deneb Algedi (the Goat's Tail) – beneficence and destructiveness, sorrow and happiness, life and death.

On the MC: great glory, fame, wealth, dignity and authority by the help of an old clergyman or influential person.

With the Sun: loss through false friends, high position but final disgrace and ruin, loss of money or property, sickness, worry through children.

With Moon: great difficulties in everything, success after patient plodding but final loss of position.

With Mercury: melancholy, quiet, solitary, unkempt or ragged, student of nature, science or philosophy, engaged in trapping animals, reptiles, snakes or poisonous beetles which do not harm the native.

With Venus: some secret desire that is never gratified, domestic or family difficulties.

With Mars: danger from enemies, accidents, honour and preferment but many quarrels and final disgrace, violent death.

With Jupiter: disappointment in secret wishes, false friends, loss through the law, church and relatives.

With Saturn: great power over animals or poisonous reptiles, indifferent to study, knowledge of many secrets of nature, feared, unpleasant appearance and life, bad for gain and marriage, death of and separation from parents in youth, secluded at end of life.

Denebola (the Lion's Tail) – swift judgement, despair, regrets, public disgrace, misfortune from the elements of nature, happiness turned to anger, noble, daring, self-controlled, generous, busy with other people's affairs.

On the Asc: riches, preferment and good fortune attended by many dangers and anxieties through own folly, benefits seldom last, trouble and sickness.

With Sun: honour and preferment with danger, public disgrace and final ruin, disease, fevers, acid, acute ailments, death by suicide.

With Moon: honour and preferment among the vulgar but final disgrace and ruin, violent disease of vital organ, blindness and injuries to the eyes, accidents, losses through servants, domestic quarrels, temporary separation from marriage partner.

With Mercury: many losses through agents or servants and through writings, bad for gain, loss of one of the family though malignant or contagious disease.

With Venus: strong passions, led astray early in life, ruined through love affairs.

With Mars: bitter, vindictive, cruel, unpopular, loss of position and public disgrace.

With Jupiter: pride, hypocrisy, disappointed life, troubles abroad or through relatives, secret enemies, danger of imprisonment or death by sentence.

With Saturn: critical, always complaining, many enemies, loss through servants and thieves, unfortunate life, domestic sorrow, wife afflicted or children mentally unsound or deformed.

Deneb Kaitos = Difda

Difda (also called Deneb Kaitos, the Whale's Tail) – self-destruction by brute force, sickness, disgrace, misfortune, compulsory change.

With Sun: mental disturbance, some loss keenly felt, accidents such as bums, scalds and cuts.

With Moon: pioneer, reckless, headstrong, violent temper, many quarrels, bad for gain and business.

With Mercury: active mind, writer or speaker upon subjects of public welfare, seeks to enact laws of benefit to the community, favourable for social affairs.

With Venus: reserved, passionate, many secret love affairs.

With Mars: passionate, violent, subject to accidents and injuries to the head, fevers, disgrace and ruin through own acts.

With Jupiter: high legal or ecclesiastical position but danger of reversal, treachery from secret enemies, loss through speculation.

With Saturn: impure mind, worry, secret wrongdoing, inharmonious environment.

Dirah – force, energy, power, protection.

Dorsum – misfortune, with Mars or Sun: also bites from venomous creatures.

El Nath (the Butting One) – fortune, eminence, neutrality for good or evil.

With Sun: ecclesiastical preferment, honour through science, religion or philosophy.

With Moon: quarrels with questionable associates, business success, environment detrimental owing to wife, partner or relative.

With Mercury: favour of superiors but enmity of colleagues, rises to high position or changes vocation, favourable for gain but many small losses, domestic expenses, often obliged to support an invalid.

With Venus: favourable for gain, enemies who are powerless to injure.

With Mars: good lawyer, speaker and debater, quick-witted.

With Jupiter: success in legal and ecclesiastical affairs, favourable for gain and inheritance.

With Saturn: cautious, thoughtful, bad-tempered, accumulates money, favourable for domestic affairs, gain through relatives, may receive start in life through a legacy.

Ensis – blindness, defective sight, injuries to the eyes, sickness and a violent death.

Facies – blindness, defective sight, sickness, accidents, violent death.

Fomalhaut (the Fish's Mouth) – very fortunate and powerful yet causes malevolence of sublime scope and character, change from a material to a spiritual form of expression.

With Asc or MC: great and lasting honours.

With Sun: dissipated, easily influenced by low companions, gain through inheritance but unproductive of good, may suffer form some crime committed, danger of bites from venomous creatures.

With Moon: secret business causing much trouble and enmity but eventual gain after difficulties.

With Mercury: many losses and disappointments, unlucky in business, better servant than master, writes or receives secret letters, worry through slander, imprisonment or damaged reputation, domestic difficulties, sickness of a Saturnian nature.

With Venus: secret and passionate love affair, some restrictions in the life, disappointments, easily led astray.

With Mars: malevolent, passionate, revengeful, many secret enemies, liable to disgrace and ruin, danger of bites from venomous creatures.

With Jupiter: sympathetic, charitable, honour in the church, freemasonry or secret societies, many voyages.

With Saturn: accidents, ailments affecting the lungs throat and feet, loss through enemies, mercurial affairs, friends, bands and companies, wrongfully accused, affairs involved at end of life, sudden death and family cheated out of their rights.

Foramen – peril, dignity, piety, usefulness and acquisitiveness, danger to the eyes.

With Sun: danger of shipwreck.

Giedi – beneficence, sacrifice and offering.

With Sun: peculiar events, unexpected losses and gains, sometimes great good fortune.

With Moon: peculiar and unexpected events, eccentric, public criticism, new and influential friends, valuable gifts, love of respectable women but difficulties and sometimes platonic marriage.

With Mercury: romantic, psychic, vacillating, bad for gain, many love affairs some of which cause notoriety, may elope with married person.

With Venus: many strange and unexpected events, peculiar and romantic marriage, may be separated for years from partner through secret government or political reason of which even native may be ignorant.

With Mars: abrupt, aggressive, much criticism, public position.

With Jupiter: government position, preferment in law or church, marriage abroad, favourable for gain and inheritance.

With Saturn: genius but kept down by circumstances, peculiar and occult early environment, birth amidst strange conditions while mother is travelling, many narrow escapes, associated with the stage, rarely marries, unfavourable for gain.

Graffias – extreme malevolence, mercilessness, fiendishness, repulsiveness, malice, theft, crime, pestilence and contagious diseases.

On the Asc: riches and preferment attended by danger, violence, trouble sickness, benefits seldom last.

With Sun: materialistic, too active a mind, ecclesiastical difficulties, bad health, otherwise similar to the effect of rising.

With Moon: great power, honour, wealth, gifts, difficulty in obtaining legacy, materialistic, interested in unpopular ideas, criticized, success after many difficulties, otherwise similar to the effect of rising.

With Mercury: dull-mind, difficulty in expression or defect in speech, gifts, difficulty in obtaining legacy but final success.

With Venus: dishonest, self-seeking, energetic, able, favourable for gain.

With Mars: athletic, suffers from over-exertion, goes to extremes, active mind, favourable for money matters but extravagant and has many debts.

With Jupiter: hypocritical, real or pretended religious zeal, legacies attended by legal difficulties.

With Saturn: cautious, cunning, self-seeking, deceitful, dishonourable, progressive ideas, religious but hypocritical, proud of home, loss by fire or water, gain through marriage and partnership, few children, long life.

Hamal (the Death Wound, the Following Horn) – brutishness, violence, cruelty, premeditated crime.

With Sun: dissipation, evil associates, loss, disgrace.

With Moon: patient, slow success through hard work, trouble through love affairs but favourable for marriage, marriage partner gains by business or speculation.

With Mercury: dull mind, many friends, great determination, tactful, greatly influenced by marriage partner.

With Venus: handsome, quiet, envious, jealous, domestic trouble, jealous, ill-health to native or family.

With Mars: violence, criminal tendencies, influential position but final disgrace and ruin.

With Jupiter: dissipated, hypocritical, legal or ecclesiastical preferment, loss by speculation.

With Saturn: cautious, thoughtful, critical, sarcastic, materialistic, interested in geology or agriculture, some domestic happiness, favourable for gain.

Han – trouble, disgrace.

With Sun: sickness, disgrace, ruin.

With Moon: disgrace, ruin, ailments affecting those parts ruled by Sagittarius.

Hyaden – see Prima Hyadum

Isidis – sudden assaults, malevolence, immorality, shamelessness.

With Sun: immoral, dissipated, low associates, many sorrows.

With Moon: reserved, suspicious, bad for business success, disgrace, loss by horses and cattle.

With Mercury: hypocritical, evil mind, low associates, imprisonment, malignant disease but chances of recovery, criminal, secrets in connection with life or parentage, domestic disharmony.

With Venus: quiet, reserved, jealous, selfish, favourable for gain.

With Mars: immoral, criminal, violent, evil environment, sudden or violent death.

With Jupiter: deceitful, dishonest, dissipated, low companions, danger of imprisonment.

With Saturn: vacillating, strong passions, evil habits, low associates, may be disowned by family, several unhappy marriages, early death of favourite child, death from consumption.

Khambalia (the Crooked-clawed) – swift violence, unreliability, changeability, argumentative nature.

Labrum (the Holy Grail) – idealism, psychic power, intelligence, honour and riches in disgrace and purifies to salvation.

On the Asc: ecclesiastical preferment, very good fortune.

Lesath (the Sting) – danger, desperation, immorality, malevolence, acid poisons.

Manubrium – blindness, explosions, fire, flaring heat, heroism, courage, defiance.

Markab – honour, riches, fortune, danger from fevers, cuts, blows, stabs, fire, violent death.

On the MC: disgrace, ruin, violent death.

With Sun: energetic, unlucky, impermanent martial honours, disappointed ambitions, accidents, sickness.

With Moon: injuries from enemies, bad for gain and domestic matters, fairly good health but many accidents.

With Mercury: good mind, rash and headstrong, quick in speech, diplomatic, capable writer, criticized, friends become enemies, bad for gain.

With Venus: evil associates, drink and other excesses, bad for gain.

With Mars: quarrelsome, violent, many difficulties and losses through Mercurial affairs.

With Jupiter: trouble and loss through legal matters, danger of judicial sentence or banishment or exile.

With Saturn: born in poverty, prison or asylum, may be abandoned, hard life, imprisoned for crime, few friends, unfavourable for domestic matters, death under similar conditions to birth.

Markeb – piety, a wide knowledge, educational work, voyages.

On the Asc: profitable journeys with Jupiterian and Saturnian people wherein native is grave and discreet but suffers much injury which ultimately turns to good.

Menkalinan (the Reinholder's Shoulder) – ruin, disgrace, violent death.

Menkar – disease, disgrace, ruin, injury from beasts, sickness loss of fortune.

On the Asc: legacies and inheritances attended by much evil.

On the MC: disgrace, ruin, danger from cattle and large beasts.

With Sun: great trouble, sickness, throat ailments, legacies and inheritances attended by much evil, loss of money, failure of crops.

With Moon: mental anxiety, hatred of the vulgar, ill-will of women, danger from thieves, sickness to natives and family, loss of marriage partner or near relative, quarrels, legal losses, legacies and inheritances attended by much evil.

With Mercury: difficulties through writings, difficulties in payment of mortgages, bad for gain, ill-health to marriage partner or relative, destruction of crops.

With Venus: strong and uncontrolled passions, jealousy, domestic disharmony and temporary separation, ill-health to marriage partner.

With Mars: evil associates, immoral, violent, murderous, violent death.

With Jupiter: deceitful, dishonest, wandering life, imprisonment, banishment, judicial sentence.

With Saturn: self-seeking, selfish, causes unhappiness to others, much sickness, bad for gain.

Mintaka (the Belt) – good fortune.

With Sun: discreet, cautious, somewhat changeable.

With Moon: active, sharp, alert in business, public position, many enemies, more successful in business.

With Mercury: studious, fond of seclusion, deliberate and fixed mind, little sympathy or disagreements with relatives, bad for gain.

With Venus: public position, enmity of women, love disappointments.

With Mars: energetic, quick mind, good speaker and debater, quarrelsome, strong passions.

With Jupiter: high position in law or church, studious and philosophical mind, gain through inheritance.

With Saturn: far-seeing, studious, good judge of human nature, psychic, domestic disharmony, sickness to family.

Mirach (Andromeda's Girdle) – personal beauty, a brilliant mind, a love of home, great devotion, beneficence, forgiveness, love, overcoming by kindness, renown, good fortune in marriage.

With Sun: trouble through opposite sex, disappointments in expectations but otherwise favourable.

With Moon: trouble with opposite sex owing to indiscretions, bad for domestic affairs, honour through martial matters.

With Mercury: vacillating, unstable, peculiar events, many travels and changes, little success.

With Venus: voluptuous, bad morals, scandal, drink or drug-taking late in life.

With Mars: ill-manners, boisterous, evil associations, may be a tramp.

With Jupiter: help from women, danger of scandal, much travel, legal or ecclesiastical difficulties.

With Saturn: strong passions, debauchery, mechanical genius, misdirected talents.

Nashira – overcoming by evil which is turned to success, danger from beasts.

North Scale (the Sufficient Price) – good fortune, high ambition, beneficence, honour, riches, permanent happiness.

On the MC or Asc: honour, preferment, good fortune.

With Sun: great good fortune, high position, transitory difficulties eventually proving beneficial.

With Moon: active mind, organizing ability, benefits through news and influential friends, valuable gifts, uses friend's name to obtain money but matter is amicably settled, high position, love of respectable women.

With Mercury: active, alert, favours from influential people, good position, much expenditure, benefits through writings.

With Venus: social success, help from women, favourable for love affairs and marriage.

With Mars: high ambition, success through energy, influential position, forceful writer and speaker.

With Jupiter: philosophical mind, ecclesiastical or legal preferment, able writer or speaker, influential friends.

With Saturn: cautious, reserved, studious, economical, analytical, good chemist or detective, good judge of human nature, early losses never fully recovered, favourable for gain and domestic matters, sickness to children in infancy.

Oculus (the Eye) – With Mercury: clever and piercing intellect.

Pelagus – truthfulness, optimism, religious mind.

With Sun: influential public position, favourable for domestic and family matters.

With Moon: successful writer on science, philosophy, education or agriculture, unorthodox in religion, defeats enemies, many friends, illness of a Saturnian nature.

With Mercury: high government position, popular criticism, wealth, anxiety on account of illness to wife or mother.

With Venus: heart rules head, favours from opposite sex, many friends.

With Mars: reserved, diplomatic, strong mind, courageous, energetic, straightforward, false friends, favourable for gain.

With Jupiter: diplomatic, philosophical mind, writer, ecclesiastical or legal preferment.

With Saturn: thoughtful, reserved, self-centred, success delayed after 50, ambition thwarted by enemies, danger of disgrace, wealth at end of life, trouble to parents, favourable marriage late in life, usually at least one child.

Phact – beneficence, hopefulness, good fortune.

Pleiades – wanton, ambitious, turbulent, journeys and voyages, success in agriculture and through active intelligence, blindness disgrace, violent death, evil, disappointments.

On the Asc: blindness, ophthalmia, injuries to the eyes and the face, disgrace, wounds, stabs, exile, imprisonment, sickness, violent fevers, quarrels, violent lust, military preferment.

On the MC: disgrace, ruin, violent death, if also with a luminary: military success.

With Sun: throat ailments, chronic catarrh, blindness, bad eyes, injuries to the face, sickness, disgrace, evil disposition, murder, imprisonment, death by pestilence, blows, stabs, shootings, beheading or shipwreck.

With Moon: injuries to the face, sickness, misfortune, wounds, stabs, disgrace, imprisonment, blindness, defective eyesight.

With Mercury: many disappointments, loss of possessions, much loss from legal affairs, business failure, trouble through children.

With Venus: immoral, strong passions, disgrace through women, sickness, loss of fortune.

With Mars: many accidents to the head, loss and suffering through fires.

With Jupiter: deceit, hypocrisy, legal and ecclesiastical trouble, loss through relatives, banishment or imprisonment.

With Saturn: cautious, much sickness, tumorous ailments, chronic sickness to family, many losses.

Polaris (the Pole Star) – much sickness, trouble, loss of fortune, disgrace and great affliction, legacies and inheritances attended by much evil.

With Sun: many troubles and evils.

With Moon: hatred of the vulgar, ill-will of women, danger of thieves.

Polis – success, high ambition, martial desires, horsemanship, keen perception and domination.

Pollux (Hercules) – subtle, crafty, spirited, brave, audacious, cruel and rash nature, a love of boxing, dignified malevolence, poisons.

On the Asc: bad eyes, blindness, injuries to the face, sickness, wounds, imprisonment, ephemeral honour and preferment.

On the MC: honour and preferment but danger of disgrace and ruin.

With Sun: occult and philosophical interests, blows, stabs, serious accidents, shooting, shipwreck, murder, extreme sickness and disease, fevers, ailments affecting the stomach, evil disposition, riches and honour but final ruin, blindness, injuries to the head and the face, quarrels, rape, banishment, imprisonment for embezzling, violent death, decapitation.

With Moon: hatred of the vulgar, ill-will of women, danger from thieves, violent death, power, pride, sickness, calamity, wounds, imprisonment, injuries to the face, defective sight, blindness.

With Mercury: unbalanced mind, unpopular and peculiar occupation, trouble with father through relatives or enemies, domestic disharmony, anxiety, loss through land, property and mines.

With Venus: strong and irregulated passion, danger of seduction if female, loss through women, danger of poison.

With Mars: violence, murder, high position but final ruin, violent death by suffocation, drowning or assassination, especially if the Moon is there also.

With Jupiter: legal losses, high position but danger of disgrace, trouble through relatives, banishment, imprisonment.

With Saturn: bad temper, bitter, sarcastic, loss of arm or leg, loss of parents or trouble through stepparents, much help from a friend, lack of education, sudden death while following occupation through horses or large animals.

Praesepe (the Exhalation of piled-up Corpses, the Manger, the Beehive, with the Aselli called the 'Cloudy Spot in Cancer') – disease, blindness, disgrace, adventure, insolence, wantonness, brutality, industry, fecundity, bloodshed, losses, fighting.

On the Asc: blindness, especially of the left eye, ophthalmia, injuries to the face, sickness, violent fevers, wounds in face and arms, stabs, violent lust, imprisonment, exile.

On the MC: disgrace, ruin, violent death.

With Sun: evil disposition, murder, blows, stabs, serious accidents, shooting, shipwreck, execution, banishment, imprisonment, sharp diseases, fevers, haemorrhage, lawsuits, danger of death from fire, iron or stones, injuries to the face, wounds, bad eyes.

With Moon: stabs, wounds, injuries to the face, sickness, blindness, eye injuries.

Prima Hyadum – Chief of the Hyades – tears, sudden events, violence, fierceness, poisoning, blindness, wounds, injuries to the head by instruments, weapons or fevers, contradictions of fortune, disappointments.

On the Asc: blindness, bad eyes, injuries to the face, wounds, stabs, imprisonment.

On the MC: disgrace, ruin, violent death.

With one of the Luminaries on the MC or on the ascendant: military leaders.

With Sun: evil disposition, disturbed mind, failure in study, muddled thinking, misfortune, murder, death by blows, stabs, shooting or shipwreck.

With Moon: tactful, fair ability, difficulties connected with writing, may forge the name of an employer or friend but finally escape punishment and retain position, liable to sickness and disgrace, danger of blindness or eye injuries.

With Mercury: quick mind, resentful, hasty temper, broods over small troubles, favourable for gain.

With Venus: many accomplishments, artistic, ability to write and paint, strong passions which influence work.

With Mars: abrupt, brave, aggressive, courageous, lacks concentration.

With Jupiter: ambitious, dishonest, legal difficulties, quarrels with relatives, judicial sentence.

With Saturn: cautious, forethought, omnivorous reader, scientific, success but little prominence, worry and annoyance from relatives.

Princeps (the Prince) – keen studious and profound mind, ability for research.

On the Asc: good fortune with troubles, discontent and fear occasioned by own temerity rather than circumstances.

Procyon – activity, violence, sudden and violent malevolence, sudden preferment by exertion, elevation ending in disaster, danger of dog bites and hydrophobia, petulant, saucy, giddy, weak-natured, timid, unfortunate, proud, easily angered, careless, violent.

On the Asc: artful, crafty, dissembling, wealth by violence and rape, lust, dissipation, waste and ruin, military preferment, quarrels, loss in trade or by servants.

With the Sun: great help from friends, gifts and legacies if not afflicted.

With Moon: occult interests, restless, never remains long in one place, quarrels with friends, partners and employers.

With Mercury: occult interest, minor position of management under government, trouble and scandal through opposite sex, favourable for health and gain.

With Venus: many benefits from influential friends, associated with the church, favourable for gain.

With Mars: cruelty, violence, scandal, slander, disgrace, ruin, danger of dog bites.

With Jupiter: many journeys, trouble through relatives and the church or law, help from friends.

With Saturn: good judgement, high position of trust, often in connection with land, may be adopted by aged couple from whom a good inheritance is obtained, benefits from elderly friends, good health, domestic harmony, marriage to one of higher station.

Propus: – strength, eminence, success.

Rasalhague (the Head of the Serpent Charmer) – misfortune through women, perverted tastes, mental depravity.

With Sun: reserved, thoughtful, studious, suspicious, solitary, reputation for athletics, little wealth, careless of public opinion.

With Moon: public prominence in religious matters, favourable for gain.

With Mercury: unpopular attitude, criticism through religion, philosophy or science, difficulties in marriage and quarrels fostered by others, trouble through opposite sex, not very good for gain.

With Venus: quick mind, well-educated, cautious, secretive, suspicious, unfavourable for gain.

With Mars: trouble through writings, public censure in connection with religion, science or philosophy, bad for gain.

With Jupiter: diplomatic, religious or legal preferment but some criticism, favourable for gain.

With Saturn: selfish, unpopular, determined, fixed opinions, successful, somewhat dishonest, domestic disharmony through jealousy, marriage partner may be invalid, loss of a Mercurial nature.

Rastanban – loss of property, violence, criminal inclinations, accidents.

With Moon: blindness, quarrels, bruises, stabs, blows, and kicks from horses.

Regulus (The Lion's Heart, the Little King) – violent, destructive, military honour of short duration with ultimate failure, imprisonment, violent death, great success, high and lofty ideals and strength of spirit, magnanimous, grandly liberal, generous, ambitious, fond of power, desirous of command, high spirited, independent.

On the Asc: great honour and wealth, but violence and trouble, sickness fever, acute diseases, benefits seldom last, favour of the great victory over enemies, scandal.

On the MC: honour, preferment, good fortune, high office under government, military success, if also with Jupiter, Sun or Moon: great honour, an ample fortune.

With Sun: power, authority, great influence over friends, honour and riches but violence, trouble, and ultimate disgrace and ruin, sickness, fevers, benefits seldom last.

With Moon: occult interests, powerful friends, danger from enemies and false friends, gain by speculation, public prominence, great power, honour, wealth, benefits seldom last, violence, trouble, sickness, high-spirited, independent.

With Mercury: honourable, just, popular, generous, abused by opponents, fame, gain through high position.

With Venus: many disappointments, unexpected happenings, violent attachments, trouble through love affairs.

With Mars: honour, fame, strong character, public prominence, high military command.

With Jupiter: fame, high preferment especially of a military nature, success in the church.

With Saturn: just, friends among the clergy, success in church or law, scholarly, wealth, gain through speculation, companies or friends, proud of home and family, good health, heart trouble at end of life, also on angle: public honour and credit.

Rigel (The Foot) – benevolence, riches, happiness, glory, renown, inventive or mechanical ability.

On the Asc: good fortune, preferment, riches, great and lasting honours.

On the MC: great military or ecclesiastical preferment, anger, vexation, magnanimity, much gain acquired by labour and mental anxiety, lasting honours.

With Sun: bold, courageous, insolent, unruly temper, hasty action, bloodshed, many enemies, great good fortune, military success.

With Moon: much worry and disappointment, injuries to life and fortune, sickness, bad for gain, ill-health or death to wife or mother.

With Mercury: prominent position in connection with Mercurial matters or in science.

With Venus: honours or favours in middle life, good and influential marriage especially if female.

With Mars: unruly, ingenious, occupied with mechanical matters, great military preferment.

With Jupiter: great legal or ecclesiastical preferment, many journeys, benefits from foreign affairs, favourable for marriage.

With Saturn: benefits from elderly people, clergy and lawyers, just, discriminative, good for legacy and inheritance, domestic harmony, good health, long life.

Sabik – wastefulness, lost energy, perverted morals, success in evil deeds.

With Sun: sincere, honourable, scientific, religious and philosophical interests, unorthodox, heretical, moral courage, bad for gain.

With Moon: secret enmity and jealousy, trouble through relatives, successful but not wealthy, success in breeding stock.

With Mercury: injury from open enemies, little help from friends, failure in business, fairly good for gain but legal losses, scandal through relatives or marriage partner.

With Venus: musical and artistic ability, not very favourable for gain.

With Mars: unorthodox or heretical religious views that may cause trouble, domestic harmony, trouble through love affairs, bad for gain.

With Jupiter: material success, preferment in church or law but criticized, gain through large animals, trouble through relatives.

With Saturn: industrious, persevering, economical, strong passions, trouble through some active indiscretion affecting whole life, trouble and disappointment in love affairs, secret help from female friends which may cause scandal, success especially in latter part of life in affairs of an earthy or Sagittarian nature.

Sadalmelik – persecution, lawsuits, extreme and sudden destruction, death penalty.

With Sun: occult interests, prominence in occultism, gain through companies.

With Moon: prominence in occult matters, success in large companies, favourable for gain.

With Mercury: occult interest and research, criticized, favourable for friendship, success in large companies, loss through servants.

With Venus: favourable for occult investigation, gain through friends.

With Mars: fame through discoveries in science or inventions, benefits do not last.

With Jupiter: ecclesiastical success, occult interests, criticized, trouble through enemies, loss though lawsuits.

With Saturn: original, inventive, psychic, careful, cautious, practical, good judgement, difficulties in putting ideas or inventions into practice, gain through companies, speculation or matters of an earthy nature, chronic illness to wife and children, favourable for gain, long life.

Sadalsuud – trouble, disgrace.

With Sun: occult interests, psychic, wealth through opposite sex involving litigation, domestic harmony.

With Moon: reputation through occult matters, respect of friends, favourable for gain, peculiar domestic conditions.

With Mercury: social success, favours from opposite sex but some transitory difficulties, retirement owing to abuse of position, sudden loss through speculation, domestic sorrow and trouble.

With Venus: strange events, romantic and peculiar marriage, entailing separation for government and political reasons.

With Mars: difficulties through occult matters, bad for gain.

With Jupiter: litigation, material and social success, difficulties in marriage, may marry abroad or to a foreigner.

With Saturn: sharp, cunning, dishonest, immoral, cold, unsympathetic, hard-hearted, disgraces an honourable father, hypnotic influence over opposite sex, many intrigues wrecking homes, death through female's revenge.

Scheat – extreme misfortune, murder, suicide, drowning.

With Sun: bad for success, danger through water and engines, liable to accidents or drowning.

With Moon: worry, loss and gain of friends through criticism.

With Mercury: many accidents and narrow escapes, especially by water, many enemies, trouble through writings, bad for health and domestic affairs.

With Venus: evil environment, suffering through own acts, danger of imprisonment and restraint.

With Mars: many accidents, bad for gain, sickness to native and relatives.

With Jupiter: many voyages, losses through law, friends and relatives, danger of imprisonment.

With Saturn: danger of death in infancy, bad for gain and pleasure, domestic trouble, colds and consumption, death by drowning or accidents.

Seginus – subtle mind, shamelessness, loss through friends and companies.

With Moon: preferment by indirect means, followed by disgrace and ruin.

Sharatan – bodily injuries, unscrupulous defeat, destruction by fire, war or earthquake.

Sinistra – immoral, mean, slovenly nature.

With Moon: lustful, wanton, infamous, scandalous, addicted to sorcery and poisoning.

Sirius – (the Heavenly Wolf) – honour, renown, wealth, ardour, faithfulness, devotion, passion and resentment, custodians, curators, guardians, danger of dog bites.

On the MC: high office under government giving great profit and reputation.

With Sun: success in business, occupation connected with metals or other martial affairs, domestic harmony, also on MC or Asc: kingly preferment.

With Moon: success in business, influential friends of opposite sex, favourable for the father, good health, beneficial changes in home or business.

With Mercury: great business success, help through influential people, worries unnecessarily, associated with the church, physical defect through accident.

With Venus: ease, comfort, luxury, extravagant, gain by inheritance.

With Mars: courageous, generous, military preferment, work in connection with metals.

With Jupiter: business success, journeys, help from relatives, ecclesiastical preferment.

With Saturn: steady, reserved, diplomatic, just, persevering, high position through friends, favourable for home, gifts and legacies, domestic harmony.

Skat – good fortune, lasting happiness.

With Sun: sensitive, emotional, psychic, criticism and persecution through mediumship but help from friends.

With Moon: new and influential friends, associated with companies, public position but little prominence, valuable gifts, love of respectable women.

With Mercury: peculiar events, occult interests, psychic, many friends.

With Venus: psychic, occult interests, friends among opposite sex, favourable for gain.

With Mars: energetic, advancement through exertions, mechanical discoveries or abilities.

With Jupiter: philosophical, occult or religious mind, social success, prominent in freemasonry.

With Saturn: trouble through opposite sex, many travels and peculiar adventures, sudden ups and downs, early marriage but may desert wife or be deserted, bigamy, separated from children, no help from friends, bad for gain and health in latter part of life, may die in workhouse, asylum or hospital.

South Scale (the Insufficient Price, the Southern Claw, Lucida Lancis) – malevolence, obstruction, unforgiving character, violence, disease, lying, crime, disgrace, danger of poison.

With Sun: sickness, loss in business, and through fire or speculation, disgrace, ruin, disfavour of superiors, suffers through wrongful accusations, sickness to family.

With Moon: trouble through opposite sex, wrongful accusations, disgrace, ruin, mental anxiety, loss of relatives, many disappointment, much sickness, disease in those parts of the body ruled by the sign.

With Mercury: crafty, revengeful, treacherous, quick mind, bad health, bad for gain, disgrace, poverty at end of life.

With Venus: bad for marriage, sudden and secret death, may be poisoned owing to jealousy of one of own sex.

With Mars: bitter quarrels entailing bloodshed or death.

With Jupiter: hypocrisy, deceit, dishonesty, pretended religious zeal for business purposes, danger of imprisonment.

With Saturn: dishonourable, often escapes justice but finally suffers, jealous, quick-tempered, domestic disharmony, bad for marriage, gain and legacies, miserable death.

Spica (the Wheat Ear of Virgo) – success, renown, riches, a sweet disposition, love of art and science, unscrupulousness, unfruitfulness, injustice to innocence.

On the MC or Asc: unbounded good fortune, riches, happiness, ecclesiastical preferment, unexpected honour or advancement beyond native's hopes or capacity.

With Sun: great and lasting preferment, eminent dignity, immense wealth, great happiness to native's parents and children, help from friends among clergy, favourable for legal or public affairs.

With Moon: gain through inventions, success, wealth and honour.

With Mercury: neat, tidy, clever, ingenious, favour of clergy and people in authority, gain through investments, responsible position.

With Venus: benefits from friends, social success, false friends of own sex.

With Mars: popular, social success, may have good judgement, quick decision, violent in dispute, rigid.

With Jupiter: popular, social success, wealth, ecclesiastical, honour and preferment.

With Saturn: apt to be suspicious, sharp or rugged but does much good, occult interests, good speaker, popular, many friends, gain through legacies but extravagant, good health, favourable for domestic matters.

Spiculum – blindness.

Tejat – violence, pride, over-confidence, shameless.

Terebellum – fortune with regrets and disgrace, cunning, repulsiveness, a mercenary nature, fateful events in connection with prophecies.

Unukalhai (the Serpent's Heart) – immorality, poison, violence, accidents.

With Sun: many quarrels and disappointments, unfortunate life, seriously affected by death of family or friends.

With Moon: clever, evil environment, hatred of authority, involved in intrigues and plots, banished, imprisoned or hanged for crime, probably by poisoning.

With Mercury: dishonourable, accused of forgery or theft of papers, ill-health, narrow escapes, danger of bites from poisonous animals.

With Venus: enmity, jealousy of own sex, bad for domestic matters, favourable for gain, secret death, probably by poisoning.

With Mars: violence, quarrels, lying, crime, violent death probably by poison.

With Jupiter: hypocrisy, deceit, banishment, imprisonment, exile.

With Saturn: secret insanity, drug taker, secret crime and poisoning often for no reason, shrewd, cunning, intelligent, studious, often physician or nurse, usually unmarried, may commit suicide or be confined in asylum or prison.

Vertex – blindness, injuries to the eyes, sickness and a violent death.

Vindemiatrix (the Sorcerer's Apprentice) – falsity, disgrace, premature harvesting, stealing, wanton folly, widowhood, arrogance, overestimation of one's powers, harming one's environment.

With Sun: worry, depression, unpopular, failure in business, harressed by creditors.

With Moon: worry, many disappointments, loss through law or writings and theft, bad health, failure in business.

With Mercury: impulsive, too hasty, loss through writings and business.

With Venus: trouble through love affairs, loss of friends, danger of scandal.

With Mars: rash, headstrong, indiscreet, energetic, trouble through law, business and friends.

With Jupiter: trouble through law or church, much criticism, many journeys.

With Saturn: cautious, thoughtful, reserved, materialistic, hypocritical in religion, loss through speculation, success in business, secret difficulty with marriage partner.

Wasat – violence, malevolence, destructiveness, chemicals, poison, gas.

Vega (the Falling Grype) – beneficence, idealism, hopefulness, refinement, changeability, grave, sober, outwardly pretentious, lascivious.

With Sun: critical, abrupt, reserved, unpopular, fleeting honours, influential position, insincere friends.

With Moon: public disgrace, probably through forgery, loss through writings, some ill-health, success in business, gain through an annuity or pension.

With Mercury: suspicious, reserved, bitter, thwarted ambitions, double dealing, secret enemies in influential positions, trouble with the mother, loss in business.

With Venus: hard-hearted, cold, miserly, ill-health, ugliness, deformity.

With Mars: scientific interests, unpopular opinions, moral courage, favourable for gain.

With Jupiter: loss through legal affairs, favourable for gain, danger of imprisonment.

With Saturn: strong passions, opinionated, original, many Mercurial difficulties, reputation suffers through wrongful accusations, trouble with superiors, domestic difficulties, few if any children, latter half of life more favourable, sudden death.

Yed Prior (the Left Hand) – immoral, shameless, revolutionary.

Zaniah – refinement, honour, congeniality, order, loveable nature.

With Sun: educational and studious interests, popular, social success, much pleasure, favourable for marriage.

With Moon: worry, loss through legal and Venusian affairs, trouble through writing, led astray by sympathies.

With Mercury: musical or artistic ability, gain through writing short stories, popular, social success, many friends especially among opposite sex.

With Venus: quick in learning, musical and artistic ability, fond of society, many friends, favourable for gain.

With Mars: active, energetic, loss through lawsuits, trouble through opposite sex.

With Jupiter: religious and philosophical mind, social success, many friends.

With Saturn: sober, industrious, many influential elderly friends, gain through old people, grandparents and marriage.

Zavijava – beneficence, force of character, strength, combative movements, destructiveness.

Zosma (the Lion's Back) – benefit by disgrace, selfishness, egotism, immorality, meanness, melancholy, unhappiness of mind, fear of poison, unreasonable, shameless.

Appendix B – The 48 Traditional Constellations

In modern times, especially in the 17th and 18th century, many new constellations were invented, but astrologically only the 48 real constellations are important, as only the traditional constellations are part of the proper mythical stories. That we can leave out the Pendulum Clock, the Printer's Office, the Camel, the Balloon and the Oven, without losing anything essential, will be clear.

There are 48 real constellations and twelve of these are of course zodiacal which means that they are placed on or near the zodiac, and these twelve zodiacal constellations correspond to the signs. It was explained in Chapter 2 that despite the fact that the sign and the constellation have the same name they are something very different. If this important distinction were made clearer in astrology a lot of misconceptions like the Age of Aquarius and the 'thirteenth' sign Ophiuchus would not arise.

Apart from the 12 zodiacal constellations there are 21 constellations placed north of the zodiac, those with a clear astrological effect have been italicized:

Andromeda – *Aquila* (Eagle) – *Auriga* (Charioteer) – *Boötes* (Herdsman) – Cassiopeia – Cepheus – *Corona Borealis* (Northern Crown) – *Cygnus* (Swan) – Delphinus (Dolphin) – Draco (Dragon) – Equuleus (the Little Horse) – Hercules – *Lyra* (Lyre, Falling Grype) – *Ophiuchus* (Snakebearer) – *Pegasus* – *Perseus* – Sagitta (the Arrow) – *Serpens* (the Snake) – Triangulum (Triangle) – Ursa Major (Greater Bear) – Ursa Minor (Lesser Bear).

There are 10 northern constellations too far away from the zodiac or too weak to be taken into account in practical astrology. A special case is the Dolphin which works out through a lunar mansion but not directly though a star (although several authors do mention the effects the constellation is supposed to have).

Appendix B – The 48 Traditional Constellations

Furthermore there are 15 southern constellations:
Ara (Altair) – *Argo Navis* (Argonauts's Ship) – *Canis Major* (Greater Dog) – *Canis Minor* (Lesser Dog) – *Centaur* – *Cetus* (Whale, Seamonster) – Corona Australis (Southern Crown) – *Corvus* (Crow) – *Crater* (Cup) – *Eridanus* (River) – *Hydra* (Watersnake) – Lepus (Hare) – Lupus (Wolf) – *Orion* – *Piscis Australis* (Southern Fish).

There are 4 constellations of this group of 15 too weak to have an astrological effect. Of the total of 48 constellations 33 are important in practice.

Appendix C. The Arabic Lunar Mansions

Information about the Arabic-western lunar mansions is limited and it is far more practical to use the semi-V system presented in Chapter 5. The list below gives the 28 unequal Arabic mansions with their zodiacal degrees (in 2000) and their ruling stars.

Al Sharatain – 3 to18 Taurus – Sharatan/Mesarthim, the Ram's Horns
Al Butain – 18 to 29 Taurus – Botein, the Ram's Tail
Al Thuraiya – 29 Taurus to 10 Gemini – the Pleiades
Al Dabaran – 10 to 24 Gemini – Aldebaran (the Bull's Eye)
Al Haqa – 24 Gemini to 9 Cancer – Meissa (in Orion's Head)
Al Hana – 9 to 20 Cancer – Alhena (the Feet of the Twins)
Al Dhira – 20 Cancer to 7 Leo – Castor
Al Natrah – 7 to 18 Leo – Praesepe
Al Tarf – 18 to 28 Leo – Al Tarf (in Leo)
Al Jabbah – 28 Leo to 12 Virgo – Regulus/Al Jabbah/Adhafera
Al Zubrah – 12 to 22 Virgo – Zosma/Coxa (Lion's Back)
 Al Sarfah – 22 to 27 Virgo – Denebola (Lion's Tail)
Al Awwa – 27 Virgo to 24 Libra – Zavijava (Virgo's breast and wings)
Al Simak – 24 Libra to 4 Scorpio – Spica
Al Ghafr – 4 to 15 Scorpio – Syrma (in Virgo: jota en kappa Virginis)
Al Zubana – 15 Scorpio to 3 Sagittarius – The Scales
Al Iklil – 3 to 10 Sagittarius – Acrab/Dschubba (the Scorpion's Head)
Al Qalb – 10 to 24 Sagittarius – Antares (Scorpion's heart)
Al Shaulah – 24 Sagittarius to 13 Capricorn – Shaula/Lesath (the Scorpion's Sting)
Al Naaim – 13 to 16 Capricorn – Nunki (bow, arrow and front leg in Sagittarius)
Al Baldah – 16 Capricorn to 4 Aquarius – Al Balda (hind part of Sagittarius)
Sa'd al Dhabhi – 4 to 12 Aquarius – Dabih (Capricorn's Eye)
Sa'd Bula – 12 to 23 Aquarius – Al Bali (the left hand of Aquarius)
Sa'd al Suud – 23 Aquarius to 4 Pisces – Sadalsuud (Aquarius' Shoulder)

Sa'dal-Akhbiya – 4 to 23 Pisces – Sadalmelek (the right hand of Aquarius)
Al Fargh al-Awwal – 23 Pisces to 9 Aries – Markab (on Pegasus' Wing)
Al Fargh al Thani – 9 Aries to 0 Taurus – Algenib/Apheratz (also on Pegasus' wing/in Andromeda)
Batn al Hut – 0 to 3 Taurus – Mirach (Andromeda's Girdle)

There are some mansions of 3 degrees length and some of 19 degrees length in this system; this is so because the boundaries of the mansions in the above division are taken simply from one (bright) star to another (bright) star. The ruling star with its constellation could be a starting-point for an interpretation of the mansion, although there is little information about them.

Despite the differences there are some things much the same, and this points to a shared origin between Arabic and the Vedic systems. The starting-points of the two systems for example are more or less close. In the Arabic division the position of *Mesarthim*, a ruling star of the first Aries mansion on the Ram's Horn, can be taken as a starting-point, but if the Aries constellation is projected, it begins a bit further back, roughly (as we cannot really be precise here) at the the end of the Aries sign (more or less close to 0° Aries sidereal). But comparing the Arabic and Vedic systems is awkward as the Arabic division is so strongly constellational and therefore has these unequal mansions. The Arabic system looks like a strongly corrupted version of an original system; the Vedic mansions seem to have preserved more of the original.

In the Arabic tradition there is another system of 28 mansions of equal length (12.51 degrees each) which is said to begin at 0 Aries, tropical. This however has to be seen more as a theoretical blue-print of the zodiac, and due to precession you couldn't use it – at least not as a mansion system with 0° Aries as its starting-point. The precession which increasingly separates the tropical and sidereal zodiacs has an important meaning. One of the traditional metaphysical principles is that there cannot be a closed system, so there can be no eternal return, nothing can ever be repeated exactly. The divine creativity is necessarily inexhaustible. This is what precession shows, because without precession things would in the end be repeated, the differences between the sphere 'that contains no stars' (the zodiac) and the star sphere is a visible effect of one of the metaphysical principles creation is based on.

236 Fixed Stars in the Chart

The Arabic system is of course interesting to experiment with, and if you want to do this the best option would be to start at 3.11 Taurus tropical, the position of *Mesarthim*, and give each mansion an equal length of 12.51 degrees. In this way you have taken into account the precession and retained the traditional mansion division. The boundaries of this equal-length system are given below:

Al Sharatain – 3.11 to 16.02 Taurus – Sharatan/Mesarthim, the Ram's Horns
Al Butain – 16.02 to 28.53 Taurus – Botein, the Ram's Tail
Al Thuraiya – 28.53 Taurus to 11.45 Gemini – the Pleiades
Al Dabaran – 11.45 to 24.36 Gemini – Aldebaran (the Bull's Eye)
Al Haqa – 24.36 Gemini to 7.28 Cancer – Meissa (in Orion's Head)
Al Hana – 7.28 to 20.19 Cancer – Alhena (the Feet of the Twins)
Al Dhira – 20.19 Cancer to 3.11 Leo – Castor
Al Natrah – 3.11 to 15.59 Leo – Praesepe
Al Tarf – 15.59 to 28.53 Leo – Al Tarf (in Leo)
Al Jabbah (Algieba) – 28.53 Leo to 11.45 Virgo – Regulus/Al Jabbah/Adhafera
Al Zubrah – 11.45 to 24.36 Virgo – Zosma/Coxa (Lion's Back)
Al Sarfah – 24.36 to 7.28 Libra – Denebola (Lion's Tail)
Al Awwa – 7.28 to 20.19 Libra – Zavijava (Virgo's breast and wings)
Al Simak – 20.19 Libra to 3.11 Scorpio – Spica
Al Ghafr – 3.11 to 16.02 Scorpio – Syrma (in Virgo: jota en kappa Virginis)
Al Zubana – 16.02–28.53 Scorpio – 3 Sagittarius - The Scales
Al Iklil – 28.53 Scorpio to 11.45 Sagittarius – Acrab/Dschubba (the Scorpion's Head)
Al Qalb – 11.45 to 24.36 Sagittarius – Antares (Scorpion's heart)
Al Shaulah – 24.36 Sagittarius to 7.28 Capricorn – Shaula/Lesath (the Scorpion's Sting)
Al Naaim – 7.28 to 20.19 Capricorn – Nunki (bow, arrow and front leg in Sagittarius)
Al Baldah – 20.19 Capricorn to 3.11 Aquarius – Al Balda (hind part of Sagittarius)
Sa'd al Dhabhi – 3.11 to 16.02 Aquarius – Dabih (Capricorn's Eye)

Sa'd al Bula – 16.02 to 28.53 Aquarius – Al Bali (the left hand of Aquarius)

Sa'd al Suud – 28.53 Aquarius to 11.45 Pisces – Sadalsuud (Aquarius' Shoulder)

Sa'd al-Akhbiya – 11.45 to 24.36 Pisces – Sadalmelek (the right hand of Aquarius)

Al Fargh al-Awwal – 24.36 Pisces to 7.28 Aries – Markab (on Pegasus' Wing)

Al Fargh al Thani – 7.28 to 20.19 Aries – Algenib/Apheratz (also on Pegasus' wing/in Andromeda)

Batn al Hut – 20.19 Aries to 3.11 Taurus – Mirach (Andromeda's Girdle)

All these diverse systems express something about the relation between the solar sphere of the 'Towers of the Zodiac', the signs, and the lunar level of the mansions. Every system emphasizes another aspect of this relation, somewhere between constellations and signs. The unequal mansions value the visible star at the boundary of the mansion above everything, the 28-mansions system starting at 0° Aries strives to retain a rigid theoretical structure. The division in 28 equal mansions starting at *Mesarthim*, the Ram's Horn at 3.11 Taurus, is in the middle of these extremes and seems to be the most balanced choice. It remains systematic but it does not ignore the precession.

Bibliography

Al Biruni, *Elements of the Art of Astrology* (1029), Ascella, London, England, facsimile 1934.

Titus Burckhardt, *Mystical Astrology according to Ibn 'Arabi*, Fons Vitae, Louisville, USA, 2001.

_____. *Sacred Art in East and West*, Fons Vitae, Louisville, USA, 2001.

John Frawley, *The Horary Textbook*, Apprentice Books, London, England, 2005.

_____. *The Real Astrology*, Apprentice Books, London, England, 2000.

_____. *The Real Astrology Applied*, Apprentice Books, London, England, 2002.

René Guénon, *The Esoterism of Dante*, Sophia Perennis, Hillsdale, USA, 2001.

_____.*The Great Triad*, Sophia Perennis, Hillsdale, USA. 2004.

_____. *The King of the World*, Sophia Perennis, Hillsdale, USA, 2001.

_____. *The Reign of Quantity and the Signs of the Times*, Sophia Perennis, Hillsdale, USA, 2001

_____.*Spiritual Authority & Temporal Power*, Sophia Perennis, Hillsdale, USA, 2001.

_____.*The Symbolism of the Cross*, Sophia Perennis, Hillsdale, USA, 2001.

_____.*Symbols of Sacred Science*, Sophia Perennis, Hillsdale, USA, 2004.

_____.*Traditional Forms and Cosmic Cycles*, Sophia Perennis, Hillsdale, USA, 2001.

Wiliam Lilly, *Christian Astrology*, Book 3 (1647), Ascella, London, England, 2001.

Marcus Manilius, *Astronomica*, Book 5 (2nd century).

Ptolemy, *Tetrabiblos* (2nd century), The Astrology Centre of America, Bel Air, USA, 2002.

Vivian Robson, *The Fixed Stars and Constellations in Astrology* (1923), Ascella, London, England, 2001.

Frithjof Schuon, *The Transcendent Unity of Religion*, Quest Books, Seattle, Verenigde Staten, 1993.

About the author

Oscar Hofman lives in Gorinchem, The Netherlands and practises all the branches of traditional astrology: medical, natal, electional, horary and mundane. He is the founder of the International School of Classical Astrology which offers a full training program in the tradition (on horary, electional, natal, medical and mundane, available in six languages) followed by students in more than 30 countries around the world. He travels widely to teach, especially in Eastern Europe and the German-speaking countries and has clients in many countries.

He has written four books (on classical medical astrology, the fixed stars, and on classical horary astrology), which have been published in six languages; he was the first European astrologer to be translated into Chinese.

Email: oshofman@xs4all.nl
Website (with a blog focusing on the fixed stars, in Dutch, French and English): www.pegasus-advies.com
Phone: 00-31-183-649405.

Also from The Wessex Astrologer
www.wessexastrologer.com

Martin Davis
Astrolocality Astrology: A Guide to What it is and How to Use it
From Here to There: An Astrologer's Guide to Astromapping

Wanda Sellar
The Consultation Chart
An Introduction to Medical Astrology
An Introduction to Decumbiture

Geoffrey Cornelius
The Moment of Astrology

Darrelyn Gunzburg
Life After Grief: An Astrological Guide to Dealing with Grief
AstroGraphology: The Hidden Link between your Horoscope and your Handwriting

Paul F. Newman
Declination: The Steps of the Sun
Luna: The Book of the Moon

Deborah Houlding
The Houses: Temples of the Sky

Dorian Geiseler Greenbaum
Temperament: Astrology's Forgotten Key

Howard Sasportas
The Gods of Change

Patricia L. Walsh
Understanding Karmic Complexes

M. Kelly Hunter
Living Lilith: the Four Dimensions of the Cosmic Feminine

Barbara Dunn
Horary Astrology Re-Examined

Deva Green
Evolutionary Astrology

Jeff Green
Pluto Volume 1: The Evolutionary Journey of the Soul
Pluto Volume 2: The Evolutionary Journey of the Soul Through Relationships
Essays on Evolutionary Astrology (ed. by Deva Green)

Dolores Ashcroft-Nowicki and Stephanie V. Norris
The Door Unlocked: An Astrological Insight into Initiation

Greg Bogart
Astrology and Meditation: The Fearless Contemplation of Change

Henry Seltzer
The Tenth Planet: Revelations from the Astrological Eris

Ray Grasse
Under a Sacred Sky: Essays on the Practice and Philosophy of Astrology

Joseph Crane
Astrological Roots: The Hellenistic Legacy
Between Fortune and Providence

Bruce Scofield
Day-Signs: Native American Astrology from Ancient Mexico

Komilla Sutton
The Essentials of Vedic Astrology
The Lunar Nodes: Crisis and Redemption
Personal Panchanga: The Five Sources of Light
The Nakshatras: the Stars Beyond the Zodiac

Anthony Louis
The Art of Forecasting using Solar Returns

Oscar Hofman
Classical Medical Astrology

Bernadette Brady
Astrology, A Place in Chaos
Star and Planet Combinations

Richard Idemon
The Magic Thread
Through the Looking Glass

Nick Campion
The Book of World Horoscopes

Judy Hall
Patterns of the Past
Karmic Connections
Good Vibrations
The Soulmate Myth: A Dream Come True or Your Worst Nightmare?
The Book of Why: Understanding your Soul's Journey
Book of Psychic Development

Michele Finey
The Sacred Dance of Venus and Mars

David Hamblin
The Spirit of Numbers

Dennis Elwell
Cosmic Loom

Bob Makransky
Planetary Strength
Planetary Hours
Planetary Combination

Petros Eleftheriadis
Horary Astrology: The Practical Guide to Your Fate

Nicola Smuts-Allsop
Fertility Astrology: A Modern Medieval Textbook

Cornelia Hansen
Kidwheels: Finding the Child in the Chart

www.ingramcontent.com/pod-product-compliance
Lightning Source LLC
Chambersburg PA
CBHW052049220426
43663CB00012B/2494